No. 30035
$28.95

Credit and Collections

for Your Small Business

Cecil J. Bond

LIBERTY HOUSE®

FIRST EDITION
FIRST PRINTING

Copyright © 1989 by TAB BOOKS Inc.
Printed in the United States of America

Library of Congress Cataloging in Publication Data

Bond, Cecil J.
    Credit and collections for your small business / by Cecil J. Bond.
    p. cm.
    Includes index.
    ISBN 0-8306-9035-2   ISBN 0-8306-3035-X (pbk.)
    1. Credit—Management. 2. Collecting of accounts. 3. Small
business—Finance.   I. Title.
HG3751.B66   1989
658.8—dc20   89-31853
                                             CIP

TAB BOOKS Inc. offers software for sale. For information and a catalog, please contact TAB
Software Department, Blue Ridge Summit, PA 17294-0850.

Questions regarding the content of this book should be addressed to:

    Reader Inquiry Branch
    TAB BOOKS Inc.
    Blue Ridge Summit, PA 17294-0214

David Conti: Acquisitions Editor
Nina E. Barr: Book Editor
Katherine Brown: Production

Contents

Acknowledgments

I wish to thank all of the people, companies, and organizations whose paths I crossed over what is now more than three decades of work in the credit management profession. Whether for better or for worse, each made a contribution to the total experience.

Special thanks to my family. Thanks also to the National Association of Credit Management for working constantly and effectively to foster a climate conducive to professionalism and professional growth.

Introduction

Credit and Collections for Your Small Business is written for the owner, manager, or designated employee whose responsibility it is to make commercial credit decisions for his or her small manufacturing, distributing, or wholesaling company. It is written with the objective of helping people with little or no credit management experience to make good credit decisions and to manage successfully an important area of their company's assets: the accounts receivable. Certainly one of the key factors in the success or failure of any company is the quality of the receivables, which is in turn the result of the quality of the credit decisions. Bringing helpful information, answers, and guidance to this area of small business management is the focus of this book.

It is not the objective of this book to turn owners, company managers, or designated employees into professional credit managers. Room for such a level of specialization in a small company does not exist. In most small business environments, the credit management assignment is an "in addition to other responsibilities" task. It is routinely one of two or more responsibilities that fall to those in an office where the number of duties and responsibilities exceed the number of employees. But if we assume that the owner or designated employee keeps this book nearby, that person will have a level of reference data and guideline support that should enable him or her to develop satisfactory levels of credit and collection skills.

What is good credit management? Take heart. It is not something that can be attained only by the bigger companies. Your small company can have it too! There is, in fact, no acceptable substitute for it. Without it, a sizable portion of your company's assets (the accounts receivable) could be at serious risk. No company can have a solid foundation of good credit accounts, and fast-turning receivables, if the evaluation process that put those accounts on the books is flawed.

You must be sure that the account evaluation procedures, monitoring of accounts, collection experience, and level of management knowledge is equal to the challenge of properly managing your company's credit and collections. Your company cannot afford to grant credit to firms who have neither the ability or the willingness to pay within terms, or close to terms. If they do not handle their accounts in a responsible manner, your own cash flow will be impacted unfavorably. Internally generated cash flow (from your accounts receivable) is a great way to eliminate some of your bank borrowing and trim the costs of doing business. It is also a great comfort to you, as the owner of a small business, to know that your company's receivables dollars are as sound as good credit management can make them.

This book will help you to evaluate the effectiveness of what you are doing with your credit accounts. It will help you to locate where and what changes are necessary, if you can make those changes within your present system, and how to replace your present system with one that does not sacrifice simplicity but works more effectively for you. It also will help you to improve your levels of knowledge regarding credit so that you can deal more confidently, effectively, and efficiently with what is probably an unfamiliar responsibility. I have arranged the book to take you in sequential steps through the entire process of managing credit in a small business environment, and the index will help you locate the subjects, subtopics, forms, sample letters, and guideline data to ease the transition from your questions to the book's answers and guidance material.

An owner who makes credit decisions, or a designated employee who makes them as one of two or three daily areas of responsibility, does not need to be knowledgable in areas of credit and collections that are not normally a part of that person's daily routine. What is important is to recognize when you are not on familiar ground, and to know where to go to get the proper level of direction or answers. When you find yourself stumped by unusual problems or circumstances, refer to the index. In addition to directing you to paragraphs or pages that will deal with areas relevant to your normal work experience, the index will direct you to material relevant to topics, subtopics, situations, and procedures that are unusual for your company but are not at such a high level that you could not expect to find the information both useful and helpful occasionally.

Because a company is small does not rule out the possibility that it has growth potential or that the owner has growth plans for it. Small companies frequently wait quietly, growing very slowly as they assess the marketplace, until one day they begin to grow at a rate that seems dramatic to those who were a part of the years when annual growth was measurable but undramatic. The foundations that are established when a company is small—whether the owner does or does not have expectations or hopes for taking the company to a higher plateau of size (sales, earnings and industry stature)—is vital to either course. If the owner wants the company to experience some annual growth but wants it to remain small, it must have a solid foundation—and good management of credit accounts is a must. If the company is small but the owner looks hopefully toward the future for the market niche that will accelerate the company's growth, a solid foundation is still necessary—and good management of the credit accounts is still a must.

These pages offer the small business owner the potential for greatly improving his or her credit management skills with a minimum investment of time and dollars. What should be committed to memory? Only the basic credit and collections guidelines—the nuts-and-bolts that will enable the owner to deal more effectively and efficiently with the basic credit management process—a process that starts with the credit application and continues through the collection of credit account balances.

This book is the small-business owner's passport to better credit decisions. It offers concise guidelines to a quality of accounts receivable that should minimize the unpleasantness of uncollectible account balances and the subsequent charging of those balances to the Bad-Debt account. Remember also that you—the owner of a small business—do not have to be a credit management professional to be an effective manager of credit accounts. You must learn the basics—getting new account information, processing and evaluating it, assigning a credit line, monitoring your accounts receivable for signs of weakness, pressing for payment of account balances at a level of intensity appropriate to the individual account, and if necessary following your money through an assignment to a collection agency, a suit for a judgment in Small Claims Court, or a Chapter XI bankruptcy filing.

Listing the basics and dealing with them is hardly the same. This book will give you what you need to understand and cope with the basics to, and through, other areas essential to the successful managing of small-business credit accounts.

Chapter 1

Credit Sales—
Who Needs Them?!

IT IS A QUESTION THAT COMES VERY CLOSE TO ANSWERING ITSELF. IF YOU ARE A SMALL manufacturer, distributor, or wholesaler, you must offer your company's products to trade customers on credit terms. There is no alternative way for any manufacturing or distributing company—small or large—to survive in today's manufacturing or nonretail sales environment unless customers can buy from them on credit terms. Credit sales? The *who* in "Who Needs Them?" is you.

Small manufacturing and distributing companies share many of the same problems that plague the bigger companies. Your small company must maintain some annual percentage of sales growth to stay healthy and meet the growth expectations you have for it. Selling on credit terms opens industry markets to your company. It gives your company a chance to more fully utilize manufacturing capacity—certainly a much higher percentage of that capacity than would be possible if you did not offer credit terms or if you offered them on a very narrow basis. How many of your present customers would buy your products if they had to pay cash? Not many because just as you would be hard-pressed to deal in a supplier or raw material's marketplace where you had to pay for the ingredients for your product(s) at the time of delivery, so would they have an insurmountable problem paying cash for your products. Credit terms enable the customers of a manufacturer or distributor to buy more products, to merchandise them more aggressively, to carry more complete product inventories, and to approach customers you could not reach if products were not available to them on credit terms. Volume sales—volume for the size of your business—should enable you to reflect lower per unit manufacturing and distribution costs in better, more competitive prices to your customers. Short of national or regional economic problems, this competitive pricing should result in more business and more profits for both you and your customers.

Credit sales, based upon a solid program of basic evaluation, processing, monitoring, and collection standards, is the only way for almost any small manufacturer and distributor to be successful. All of the bigger companies offer credit terms to their customers—often offering a broad variety of credit terms. Although you might not be able to meet some of their extended terms arrangements, (example: a due date 15 to 30 days beyond your standard terms), any reasonable use of terms that are used commonly in your industry should make you competitive in that area. If your products emphasize quality as opposed to the lower-priced, mass-produced items, good credit terms will help you locate customers who favor a quality line or handle products for both the quality and mass-produced markets.

There is no acceptable rationale for any manufacturer or distributor to reject or to minimize the use of credit terms. Most companies support their monthly cash flow needs with a bank credit line—one that they have negotiated for the sole purpose of augmenting cash generated from account receivable payments. The combination of money generated from receivables plus the occasional or frequent use of the bank credit line must take care of your company's monthly cash requirements, provide money for short- and long-term commitments, and make it possible for the company to show a profit. Would all of this be possible if your company did not offer credit terms? Would there in fact be a company with any reasonable chance for survival that did not offer credit terms? Not in today's business environment.

Cash on the barrelhead is a term that once was in common usage. It stated about as clearly as any phrase could the way business was conducted in an earlier era—the years before and including World War II. Little commercial or consumer credit was available in the years preceding industry's move to mass production. In the early years of the move to mass-production techniques, any real chance for the use of commercial and consumer credit on a broad basis was stifled because people frowned upon debt—both commercial and consumer. Problems with the economy—many of which manufacturers and bankers could have solved had they been oriented to a credit-stimulated economy—never gave credit terms a real chance to change the ''barrelhead'' economy until the years after World War II. Has credit worked? Abuses will always occur, but the broad use of commercial credit (and consumer credit) has changed the way business people at all levels think and perform.

Small businesses have shared in the post-World War II growth, contributing products and services of all types in all areas of the marketplace. Could growth have happened without credit terms? Not a chance. The Industrial Revolution forced business people everywhere to consider new marketing concepts, and sales on credit terms was found to be the only way to sell the enormous quantities of products that factories could produce. It took an industrial upheaval and years of gradual adjustment to this new marketing philosophy to push credit sales into the mainstream of business life. Companies which failed to adapt to the new philosophy—companies that did not link new production techniques and capabilities with competitive, credit-inspired marketing concepts—did not survive.

It is not different in the current era. Many owners of small manufacturing and distributing businesses have major concerns regarding the risks they take when they sell on credit terms. The very nature of a credit sale involves risk, but unless he or she has enough personal wealth to subsidize his or her business venture, a manufacturer or distributor who does not offer credit terms is not destined to have a successful company.

You can minimize your company's risk by dealing with credit terms on an informed, knowledgable basis. You can minimize risk by being aware of industry and economic conditions, new products and industry trends, and changes in terms offered to trade (industry) customers, and by being alert to whether you are in an area of manufacturing that could benefit from an evaluation of the products that have long been considered ''industry standards.'' Do sales figures for your industry warn of a decline in a product's acceptance that is not yet reflected in your company's sales figures? Is your industry unusually sensitive to downturns and upswings in the regional or national economy? Of enormous importance to you personally is whether your company is continuing to experience an annual percentage of growth that is both healthy and personally satisfying.

Credit sales is a solid method on which your small company can capitalize to improve the company's long-term opportunities for success. Credit sales is the primary lubricant that allows companies with fine products and good potential to avoid seeing that potential wither and die. It is a primary ingredient in keeping the economy flowing and out of a paralyzed state. Although credit might be a shock-inducing word for consumers who receive monthly charge card reminders of their purchasing sins, users of commercial credit could not survive without it.

Is there any further doubt that you should sell on credit terms? We have already established the fact that industry practice determines whether a company or business must offer credit terms and what those credit terms will be. My question then is why wouldn't you—or any other owner of a small business—want to sell products on credit terms if you knew that credit sales would help your business to be more competitive, would produce more sales, and would help the business to become more financially successful? Why wouldn't the owner of any small manufacturing and/or distributing company want to sell on credit terms if the use of that basic marketing tool would make it possible to add customers who could not buy the company's products and services on ''barrelhead'' terms?

It is true that the additional costs of financing sales on credit terms frequently require the manufacturer or distributor to increase the size of bank and supplier credit lines to accommodate the turnaround time necessary to convert accounts receivable into cash. But this process goes on daily in the United States and most of the world's industrialized countries. Even though your company is small, bank and supplier credit should not be a problem if you are well organized, well managed, and adequately staffed. Your company also must offer a good product line; and it must have a territory and customer base that is economically solid. The bank and your other suppliers will expect you to be profitable, and you should have the same expectations for your company.

The only foreseeable problem in a company situation such as the one just described involves the effect of a sharp decline in either your regional economy or the national economy. At that point, your bank and suppliers would be expected to tighten lines of credit just as you would want to take a firmer grip on the extension of credit to your own accounts. But if we assume that the economy and your company will avoid any serious crisis—monetary or other—then we also must assume that your company will benefit enormously from the maximum use of credit sales within limitations that are both healthy and prudent for the size, financial stability, and goals of your company.

If it is true that your competitors offer credit terms to their customers, then you have no choice. Welcome to the broad opportunities that the world of credit sales offers to your business.

Chapter 2

Your Credit Department

THIS CHAPTER AND CHAPTER 3 (BEFORE CREDIT SALES—A SOUND CREDIT POLICY) will give you the tools necessary to set up or reorganize a credit department that will work for you, not against you. Keeping the department lean—only slightly more complex than bare bones—will serve you well at a time when managing credit accounts is a small part of your day or the delegated ''add-on'' task of an employee. It also will provide the foundation for department growth while reminding you of the important money decisions that you'll be making—and their potential for favorable or unfavorable impact on your profit and loss statement.

Putting your company's credit function on a solid foundation is not difficult, plus it offers the potential for well-planned growth when your company needs more than a part-time credit manager. But until your company's growth reaches that point—if that much growth is in your plans—the system will be one that takes a minimum amount of your daily time. Credit decisions are important but an owners time must be split among many areas and responsibilities. Neither you or a designated employee should have to spend a disproportionate amount of time on any one phase of the company's operation. Your small company cannot afford to have you or an employee become trapped in a process that can never become part of systematic procedures.

THE DEPARTMENT FOUNDATION

The incentive for putting your company's credit department on a solid foundation is dollars. When your company is receiving and processing credit applications and orders for release on credit terms, you put the varying amounts of your company's assets at risk. The degree of risk depends upon your experience and your knowledge of the account. When the account is new to your company, the degree of risk hinges on the quality of the customer's references, how well you have prepared yourself to evaluate data received from supplier and bank references, how much attention you pay to the financial statements, and your access to commercial credit agency reports (Dun & Bradstreet, etc.).

Now is not the time to discover that your idea of what information is needed to do a good job of handling a small volume of credit accounts is inadequate.

Your company should have a simple system for dealing with credit-related matters. This system should enable you to routinely evaluate the credit data for most new account applicants. The same simple, but thorough, system should allow you to routinely clear orders for established accounts. Don't continue to use a system (or procedures) that does not let you do your credit work in an efficient, well-programmed manner. If your system is inefficient, revise the procedures you are using or put together a new and more effective set of procedures—procedures that require less management time and that produce quality results. When the level of planning is inadequate for the needs of your company, the quality of the credit decisions can rapidly become a major concern. Your company could lose potential customers you should accept, plus it would suffer the penalties of a low efficiency level and lost receivable dollars. Every company needs a strong credit policy and good credit procedures. Both should be in place before you receive the first order, but if they are not, you should take corrective action at the earliest possible moment.

ORGANIZING OR OVERHAULING

How do you determine whether a credit function or department needs to be reorganized? Reorganization is necessary when you are doing the following:

☐ When you process an account one way then vary the procedure the next time.

☐ When too many loose ends exist before the reference data is in place and you are ready to evaluate it and make a credit decision.

☐ When there is no pattern and no consistency to the gathering, processing, and evaluating of the reference data.

☐ When you do not have the kinds of forms that make it easier and faster to gather data and put it in a useful form.

If you have been shaking your head as you read the above, it indicates that your credit activity is taking too much time and is probably not delivering the desired results. You are making credit decisions, but certainly not under the most favorable of conditions.

It is not possible for me to spend "hands on" time in your office, therefore, the medium for an easily-understood level of communication between us is these pages. Many areas of the decision-making process require a working knowledge of your company and your business philosophy. Through these pages, I can give you the types of guidelines and answers that you can apply to your company. You might not have many credit accounts but you must have a credit policy (see chapter 3) if your daily credit decisions are to be consistent with the company's goals and needs. Your credit policy may be restrictive, moderate, or liberal. You must decide what type policy you want based upon the company's need for a *fast-turning receivables base* (customers who pay within terms) and general financial needs. It might be liberal when you have a specific time frame for a projected level of growth. It might be restrictive (fast-turning receivables) when economic, industry, or company conditions cause you to stress a very conservative approach to credit.

A small company shares the same need as larger companies to know whether the credit department is organized for maximum results with a minimum expenditure of time. It must be efficient and effective because a small company does not have the luxury of a large staff. "Delegating responsibility" is a term that has a very narrow potential in a small-company environment. When the office staff is two, three, or even as many as a half dozen, there is plenty of work to go around. An efficient credit operation is a must to ensure that the person who has the responsibility of making credit decisions— whether it is the owner or a designated employee—has the necessary level of decision-making knowledge and the variety of tools necessary to make good decisions.

Bad-debt losses and their impact on your company is not the subject of this chapter, but the possibility of this type of loss is inevitably linked with the credit decisions made by you or your designated credit manager. You have other business management worries. You do not need the additional aggravation of seeing too many of your accounts receivable dollars deteriorate and slide into the category of uncollectible bad-debt items. For example: an account is approved for an opening order of $800. It makes one $200 "on account" payment, closes the place of business overnight, and the firm's owner disappears. You assign the account to your collection agency but they are unable to trace the owner or find any attachable assets. Prior to the end of your company's fiscal year, your accounting firm will review receivable balances. At that time, they will advise that you should charge this uncollectible item against the Bad-Debt account. This account reduces the annual profit figure for your company by the amount involved.

Take a hard look at the procedures you currently use to process new accounts, assign credit limits, monitor accounts receivable, control credit limits, and follow up on in-house and third-party collection efforts. If a review of your current procedures indicates that you need to reorganize them, now is the time to begin.

Reorganization Steps

Begin with a simple physical layout which includes the amount of space you will allot your credit department based upon the size of the equipment, the type and variety of the equipment, and the number of people who currently occupy or will occupy the space. The next step should be an evaluation of your present system for processing data. If it is not a computerized system, you should incorporate into your thinking and planning the question of whether your company should-or-will be soon considering the change.

Office Equipment: If the company has a maximum of 100 active or *semi-active accounts* (one or more credit sales every three months) and the responsibility for credit decisions rests with an owner, partner, or designated employee, a three-drawer file offers enough space for customer files, credit department forms, current and recent accounts receivable, aged trial balance reports, third-party collection assignment forms, and any books or publications relating to credit. If the credit department has a level of activity that indicates a rapidly approaching need for a full-time credit manager, additional space will be necessary. The minimum allotment of footage for office space should be enough for a desk, a chair, a three-drawer file cabinet, a typewriter, a typewriter stand, a small electronic calculator, a two- or three-tier desktop file, and if overhead lighting is not good, a desk lamp.

Personnel: Depending upon the activity level of credit accounts versus the experience level of the person handling these accounts, the company's receivables will demand a substantial percentage of that person's time. Two hundred active accounts (same criteria as stated above for determining "active") should be a manageable load for a person whose experience is limited. What about a company who has three, four, or five hundred accounts? These numbers are well above the number of accounts most small manufacturing companies would have, and they are several times the number that an inexperienced credit manager should handle. An experienced professional credit manager should be able to handle five or six hundred active accounts, plus some-or-all of the clerical work that such a responsibility entails, but not an inexperienced credit manager. Problems develop rather quickly when a less-experienced person is pressured to make prompt and sound decisions and doesn't have the time to give an appropriate amount of attention to each account. Never allow such a situation to occur or develop. You—the company's owner—should promptly assign another employee to provide clerical support for your credit supervisor before that person gets into trouble along with your receivable dollars. If you are handling the credit policy, you'll begin to feel the pressure. You'll begin to feel the extra demand of time that credit is asking of you, and the fact that it narrows the time you have to devote to other equally important company tasks. Don't let it get out of hand. Promptly assign someone to give you backup support. When the credit supervisor is an employee, don't hesitate to assign clerical help for filing, typing, payment-related correspondence, and other clerical tasks that will allow the credit supervisor to concentrate on the direct, dollars-related aspects of credit management. As an employee's management skills increase, you will be able to cut back on the hours of clerical support you now require, or if there is rapid company growth, you will be able to defer any need for additional support help for a longer period of time.

Computer Processed Data vs. Manual Processed Data: If your company uses computer-processed data, is it done on in-house equipment (leased or purchased), on a *time-share basis* (in-house keypunch operator but the data processing equipment is located elsewhere), or does your company contract with a data processing service? If your firm is not into one of these data processing formats, we must then talk about manual, grind-it-out data processing on an adding machine or calculators. This manual data processing might continue to be cost effective on a short-term basis, but I would urge you to watch these costs versus the possibililities for getting your company into computer-processed data with a very minimum investment in equipment. No investment at all is required if you contract with a data processing company, but be sure that your costs between manual and computerized data processing are in line with what your company should spend for the service.

It would be inappropriate for me to try to get into specific recommendations for data processing equipment or programs. My function is not to tell you or your accountant when the timing is right for your company to go to a computerized data processing system, a data processing service, or some form of time-share system. I don't know any facts regarding your company, your goals, your financial commitments, or your financial capabilities. My primary objective is to encourage small companies to consider whether their objectives might be attained more easily if they used a computerized system. Hardware and software change so rapidly and the requirements of one company differ so greatly from those of another that specific recommendations would be unwise. Brand name recommendations that I might make today—especially in the area of software—could become outmoded for your company's purposes within two or three years. So, let me stay away from specifics and instead suggest that you consider the following: If your company does not have an in-house system and data processing is done by a company keypunch operator who accesses time-share equipment at an off-site location, a professional programmer should evaluate your company's future needs. Your accountant also should be a good source of information regarding hardware and software items most suitable for your company.

You, as an owner, have one distinct advantage over the bigger companies. When the time comes for you to seriously consider a data processing system for your company—a system that can do accounts receivable aging reports, billing, inventory control, raw materials reports, payroll, etc.—the only person you must sell on the merits of one system over another is yourself. It's an enviable position, but it also imposes a real responsibility. You will want input from the best and most knowledgable people as it relates to your company's needs and situation. You also will want to give strong weight to the recommendations of your accountant, programmer, or data processing advisor. But, when you have all of the facts, it will not be a "decision by committee." The decision will be yours.

This section of the chapter is not intended to push every small manufacturer or distributor into looking at the latest in high-tech hardware and software. I am several years past a vested interest in Silicon Valley's companies, products, and high-tech stocks. Not every small business firm has gone to computerized data processing nor should they be in a rush to do so. Many small businesses continue to process their data the old fashioned way—they do it manually. The important thing is to be aware of what your company is doing, how rapidly it is doing it, whether some form of data processing would pay dividends for your company, and what time frame would be right for the change. Manufacturers and distributors who are not trying to play catch-up in a syndrome of accelerated growth have time to develop their timetable. The small company that is experiencing approximately a five percent "real growth" per year might have no desire to be more than a comfortably successful minor player in its industry. A very small customer base (as few as 10 to 25 accounts) might represent ninety-plus percent of the company's annual sales, and the company might have been successful at this modest level for several years. If this company also has a consistently tight cash flow, an economically depressed sales or service area, a manufactured product that has no *exclusivity* (is constantly elbowing other manufacturers and distributors of similiar products for shelf space or market share), it should not consider a near-term change to computerized data processing. This company will probably continue to manually process data for a very long time.

Whether your company processes data manually or electronically will determine the type of aging reports you will use to monitor accounts receivable balances. *Accounts Receivable Aged Trial Balance Report* (referred to in these pages as an "aging sheet" or "aging report") is an ongoing list of all open accounts. The total dollars owed by each account is broken down into categories of aging. It is usually broken down via columns that reflect balances ranging from current, 0 to 30 days past due, 31 to 60 days past due, 61 to 90 days past due, and 91 days and over past due. The appropriate dollar amount is listed under the applicable category of aging. The report changes daily with the payment of some of the account balance or the payment of an account total. These payments are usually entered on the aging sheet to reflect what customers have paid and what is still open. Billings (invoices) become part of a new aging sheet—one that you might prepare manually or on a computer. If you prepare the report manually, the number of listed accounts on each aging report should not exceed 25 or 30, most of which have purchase activity at least once a week. When the number of *open accounts* (accounts that have current and past due balances) is less than 25 or 30, you should not prepare a manually-prepared aging report more frequertly than once every week or ten days. The owner should have aging reports prepared by a clerk who is good with figures—someone who can take account totals, break them into the appropriate sections of aging, reconcile individual column amounts to the account total, and spend a minimum amount of time turning individual accounts data into a new, current aging report.

During the time period a currently applicable aging report is in use, the daily procedure of hand-recording payments to individual account balances allows the owner—who in this example is making the credit decisions from receivables aging reports prepared by a figures-oriented employee—to monitor the current or past due status of customer accounts. No invoices (charges) are added to an aging report after the owner or credit manager receives it unless he or she must decide whether to release an in-house customer order. The owner should ask the employee who keeps individual accounts receivable records to bring the customer's balance owing to a currently applicable figure, then break the figure into the applicable columns of aging. The owner can then decide

ACCOUNTS RECEIVABLE AGING SHEET

Date_____

Account No.	Amt. Owing	Current	Past Due 1-30 Days	Past Due 31-60 Days	Past Due 61-90 Days	Past Due Over 90

(You can determine the percentages for each column by dividing the total Amount Owing into each of the five other columns.)

FIG. 2-1.

whether a payment must be received before more products are released. (You can manually prepare the sample Accounts Receivable Aging Sheet shown in FIG. 2-1 or adapt it to an older bookkeeping machine. The sample Accounts Receivable Aging Sheet shown in Chapter 7 is for use when report data is computerized).

Thousands of owners bring their small companies through the early, tentative months of credit sales, basing their decisions primarily upon quality input from the applicant's bank and supplier references. Don't let feelings of doubt and insecurity muddy your credit decisions. You should not experience unusual problems if you apply to each credit decision your knowledge of the industry, personal knowledge of certain applicant companies, your best judgment as it relates to your company's credit policy and financial needs, and if you follow the procedures and other guideline data contained in this book. Do nothing in a hasty or precipitous manner. Allow yourself and the credit function to grow and mature with your company—to grow from a few accounts into a credit department. When there is an obvious need for change in any phase of your credit function, don't make it a sudden or disruptive change. A credit function that you are easing into the maturity of a credit department needs an even, steady hand.

Hiring a Credit Manager: Growth puts an increasing variety of responsibilities on the shoulders of the company's owner. There comes a point when it is no longer possible to talk about the entrepreneur who has the time to be involved in every facet of the company's operation. The talk must center around filling a growth-related need—a need that a strong assistant credit manager can fill. A credit manager who learned the profession at a larger firm is now ready to put together a credit department and run it effectively. Many credit assistants who come from large companies are excellent manager candidates for the business whose sales and number of accounts has reached a level that requires a full-time manager. If one day you find that your company is no longer small, consider hiring a young credit professional who has learned his skills at a larger company. An owner doesn't have to be told when it's time for such a move. An owner knows the time is right when the number and complexity of credit decisions is adding up to more hours than he or she has available to manage credit accounts. Be cautious and thorough when you evaluate a credit applicant and do not have any doubts about the applicant when you arrive at a decision.

The Customer Credit File: One of the more important considerations when you are setting up or rebuilding your company's credit department is to establish a format for good customer files. It isn't good enough to use manila folders, type customer names on a colored tab, then have a disorganized jungle of papers on the inside. You should have a systemized sequence for filing the various forms, credit reports, letters, and other material relevant to the account. Information is the key ingredient when a creditor/customer relationship is getting its start. The emphasis shifts gradually to experience as the creditor company builds a base of personal experience with the customer company—a base that can become a useless mass of nonrelated, nonintegrated material if it isn't put together in manageable form.

The following is a practical guide for systematizing the contents of your customer credit files. Some account folders will expand more slowly after the initial input of forms, reports, and letters; others will quickly expand to the point where they become candidates for a Weight Watcher's program. Important points to remember: properly set up the file folders; add papers and letters in a systematic rather than a haphazard manner; make dated, clear-and-accurate notes regarding any discussion, telephone conversation, or subject that might have future relevance or importance, and *never* allow yourself to wonder if the time spent maintaining good-and-complete files is a waste. Let me assure you that it is not.

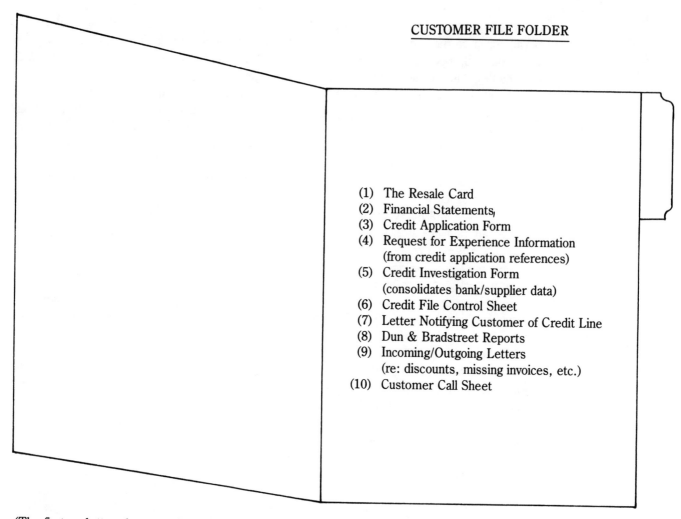

CUSTOMER FILE FOLDER

(1) The Resale Card
(2) Financial Statements,
(3) Credit Application Form
(4) Request for Experience Information
      (from credit application references)
(5) Credit Investigation Form
      (consolidates bank/supplier data)
(6) Credit File Control Sheet
(7) Letter Notifying Customer of Credit Line
(8) Dun & Bradstreet Reports
(9) Incoming/Outgoing Letters
      (re: discounts, missing invoices, etc.)
(10) Customer Call Sheet

(The first or *bottom* document is numbered (1). When you open a customer's file folder, the *top* document should be the Customer Call Sheet)

FIG. 2-2.

The first (or bottom) document is numbered (1). You should set up file folders with documents in the following order:

- ☐ (1) The Resale Card (Sales Tax Exemption Number)
- ☐ (2) Financial Statements (first-and-updates filed together)
- ☐ (3) Credit Application Form
- ☐ (4) Request For Experience Information (from Credit Application references)
- ☐ (5) Credit Investigation Form (consolidates bank/supplier data)
- ☐ (6) Credit File Control Sheet
- ☐ (7) Letter Notifying Customer Of Credit Line
- ☐ (8) Dun & Bradstreet Reports (if any)
- ☐ (9) Incoming or Outgoing Letters (re: discounts, missing invoices, etc.)
- ☐ (10) Customer Call Sheet

Documents and correspondence not listed above (Chapter XI filings, third-party collection assignments, etc.) may become part of a customer's file. If the file folder is set up properly, you should have no difficulty fitting a new category into the appropriate location (FIG. 2-2).

Active and Inactive Files: The type of merchandise or product you sell has some bearing on the frequency that some customers will buy from you. In most situations, if a customer does not buy for a period of six months, you should consider the account inactive and put it in a special "inactive" section. When you have a customer or customers who buy *sporadically*—no particular pattern but you seem to get an order every few months—continue that type of account in your active file.

Customers who are volume merchandisers or major players in their field and territory normally will buy much more frequently than the smaller, less aggressive accounts. When an account that has done a good job for your company has not bought any of your products for an unusually long period of time, discuss it with your sales people. See what you can do to help re-establish a relationship with the account. Perhaps you should send a letter to the former customer's purchasing manager citing the long relationship between your two companies, stating the amount of credit available to his company, and encouraging him to use it.

Chapter 3

Before Credit Sales—
A Sound Credit Policy

A WRITTEN CREDIT POLICY IS AS IMPORTANT TO AN OWNER-MANAGED CREDIT DEPART-
ment as it is to a bigger company. An owner might know the types of credit accounts that
are best for his or her small company but the pressures and distractions of other decisions are ever present. The absence of a concise credit policy could cause an owner to
make decisions that violate the company's standard for acceptable credit accounts.

The credit policy should be one of a small company's key guidelines, helping to
channel the owner's thinking toward more fixed and uniform procedures in other company areas as well. A bad credit policy—or none at all—can lead to credit decisions that
deliver too many slow-pay accounts. When that happens, your monthly projection for
cash flow (money received from receivables payments) will fall consistently short of your
projection, making it necessary for you to increase debt with additional borrowing
against your bank credit line. It is a sequence of events that is loaded with the potential
for serious company problems. You don't want to increase sales and production only to
find that the money in your accounts receivable is increasingly centered in the past-due
columns of your aging report.

When your credit policy isn't a written one, you really have no proper handle on the
day-to-day uniformity of credit decisions. You must have a credit policy that sets the
guidelines within your company so that you or a designated employee can work effectively. Review the results of what you are presently doing. Is the quality of your receivables consistent with what you think it should be? If it isn't, every credit decision that
finds its way onto your accounts receivable aging report has more potential for becoming
a bad-debt loss than you should be experiencing.

An effective credit policy combines current and projected financial needs with the
need to compete for customers in a particular industry or geographic area. You write the
credit policy in the most concise, all-inclusive format that your good-business sense tells
you will help your company to meet its objectives. It can be a minor masterpiece, but
unless you translate the words into everyday guidelines for credit decisions, it will be

worthless. Your attitude toward credit accounts and credit decisions must remain consistent with the guidelines that form your company's credit policy. If business conditions change and it becomes obvious that your credit policy is too restrictive, change your written credit policy to reflect the changes in parameters for an acceptable account. A credit policy is never totally rigid; you must write some flexibility into every policy or plan. A company locked into rigid policies and guidelines that have no provision for the occasional exception is a company destined to immobilize itself in the web of its own constraints. Plans and policies—for your credit department and for the other areas of your company—will help you to focus your time, talents, and energies into a work pattern that will give your company its best chance for success.

THREE BASIC CREDIT POLICIES

The three basic types of credit policies are: restrictive, *moderate* (middle-of-the-road decisions), and liberal. Each type of policy involves a different mix of ingredients, a somewhat different business philosophy and goals, different financial needs, or a combination of the three policies (something from one policy, a few things from another policy, and one or two guidelines from the third policy). A credit policy tailored from one or more of the basic policies is acceptable. The test of a credit policy is whether it does an effective job for a specific company. If it does, the policy is sound.

Restrictive Credit Policy

A restrictive credit policy is usually the policy of a company that has no plan to grow at a rate that is more than minimal. The company usually is unwilling to take more than minor risks, preferring instead to deal with customers whose paying habits stay in a tight little area between discount and discount/prompt. An account might occasionally run a few days beyond the due date but this would be the exception rather than the rule.

Obviously, this account category represents management that is ultraconservative in its attitudes toward business and business practices. It is almost invariably on a solid financial footing; it intends to remain there; and it uses little or no bank support to augment the adequate flow of cash received from rapidly-turning receivables. More aggressive companies look upon this level of conservatism with considerable disdain, however, many very conservative business people have survived long after the more aggressive companies have gone the way of a Chapter XI filing (see chapter 9). Although an ultraconservative credit policy is intended to protect the business, it is not without danger. Just as a policy of excessively liberal credit can destroy a company, so a policy of restrictive credit can stifle all growth to the point where momentum necessary to maintain position is lost. When a business is not aggressive enough to replace lost accounts, the company's receivables base gradually will erode to a dangerous level. A restrictive policy should never be allowed to become a policy that stifles "normal growth" as individual companies apply their interpretation to the phrase. (Example: A small manufacturer supports cash flow needs from fast-turning receivables. A potential customer—one who has been in business for several years, who is marginally profitable, and who does a volume of business that requires suppliers to wait 40 to 55 days for receivables payments—asks the company to set up a credit line that would make it one of the manufacturing company's largest accounts. After evaluating the payment information received from the potential customer's supplier references, the company decides that it cannot handle the potential customer's credit requirements. Payment for products would not be prompt enough to meet the manufacturers credit policy and cash flow requirements. Under other financial circumstances and with a credit policy that provided for some slower-turning accounts receivable, the manufacturer would have granted the requested credit line. In this example, the request for a credit line did not fit the company's credit policy or the company's monthly financial requirements).

Moderate Credit Policy (Middle-of-the-Road)

This policy mixes good accounts, average accounts, and some accounts that are consistently slow to 30 days. It is a more conventional mix of credit risks than the conservative or the liberal approach to credit. The small company's money is at a somewhat greater risk than the money of a company selling only to accounts that are well established and pay within terms. It is, however, a much safer footing than the creditor whose liberal policy easily could become reckless. Some bank support usually is combined with monthly receivables collections to provide an adequate flow of cash. Financial strength might be more shallow than companies that practice a restrictive policy, a fact that translates into a pattern of payable payments which rarely include the discounting of invoices. Some of these customers take the higher percentage discounts and let the accounts of other suppliers drift from a few days past due to 20 or 30 days. Suppliers who have this experience with an otherwise strong customer dislike the earlier payment of these accounts but are not concerned with the level of past-due aging. It only becomes a major concern when the monthly payment response becomes less and less prompt. (Example: A potential customer who has been in business for several years, who has established a good reputation in the trade, who has been growth oriented, and who has paid trade accounts consistently between prompt and 30 days slow (past due) has asked a small manufacturer for a credit line. No unusual risk is involved. Profit and loss statements and the applicant's bank indicate that the business is well managed and profitable. Because profits are being put back into the business, suppliers are not paid within sales terms. The small manufacturer has adequate cash flow and financing to support the company's credit policy (moderate) and the prospective customer meets the criteria for the requested credit line. The manufacturer goes into the relationship knowing that the customer payments will not be within terms, and that is acceptable).

The Liberal Credit Policy

This policy is much more dangerous than the other two because it forces the credit manager to walk a decision-making tightrope over a pit filled with the bones of companies who were once high fliers. These bones represent companies so eager to move forward that they propelled themselves well beyond the point of sound business judgment before they stopped, realized where they were, then went straight into the pit with other Chapter XI victims. A liberal credit policy can be—or can become—a high-risk policy. Risks are high, the loss of receivables dollars can be heavy, and the danger to company survival can be very real. When a company that has a liberal credit policy loses a major customer to business failure, it can be a catastrophe for the creditor. Unlike the preceding two credit policies, many of these creditor companies are big risk takers in every area of their operation. They expand much too rapidly for the size and worth of the company. Rapid growth too often dictates accepting accounts unworthy of the credit line they receive. These liberal credit grantors are not companies who can afford any combination of major losses and slow-turning receivables.

A liberal credit policy too often gives a company both of the above problems plus undercapitalization and sporadic cash flow, two other negatives that plague many companies who promote their liberal credit policy. When the delicate balance is working, these companies can project an exciting image of success. When the apparent success begins to unravel, major crisis follows major crisis until the company collapses under the weight of its own uncontrolled, unrealistic drive for big success. Occasionally, a company can walk multiple tightropes and succeed—a liberal credit policy, a high-profit product line that finds an instant market, and high enough bank balances to support runaway growth. It's a rare company that can overcome the multiple problems of uncontrolled growth just as it is a rare credit manager/owner who can handle the pressures of constantly performing on a tightrope. (Example: The small company in this example is interested in rapid growth. The owner has not bothered to evaluate whether the company can afford to take the risks in accounts receivable that cover a spectrum of payment records that range from good thru slow 60 to 75 days. A credit applicant who has been in business for three years and who's profitabliity is borderline, applies for a substantial credit line. The aggressive, chance-taking manufacturer is focusing first on sales growth and second on quality of the accounts. Although other suppliers report that this applicant pays 40 to 60 days slow (past due), and often pays only after one or more reminder calls, the manufacturer accepts the account. This illustration is an example of a liberal credit policy extended to the point where it has become liberal/foolish).

At the end of this chapter (FIG. 3-1) I have included a sample company credit policy. It is concise, covers all relevant areas, and should be helpful when you tailor one to your own company. Remember, however, that you should shape any credit policy to conform to the requirements and goals of your company. A company with a moderate or middle-of-the-road policy toward credit sales would structure their credit policy similar to the sample policy. Add nuances peculiar to your company to bring our sample credit policy into line with your company's requirements.

GOOD CREDIT DECISIONS

Every person who makes credit decisions, whether the owner of the business, a partner, or a designated employee, goes through a period of basic training. The scope of the credit manager's decision-making knowledge depends only upon the types of decisions the owner or designated manager must make. Some people are fortunate in that they learn the decision-making basics from an experienced credit manager. Others do it on their own—reading, practicing, and learning as they go. They approach each new level and area of risk with a level of respect appropriate for the new elements of danger. Either route works if the person who is learning credit management is conscientious in his or her approach to the challenge.

The goal in any credit management environment is the same. The company owner who handles credit matters wants to learn how to gather and evaluate the data necessary to make quality credit decisions. He also wants to go through the learning process at a minimum cost of time, confidence, and the company's receivable dollars. Be neither defensive nor aggressive toward decisions and decision making. Be guardedly confident as you move through the various stages of the learning process. A guarded level of confidence should impose levels of restraint compatible with what you should use in the daily process of credit management. When one of your decisions becomes a loser, convert it into a long-term winner for you and your company by analyzing what happened. Was there something you should have seen early in the account's trip across your aging report? Did it become a trouble account so fast that you had no warning? Did on-account payments continue almost to the week in which you received the notice of a Chapter XI filing? Were other and more experienced credit manager's caught for as much or more than the amount owed to your company? Be realistic, my friend. If your relatively limited credit management experience puts your company in a position with a debtor that is no worse than most of the other suppliers, there is no basis for suggesting that you did not do a decent job in judging the account. If you are caught with many more outstanding receivable dollars than the debtor's other suppliers, then it might be time to review your procedures for assigning credit lines to new accounts, for monitoring your receivables balances, and for approving orders to active accounts. An owner who does no worse than the experienced professionals at bigger companies—particularly those managers who are operating within a comparable credit policy—has reason to be encouraged. The key to successfully managing your credit accounts is to avoid being sandbagged a second time from the same direction. Learn from every experience and you will minimize your losses.

CREDIT PROCEDURES

Do not confuse credit policy with credit procedures. *Credit policy* is the basis or criteria for determining which types of credit accounts offer a manufacturer and/or distributor the mix of financial and business strengths that are compatible with the company's credit policy—restrictive, moderate, or liberal. Other factors might enter into a decision to accept or reject a prospective customer's application for a credit line—a good customer already in the applicant's sales and service area, or a questionable reputation among trade members. Your company should write a good credit policy in such a way that it tells you and your employee what your credit department should do, not how you should do it.

Credit procedures are an adult version of show-and-tell. They show you the tools (forms, letters, and reports) that are necessary to do a good job, and they tell you the proper sequence for using the forms and letters needed to gather and evaluate information from the applicant's bank and suppliers (see Chapter 5: Useful Tools for Gathering Necessary Information). These tools are the credit department's internal guidelines for doing the total job of credit management. Good credit procedures eliminate many of the elements that lead to costly mistakes)—elements associated with a nonroutine, haphazard approach to decision making. Your company does not need the extra risks that you can expect when there are no effective procedures—no step-by-step building of a case for or against the granting of an applicant's request for a credit line. Good credit procedures involve a conscious effort to repeat successful and sequential procedures until the person who handles credit decisions is immediately aware when any step in the process is missing or incomplete. Procedures should interface comfortably with your company's credit policy and should result in a contribution to the company's goals as stated in the credit policy.

Can a credit department be effective with a policy and no procedures—or procedures and no policy? A small company's credit decisions, whether made by the owner or an employee, are as vulnerable as those made by a professional at a larger company. Would you operate your car for more than a few blocks if it had small emergency-type tires and rims on the left front and right rear wheels and standard-sized rims and tires on the right front and left rear wheels? This tire design would result in a lopsided ride. Suppose you add 100 bone-jarring miles every morning and evening over unpaved, poorly maintained roads, at 65 or 70 miles an hour. You would be unable to keep up with other vehicles and your car would develop serious structural and engine problems.

Your credit department needs the disciplined approach to credit management that a good sequential approach will give you. Safe shortcuts are not available. You cannot eliminate one or two of the fact-gathering or fact-evaluation steps and still expect to arrive at a good decision. Do it the sensible way; administer your credit accounts by plan, not by chance.

Following are two examples of planned, sequential procedures. The first gives you the step-by-step method for obtaining credit information from an applicant, how you should evaluate the information, and when you should assign the credit line (or approve a first order):

☐ Send the prospective customer a New Account Information Form and include a self-addressed, stamped, return envelope.

☐ Attach the New Account Information Form to a cover letter (FIGS. 5-4, 5-5, 5-6, 5-7) and ask for a current financial statement.

☐ Contact credit references (from data on the New Account Information Form) by telephone or letter (FIG. 5-1).

☐ Enter information gathered from the applicant's references (suppliers and banker) onthe Credit Investigation Form (FIG. 5-10).

☐ Consolidate and refine the information as indicated on the Account Information Sheet (FIG. 5-1).

☐ Compare the dollar total of the applicant's pending first order or requested credit line with the experience of the suppliers, banker, and financial statement information. If suppliers and banker experience continues to be good, is at-or-above the high credit you are being asked to carry, then the account should qualify for the requested credit line. If the accumulated data indicates a slow-pay account with trade payments becoming increasingly slower, the account could be sliding into serious trouble. You should not sell this account on credit terms.

☐ Send the customer a letter stating that you have approved a cedit line for the requested or a lower amount. If the amount is lower than requested, your explanation should not reflect unfavorably on the new customer. Cite the fact that your company is a grantor of minimum credit amounts until you have accumulated more experience with their company. Mention that you feel sure the customer's company is equally prudent in its approach to credit matters; express your appreciation for the opportunity to be of service; and close with the statement that you are available to help if there is ever a problem—in your area or another area.

The second example moves forward to the point when account balances have been appearing on the Accounts Receivable Aged Trial Balance Report for several weeks. The oldest open balance has now moved into the first past-due column (1 to 30 days), and at 10 days past due, you begin the following collection sequence:

☐ Make the first reminder telephone call to the accounts payable person who handles your account.

☐ If there is no payment response, make a second call to the same person seven to ten days after the first call. Get a firm payment commitment (check to be released the day you call, the day after you call, on Friday of that week, or some specific near-term date).

☐ When the account is 20 to 30 days past due, confirm that the person who processes your invoices has written the check or has forwarded payment data to the data-processing department for the weekly or twice-monthly writing of checks. If he/she has done that, or has taken the next step of contacting the controller and has been told that the check is being held for a few days, ask to talk with the controller. Make your case for a prompt release of the check; nail it down to a specific release date (within seven days of your call). You also might tell the controller that you will be unable to ship his (or her) company any products until they have paid the past-due balance (state the amount).

☐ If the check does not arrive within two or three days after the promised date, notify the company by letter (attention of the controller with a copy to the purchasing manager) that you will be unable to favorably consider offering credit terms on future orders if the past-due balance is not paid within 10 days of the date of your letter.

☐ If there is no response and no satisfactory explanation, decide what final action you must take. You can assign the account for third-party collection (to a collection agency or an attorney who specializes in collection matters), or if the balance is less than $1500, you can sue for a judgment in a Small Claims Court. At this point, there is no interest in again selling the account on credit terms. Your only concern is to collect your company's money and move on to other better customer relationships.

Credit policy and credit procedures are blood relatives in the context of interlocking guideline material for every owner of a small company who wants the best and most effective credit department for his or her company. It is a very attainable goal, a goal that will keep accounts receivable dollars out of the bad-debt account and put them where they belong—in the profit figure on your financial statement.

SAMPLE CREDIT POLICY

The XYZ Company is committed to a growth pattern that is moderate in terms of our industry's standards. We do not seek to take unnecessary or unusual financial risks. Nor do we wish to promote growth at levels beyond our financial capabilities; beyond the capabilities of our present plant facility, or beyond our ability to add good, productive people. Our company is dedicated to a pattern of solid, steady growth, and to a company policy that incorporates the highest standards of personal and business ethics in our relationships with fellow employees, all segments of the general public, our customers and our suppliers.

It is our commitment to manufacture products of the highest quality for the targeted market level and to act responsibly and positively in our relationships with other members of our industry. We do not intend to become a major player in our industry, but it is our goal to make the XYZ Company a positive factor in how the comsumer perceives our industry. In a phrase, we are not a "fastbuck" company. We are in business for the long haul and we expect this attitude to guide and motivate the actions of employees interaction with each other, in their contacts with the public, and in every decision-making and production area of our company.

The following guidelines will help the Credit Department to channel its efforts toward making an appropriate contribution:

☐ Credit terms should not be offered to accounts that do not meet the criteria for a low-risk receivables base.

☐ Account evaluation procedures shall be geared to an annual bad debt loss (percentage of sales) that is not in excess of the average for our industry.

☐ The credit manager's decisions regarding any sales or credit line situation may be reviewed by the Treasurer (or VP of Finance) if requested to do so by the Sales Manager (or VP of Sales).

☐ The credit department shall work effectively with all departments and levels of company management to ensure a continuity of company objectives.

☐ Any question that the credit manager might have regarding the application of this credit policy to a specific account is to be discussed with the Treasurer.

☐ Credit policy will be reviewed periodically by senior management to ensure that the company's goals remain unchanged as they impact the credit department.

☐ Credit department personnel should, whenever possible, be a positive force in our effort to build strong customer loyalties and relationships.

☐ The Credit Department shall expedite the processing of credit decisions, within the context of an appropriate input of necessary data and an appropriate time frame in which to evaluate that data.

The Treasurer (or VP of Finance) will monitor the effectiveness of methods used by the credit department to achieve its' goals.

_____   _____

       (date)   (title)

Chapter 4

Some Terms and Conditions for Sales

AT MANY SMALL COMPANIES, THE OWNER MANAGES SALES AND CREDIT. IT ISN'T THE type of arrangement that I encourage but if you are the only one who is qualified for either job, then you should manage both. Balancing both responsibilities is delicate—too delicate for some owners to handle successfully—but most manage somehow to effectively present their products to purchasing managers while still maintaining credit standards that are in harmony with the company's credit policy.

The terms and conditions that apply to many sales are not always the preferred choice of the manufacturer or the buyer. Once again, it is "industry practice" that puts a paternal hand on the actions of individual industry members. Just as it casts a long shadow in making credit sales mandatory for almost all commercial transactions, so it is the primary force for determining which of many sales terms you should consider "industry standards."

You can identify some sales terms more closely with one industry than with others. Suppliers of food and beverage items sell their products on very short terms—usually Cash when the account is not known or is known to be a high risk, Net 10 Days (from date of invoice) when the account is thought to be a normal risk, and an additional 10 or 15 days if the company is big, a volume buyer, and a prompt payer. Floor-covering manufacturers and distributors offer a wider variety of terms including *C.O.D.* (Cash on Delivery) when the account is unknown or known to be a poor risk, Net 30 or Net 45 Days if you do not offer a discount but the customer qualifies for "standard terms", and either 2 percent 10 Days/Net 30 or 2 percent 10th Prox/Net 30 when the manufacturer or distributor offers a discount. Buyers in the dry goods and ready-to-wear lines are often the beneficiaries of long dating or seasonal dating. It is the practice in the garment industry for terms to run 60 days to several months. The buyer also enjoys the dual benefits of buying merchandise at an early, fixed price and being able to take delivery months before payment is due. Many other manufacturers and distributors offer some discount incentive with payment due on terms consistent with industry practice. These terms are not inflexible. A company can be as creative as a particular sale or relationship dictates just as long as the terms do not give preferential treatment to one customer over others in a particular category of sales. (See Robinson-Patman Act discussed later in this chapter.)

If you are not currently offering your customers a discount, should you? Do others in your industry offer discounts? Have you ever questioned whether a discount does or does not give them a competitive edge? Discounts in the various industries can vary from ½ percent through 5 percent, but the motivation for offering a discount is not because the owner has nothing better to do with the company's money. The owner offers a discount in the hope that a large enough number of customers will pay early (discount their invoices) to make the program worthwhile. If a small percentage of customers discount their invoices and that small percentage is confined to accounts that buy small quantities, the discount program is not a success. The only way a discount program works for a company is when several of its volume customers discount their invoices. When that happens, the program should generate substantial earlier amounts of cash at a cost of whatever the discount rate is for the gross total of the discounted invoices (less sales tax).

Industry practice, the profit margin on your product(s), and the urgency of your company's need for a rapid turnover of receivables will influence your decision regarding discounts. Another major consideration when considering a discount program is the profit margin on your product(s). If the profit margin is so narrow that a 2 percent discount (or more) would decrease an already slim margin to an unacceptable level, then you must weigh very carefully the potential benefits of faster-turning receivables over a lower margin of profit. Do your products deliver a profit margin that poses no problem? Then you can look at the questions of industry practice, competitive advantage, and the potential for accelerating receivables-generated cash flow.

SALES TERMS

Following are some of the more commonly used sales terms. The terms we have listed vary from across-the-board usage in many industries to others that have a much narrower application. If you are in an industry that offers discounts or where some companies offer a discount, two or three sales terms should be regarded as industry standards. Sort out your industry and company options, then go with what your knowledge of your industry, your customers, and your company tell you should be most effective.

☐ *Cash*—synonymous with personal check, certified check, cashier's check, bank money order, post office money order, or other money order.

☐ *C.W.O.*—Cash With Order. Many of the previously-listed cash payment options also are acceptable here.

☐ *C.B.D.*—Cash Before Delivery. You may modify this sales term to a specific percentage of the total amount of the order. The time frame in which one or more of these C.B.D. payments is due depends upon the specific agreement between buyer and seller (Example: the seller might insist that payment, if it is to be in the form of a check, must be in the seller's hands a minimum of 10 days before delivery (or release) of the goods. This early receipt will enable the seller to deposit the check and allow time for it to clear before they release the product.

☐ *C.O.D.*—Cash On Delivery. This term is not a particularly popular sales term with most companies. You should use it only if the customer is not credit worthy at the level of the order or if you have not received and processed credit information. Some customers prefer to pay on C.O.D. terms, however, this practice is rare. Remember the risks involved in accepting company or personal checks. Remember also that if the customer refuses to accept the merchandise on C.O.D. terms (even after agreeing to do so), you might have to pay two-way shipping charges. Get your shipping costs up front or be sure the customer knows that you will be sending the shipment C.O.D. Also make sure he is willing to accept it on those terms, that he knows whether a company or personal check will or will not be acceptable, and that he knows the dollar amount of the shipment and the date on which you intend to ship the product(s). (The shipping date is particularly important if the customer must pay for the shipment with a cashier's check or money order).

☐ 2 percent 10 Days/Net 30—This sales term offers a 2 percent discount if your customer pays the invoice within 10 days from the invoice date. Net 30 Days means that the customer has 30 days from the date of the invoice to pay the total amount.

☐ Net 30 Days—This term is about as bare bones as terms can get. The supplier does not offer a discount and the customer has 30 days from the invoice date to pay the invoice total.

☐ E.O.M.—End of Month. Payment is due by the end of the month following the month in which the buyer purchases the merchandise. The supplier does not offer a discount if the sales term is stated in this language. The seller might, however, link this term with a discount if he so desires.

☐ 2 percent 10th Prox/Net 30—The seller offers a 2 percent discount if the invoice is paid by the 10th of the month following the month in which purchase(s) is made. If the discount is not taken within this time frame, the full amount of the invoice becomes payable prior to the last day of the month following the month in which the buyer purchased the product.

☐ R.O.G.—Receipt of Goods. This term is a different approach to defining the point when the discount period starts. In other sales terms, you calculate the discount period from the date of the invoice. When R.O.G. becomes a part of the sales term, the discount period does not begin until the customer has received the merchandise. Depending upon the distance between seller and buyer, and the direct or indirect nature of freight service, the buyer could gain several days with R.O.G. over date of invoice.

Sales terms are available that require a minimum of part cash with the order before any action is taken to process the order. Suppliers use this term especially if they must manufacture, process, or package the product or item in a manner that would make it unsalable to another customer. Often such an order involves additional expense such as purchasing special ingredients and/or packaging materials, rearranging production schedules, and straining warehousing capabilities. It also might involve a certain amount of in-house research and development and levels of quality control that impact, or could impact, the scheduling of other products. Under conditions that commit time, money, and effort to a custom product, a minimum payment of 50 percent with the order is realistic if that figure is high enough to cover your manufacturing costs. You will receive the remaining 40 percent when you deliver the order, or if there is enough latitude between production costs and the customer's cost, the manufacturer or processor might require a payment of 25 percent of the order total when they deliver the order and the final 25 percent within 30 days of the delivery date or the invoice date.

If a customer wishes to place an order with your sales manager or sales department but your standard terms (Net 30 Days, etc.) are a tighter time frame than the customer can handle, a discussion between key company personnel must ensue. When any two people in your company are involved in a discussion leading to a decision involving anything relating to a substantial amount of money or product (for your company), the final decision should be in writing. In this instance, the person who has sales responsibility should complete the Request For Special Terms form (FIG. 4-1), go over the acceptable

REQUEST FOR SPECIAL TERMS

Date: _____

To Be Completed By Sales:

Customer Name: _____

Customer's Address _____

_____

Terms Requested: _____

On (P.O. or Invoice Number): _____

Reason: _____

_____

_____

Requested by: _____

- -

To Be Completed By Credit Department:

Date Account Opened: _____

Financial Statement (Date): _____

D & B Rating: _____

Payment History With This Company: _____

_____

Comments And Recommendation: _____

_____

_____

Approved: _____ ____   Approved: _____ ____
          Sales Manager   Date   Credit Manager Date

Comments: _____

FIG. 4-1.

payment options with you (the owner), then relay that information to the customer or prospective customer. The customer's request was put on paper, there was a discussion regarding terms, and you and the sales manager arrived at special terms that fit the customer's needs. The decision is on paper, the Request For Special Terms form is filed in the customer's file folder, and there can never be any question regarding the circumstances that prompted the decision. This example shows a procedure used properly, used at the right time, and used under the right circumstances.

REVOLVING LETTER OF ASSIGNMENT

The Revolving Letter of Assignment can be described best as the domestic version of an International Letter of Credit. It involves a written agreement (initiated by the supplier) between the customer, the customer's bank, and the supplier whereby the supplier submits invoices for material or products to the customer's bank for payment. The bank pays invoices against the customer's credit line for the period of months and maximum dollar amount specified in the assignment letter. If the Revolving Letter of Assignment is for $100,000, the dollar value of unpaid invoices should never exceed that figure. As the bank pays invoices, that amount is again freed for use under the agreement—hence the term Revolving Letter of Credit. The supplier is able to sell a customer who might be difficult or impossible to carry under other conditions. The customer is able to purchase the supplier's goods—perhaps a particular type or brand of goods specified by an architect for a development of expensive oceanside condominiums—under material release and payment conditions not acceptable to the supplier under any other form of secured position. A unique situation often calls for an equally unique or innovative solution. Although it is used infrequently, the Revolving Letter of Assignment can be a very effective way to save a good piece of business.

A word of caution: Do not let yourself get involved in an ongoing control situation of this type unless you have the background and experience to properly handle it. The banker monitors the dollar amount of unpaid billings in his office at any given time vs. the dollar amount stated in the Assignment. He is taking care of his bank's position only, not yours. You must know at all times the dollar value of invoices submitted and unpaid and the amount of credit still available between the total unpaid invoices and the credit line figure in the Assignment. Closely monitoring the status of this type of arrangement is your responsibility—a responsibility that you must handle with care to ensure a satisfactory, profitable experience for your company.

IRREVOCABLE LETTER OF CREDIT

The Irrevocable Letter of Credit represents the issuing bank's guarantee of payment for goods shipped to a buyer in a foreign country, subject to the supplier or the supplier's representative (an international freight forwarder, etc.) complying with terms and conditions as specified in the Irrevocable Letter of Credit. Payment should not involve any unanticipated delay if you present the credit and required support documents for payment prior to the credit's expiry date. Any attempt by one or more of the parties to amend the original credit is an action that should be taken prior to shipping the goods and will not be binding unless there is unanimous agreement to the change(s).

The supplier and/or the supplier's representative must prepare many documents prior to delivery of the goods at the dock or airport for shipment to the foreign buyer. The documents include insurance documents, certificate(s) of origin, consular invoices, commercial invoices, specific documents that include the type and quantity of goods you are shipping, the name of the vessel (or air freight carrier and flight number) on which the goods are loaded and shipped, the port and date from which the vessel will depart, and some additional details and data. The entire package—shipment of the goods by a specific date and presentation of the Credit and documents required for payment—must be accomplished within the time frame of the credit's effective date and its date of expiry. An extension of the expiry date might be possible depending upon the circumstances and the importance of the goods arriving in the foreign country by the specified delivery date. The shipper can request an extension of the expiry date and it could be granted unless it is a key consideration of the agreement that you must make delivery by the specified date to preserve the integrity of other contractual arrangements. If you find yourself in a situation where an Irrevocable Letter of Credit is the only way to go, be very sure to abide by all of the terms, directions, and guidelines contained in the document. If you aren't experienced in this area, get help from your banker or a bonded, experienced, international freight forwarding firm with offices and agents in all the principal cities and areas of the world.

REVOCABLE LETTER OF CREDIT

I can think of no persuasive reason for a supplier to sell goods to an overseas buyer if the offered payment is in the form of a Revocable Letter of Credit. The seller has no leverage. All of the control, including control over the seller's goods and the right to revoke the Letter of Credit, rests with the buyer. If your company made such a sale, you virtually would be in the same position as if you had made an open account sale to a customer you probably know very little about, in a country whose laws generally make it very difficult for a foreign supplier to collect a debt. Your product(s) could be in a foreign country, already unloaded and delivered to the customer, and you would have no protection against the customer instructing their bank to revoke the Letter of Credit. Certain conditions might make it possible for your company to receive payment before the *issuing bank* (the bank that issued the Revocable Letter of Credit) had time to notify branch banks and other banks that the Credit had been revoked, but you would not want your company's money to be riding on such a remote chance.

Never allow your company to become involved in any payment(s) situation that dangles the word "revocable" unless you—or you and your attorney—have assured yourselves that it is not an agreement that could be yanked out from under your payment expectations. And never, **never** go into a transaction that calls for a Letter of Credit if the words Letter of Credit do not have the magic prefix—Irrevocable.

QUANTITY DISCOUNTS

The criteria for granting a quantity discount to one of your customers is simple but requires close attention to the circumstances of the sale. The practice of allowing a quantity discount has never led to serious problems in the courts (charges of unfair trade practices, restraint of trade, etc.) when you can show that you have applied this discount in such a manner and in specific situations that reflect an "actual cost saving to the seller." If that seemingly simple criteria cannot be met, or is not met, then such discounts could be a violation of the Robinson-Patman Act. To be unlawful under the Act, the effect would have to substantially decrease in interstate commerce, regardless of whether any competitive damage or harm could be shown. The act of offering a discount or discounts that do not reflect direct cost saving to the seller—your company—is the violation, not whether competitors of the customer who bought from you on quantity discount terms were harmed or damaged. It doesn't matter that you are a small player in your industry. You might inadvertently be in violation of the Act if you aren't wary of special terms and arrangement.

The Robinson-Patman Act

The Robinson-Patman Act is a long and complicated piece of legislation—a delight for attorneys and a horror for most litigants. It is designed to protect individual competitors against the unfair or discriminatory trade practices of other competitors. It's goal is the protection of small businesses against their larger competitors, to preserve competition generally, and to prevent practices of a discriminatory nature that might have an adverse effect on the free enterprise system of competition. The owner of a small company is responsible directly for the sales policies over which Robinson-Patman casts a watchful eye. Every owner should know how the Act relates to the marketing and sales policies of his or her company, and know how Robinson-Patman reaches out to protect companies that might become the victims of unfair practices.

PROMOTIONAL DISCOUNTS

Promotional discounts are a form of discount used primarily to introduce a new product, to try to increase sales of existing products, to reduce the inventory level of a particular product or products, and to motivate customers to buy an extra order or increase the size of a regular order to a level where it will qualify for the discount. Many companies use this tactic if their product(s) have seasonal peaks and valleys. A promotional incentive is another calculated risk that must deliver a higher level of orders from customers who don't usually buy at that level. If the only result is to motivate volume buyers to put a large supply of discounted product(s) in their warehouse, and reduce the size of the next few orders until they have sold the discounted product, then the promotion has failed to deliver the desired results.

When problems—particularly those of communication—occur during the course of a promotion, the person who is the credit manager (owner or designated employee) will be spending too much extra time responding to the oral and written questions of customers. At this point the owner or designated employee must adjust his or her customer relations hat and move into damage control before it becomes a more serious problem.

Example: I became involved in the fallout from one promotion while doing in-house consulting for a small-business client. The problem surfaced when customer payments began arriving that the credit department could not reconcile with referenced invoices. Not until someone in the office remembered seeing a letter sent out by the owner that announced an additional discount of 3 percent for a period of 90 days on a specific product, did I begin to understand the problem. Telephone calls to several accounts quickly confirmed that many customers were participating in the program, many were taking normal discounts PLUS the additional 3 percent, and many were forwarding checks for these net amounts. Good? Not really. The promotional discount was not supposed to work that way.

The crux of the problem was the owner's original letter to customers and prospective customers in which he outlined the requirements for qualifying for the promotional discount. He had failed to clearly state that he would apply the promotional discount—the additional 3 percent—in the form of a customer credit to respective customer accounts, based upon the total amount of promotional discounts earned during the 90 days of the promotion. Customers had no problem accepting the offer of an additional 3 percent discount. The problem took shape because the owner left the matter of computing the discount to the company's customers. (See FIGS. 4-2, 4-3, 4-4)

The owner's failure to clearly define the guidelines by which his company would compute promotional discounts generated a small mountain of extra paper work. His company had to send letters of explanation, credit memorandums, and/or invoices to

August 10, 1988

Henry Parnell
The Parnell Company
5631 Barnhart Avenue
Roanoke, VA 24014

Dear Mr. Parnell:

You will want to compare the attached application of payments against the notations that were on The Parnell Company's checks 1261 and 1262.

A second 3% discount was deducted from certain of the invoices listed on your checks. Because it was not an applicable deduction (only one 3% discount is allowed), it was necessary to adjust the amount of money applied and change the mix of invoices involved.

We hope the attached detail sheet will allow you to adjust your records to coincide with ours, and that it does not impose an unreasonable burden.

Sincerely,

Cecil Bond
Credit Department

FIG. 4-2.

August 17, 1988

Henry Parnell
The Parnell Company
5631 Barnhart Avenue
Roanoke, Virginia 24014

Dear Mr. Parnell:

Many thanks for your call. After our conversation this forenoon,
I reviewed the problem with Ed Wilson, the company's sales
manager.

Ed's May 8th letter to our dealers did indeed state that an
additional promotional credit of three percent (3%) could be
earned on net invoices on all purchases above stated figures
during the period April 1 through July 31, 1988. The Parnell
Company's base figure upon which the promotional credit could
be built was $131,418.00

Unfortunately, Mr. Wilson inadvertently omitted from the May 8th
letter the information that our company will prepare credits
for each dealer account. Sales figures for the subject period
will be the basis for determining credit amounts and should
pose no computation or reconciliation problem for our dealers.

The inconvenience is regrettable but we must ask you to continue
to pay invoices in the normal manner, applying the promotional
credit only after the specific figure has been received from
us.

Sincerely,

Cecil Bond
Credit Department

FIG. 4-3.

August 25, 1988

Cecil Bond
Credit Department
Ziegler & Company
5932 College Avenue
Santa Clara, California 95131

Dear Mr. Bond:

Thank you for your two recent letters. I have taken your
letter of August 17 to heart and will proceed to pay invoices
taking only my 3%. I place my additional 3% in your capable
hands. How's that for blind faith?

Enclosed please find check for invoice 4891, less 3%. I
understand that our most recent shipment has been found in
the wilds of North Carolina, so you will have more checks in
the near future.

It is very reassuring to know that Ziegler & Company has a
competent credit department working for its' business success,
and your distributors' success too.

Sincerely,

Henry Parnell
President

FIG. 4-4.

customers correcting the amount of discounts taken by the customers. Eventually, a letter followed prepared for the owner's signature, that was both an apology for the ambiguity of the original letter and a restatement of the promotion. The fact that the offer should not have generated such complications became lost in the flurry of extra letters, telephone calls, and related work that diverted the time and attention of a four-person office staff. The confusion generated because of the absence of a key piece of payment information diminished some of the positive aspects of the promotion, especially for those customers who had thought they were abiding by the guidelines only to find themselves adjusting payment records, paying more money, or waiting for the credit or invoice to adjust their records.

Whether you handle sales or credit, you must be sure that any correspondence is well constructed. It must not develop into a similiar situation as I described in the example. Credit is squarely in the middle of any confusion that results from any mass-mailed, special sales offer that invites extensive misinterpretation. Save yourself and your company the aggravation of having to cope with problems that are avoidable.

CONDITIONS OF SALE—PROTECTIVE FILINGS

Manufacturers and distributors frequently protect their interest in products, merchandise, or construction materials with a Uniform Commercial Code filing (UCC) or a filing under the Mechanic's and Materialmen's Lien Laws. A *perfected filing* under the UCC (a filing properly prepared, notarized, and filed with the appropriate state jurisdiction) can, in a bankruptcy situation, be for secured creditors the difference between getting most of their money or being with the great mass of general or unsecured creditors, and getting little or nothing. The pages that follow explain the purpose of the UCC and the Lien Laws, how they differ, and why you should not hesitate to use one or the other to ensure an appropriate level of protection.

Priority Tax Liens

Any supplier or creditor who perfects a properly prepared Uniform Commercial Code interest in goods or merchandise will collect his or her company's money ahead of government agencies, if the company's security interest was perfected before the federal government filed its tax lien. The person or company who perfects a security interest (UCC, Mechanic's Lien, Judgment Creditor or Purchaser) has priority over the federal tax lien.

Uniform Commercial Code Filings (UCC)

The UCC has for a varying number of years been in effect in every one of the 50 states. Although the various state legislatures did their best to put a personal imprint on the resulting legislation—thereby somewhat diluting the original concept of a "uniform code" among the 50 states—it is much more effective than were previous controls. Suppliers are now able to protect their intra- or interstate interests in goods via a Purchase Money Security Agreement with a subsequent UCC-1 filing (FIG. 4-6). This procedure not only gives the company or individual a security interest in their goods until they have received payment and cancelled the filing, but it also gives protection for an appropriate dollar interest in the proceeds from the sale of those goods. Another comfort for the manufacturer's or distributor's owner/credit manager is the knowledge that merchandise shipped after the first order—goods identified by the term *after-acquired merchandise*—is covered by one (the original), properly perfected, UCC filing.

Each of the 50 states has its own UCC forms. To ensure that your filing is in compliance with the statutes of a particular state, request a set of the appropriate filing forms from the office of the secretary of state in which the filing is to be made. Also, be aware that filing locations and jurisdictions vary from one state to another, and from one type of collateral to another. Information relevant to a proper UCC filing in each of the 50 states is available in a current edition of the National Association of Credit Management's Credit Manual of Commercial Laws. (California's forms are used here to illustrate. All references to specific time frames pertain only to California's UCC statutes.)

☐ Information Request (FIG. 4-5): A form sent to the filing officer requesting copies of any currently effective financing statements which name your customer as the debtor. (Very important for you to know how many suppliers would have an earlier or prior claim over yours). The form requests names and addresses of the secured parties, file number, date and hour of the filing.

☐ Security Interest (not a form): The secured party can protect his or her Security Interest by taking possession of the collateral or filing notice that he or she has a Security Interest in the property covered by the Security Agreement with the appropriate filing officer. This protection is secured by filing a Financing Statement.

☐ Financing Statement (FIG. 4-6): A Security Interest is protected against the claims of third parties when the secured party takes possession of the collateral or files notice with the appropriate filing officer that he or she has a Security Interest in the property or goods covered by the Financing Statement. A Financing Statement might or might not state a maturity date. If the maturity date of the secured transaction is less than five years, the filing will remain effective for 60 days after the maturity date. If the filing has no stated maturity date, it is good for five years from the date of filing.

☐ Financing Statement Change (FIG. 4-7): The Financing Statement Change is a multi-purpose form covering any one of the following: continuation of the original Financing Statement between a debtor and secured party (file number and date); release by secured party of the collateral covered by an earlier filing and described in another section of the form; assignment of the secured party's rights to an assignee named in an earlier section of this form and including original Financing Statement file number and a description on this form of the collateral; termination of the security interest in a named Financing Statement, including the file number; amendment to a Financing Statement bearing a stated file number and setting forth the terms of the amended Financing Statement.

The Uniform Commercial Code is a complex and lengthy piece of legislation and, as stated previously, it differs in varying degrees throughout the 50 states. Unless you have had experience in the preparation and perfecting of UCC filings, have your attorney go over the completed forms before you forward the package to the appropriate filing authority. Don't assume that you have met the criteria for a perfected UCC filing in a specific state if you are not qualified to properly interpret the statutes (UCC and other) of that state. How bad can the penalty be for your company if the UCC filing is flawed? For openers, a creditor who secured his/her company's position after yours can challenge your imperfect filing. The bottom drops out of your company's position if the referee in bankruptcy rules that yours is not a perfect filing. From what should have been a perfect filing (all required information correctly stated and placed, and a provable Security Interest), your company joins the unsecured creditors—the absolute depths of the pit as it relates to your chances for salvaging meaningful receivables dollars. (See FIG. 4-8)

REQUEST FOR INFORMATION OR COPIES. Present in Duplicate to Filing Officer

1. ☐ INFORMATION REQUEST. Filing officer please furnish certificate showing whether there is on file any presently effective financing statement naming the Debtor listed below and any statement of assignment thereof, and if there is, giving the date and hour of filing of each such statement and the names and addresses of each secured party named therein.

1A. DEBTOR (LAST NAME FIRST)		1B. SOC. SEC. OR FED. TAX NO.
1C. MAILING ADDRESS	1D. CITY, STATE	1E. ZIP CODE

1F.

Date_____19____ Signature of Requesting Party_____

2. CERTIFICATE:

FILE NUMBER	DATE AND HOUR OF FILING	NAME(S) AND ADDRESS(ES) OF SECURED PARTY(IES) AND ASSIGNEE(S), IF ANY

The undersigned filing officer hereby certifies that the above listing is a record of all presently effective financing statements and statements of assignment which name the above debtor and which are on file in my office of _____19____at_____ ___M.

_____19_____
(DATE)

_____
(FILING OFFICER)

By:_____

3. ☐ COPY REQUEST. Filing officer please furnish_____copy(ies) of each page of the following statements concerning the debtors listed below ☐ Financing Statement ☐ Amendments ☐ Statements of Assignment ☐ Continuation Statements ☐ Statement of Release ☐ Termination Statement ☐ All Statements on file.

FILE NUMBER	DATE OF FILING	NAME(S) AND MAILING ADDRESS(ES) OF DEBTOR(S)	DEBTORS SOC. SEC. OR FED. TAX NO.

Date_____19____ Signature of Requesting Party_____

4. CERTIFICATE:

The undersigned filing officer hereby certifies that the attached copies are true and exact copies of all statements requested above.

_____19_____
(DATE)

_____
(FILING OFFICER)

By:_____

5. **Mail Information or Copies to**

NAME
MAILING
ADDRESS
CITY, STATE
AND ZIP

UNIFORM COMMERCIAL CODE-FORM UCC-3

Rediform 5S803

FIG. 4-5.

This **FINANCING STATEMENT** is presented for filing pursuant to the California Uniform Commercial Code

1. DEBTOR (LAST NAME FIRST)			1A. SOCIAL SECURITY OR FEDERAL TAX NO.
1B. MAILING ADDRESS	1C. CITY, STATE		1D. ZIP CODE
1E. RESIDENCE ADDRESS (IF AN INDIVIDUAL AND DIFFERENT THAN 1B)	1F. CITY, STATE		1G. ZIP CODE
2. ADDITIONAL DEBTOR (IF ANY) (LAST NAME FIRST)			2A. SOCIAL SECURITY OR FEDERAL TAX NO.
2B. MAILING ADDRESS	2C. CITY, STATE		2D. ZIP CODE
2E. RESIDENCE ADDRESS (IF AN INDIVIDUAL AND DIFFERENT THAN 2B)	2F. CITY, STATE		2G. ZIP CODE
3. DEBTOR(S) TRADE NAME OR STYLE (IF ANY)			3A. FEDERAL TAX NO.
4. ADDRESS OF DEBTOR(S) CHIEF PLACE OF BUSINESS (IF ANY)	4A. CITY, STATE		4B. ZIP CODE

5. SECURED PARTY
 	
   NAME
   MAILING ADDRESS
   CITY   STATE   ZIP CODE
			5A. SOCIAL SECURITY NO. FED. TAX NO. OR BANK TRANSIT AND A.B.A. NO.

6. ASSIGNEE OF SECURED PARTY (IF ANY)
 	
   NAME
   MAILING ADDRESS
   CITY   STATE   ZIP CODE
			6A. SOCIAL SECURITY NO. FED. TAX NO. OR BANK TRANSIT AND A.B.A. NO.

7. This FINANCING STATEMENT covers the following types or items of property (if crops or timber, include description of real property on which growing or to be grown.)

$ _____

8. Check ☒ If Applicable	A ☐ Proceeds of collateral are also covered	B ☐ Products of collateral are also covered	C ☐ Proceeds of above described original collateral in which a security interest was perfected	D ☐ Collateral was brought into this State subject to security interest in another jurisdiction

9.	CODE	10. This Space for Use of Filing Officer (Date, Time, File Number and Filing Officer)
(Date)_____ 19___		
	1	
	2	
By:_____ SIGNATURE(S) OF DEBTOR(S) (TITLE)	3	
	4	
	5	
By:_____ SIGNATURE(S) OF SECURED PARTY(IES) (TITLE)	6	
11 **Return Copy to**	7	
	8	
NAME ADDRESS CITY, STATE AND ZIP	9	

(1) **FILING OFFICER COPY**

STANDARD FORM— FILING FEE $3.00
APPROVED BY THE SECRETARY OF STATE   UNIFORM COMMERCIAL CODE — FORM UCC-1

Rediform 5S801
Poly Pak (50 sets) 5P801

FIG. 4-6.

This **STATEMENT** is presented for filing pursuant to the California Uniform Commercial Code

1. FILE NO. OF ORIG. FINANCING STATEMENT	1A. DATE OF FILING OF ORIG. FINANCING STATEMENT	1B. DATE OF ORIG. FINANCING STATEMENT	1C. PLACE OF FILING ORIG. FINANCING STATEMENT

2. DEBTOR (LAST NAME FIRST)		2A. SOCIAL SECURITY OR FEDERAL TAX NO.

2B. MAILING ADDRESS	2C. CITY, STATE	2D. ZIP CODE

3. ADDITIONAL DEBTOR (IF ANY) (LAST NAME FIRST)		3A. SOCIAL SECURITY OR FEDERAL TAX NO.

3B. MAILING ADDRESS	3C. CITY, STATE	3D. ZIP CODE

4. SECURED PARTY

    NAME

    MAILING ADDRESS

    CITY   STATE   ZIP CODE

4A. SOCIAL SECURITY NO. FEDERAL TAX NO. OR BANK TRANSIT AND A.B.A. NO.

5. ASSIGNEE OF SECURED PARTY (IF ANY)

    NAME

    MAILING ADDRESS

    CITY   STATE   ZIP CODE

5A. SOCIAL SECURITY NO. FEDERAL TAX NO. OR BANK TRANSIT AND A.B.A. NO.

6.

A. ☐ CONTINUATION-The original Financing Statement between the foregoing Debtor and Secured Party bearing the file number and date shown above is continued. If collateral is crops or timber, check here ☐ and insert description of real property on which growing or to be grown in Item 7 below.

B. ☐ RELEASE-From the collateral described in the Financing Statement bearing the file number shown above, the Secured Party releases the collateral described in Item 7 below.

C. ☐ ASSIGNMENT-The Secured Party certifies that the Secured Party has assigned to the Assignee above named, all the Secured Party's rights under the Financing Statement bearing the file number shown above in the collateral described in Item 7 below.

D. ☐ TERMINATION - The Secured Party certifies that the Secured Party no longer claims a security interest under the Financing Statement bearing the file number shown above.

E. ☐ AMENDMENT-The Financing Statement bearing the file number shown above is amended as set forth in Item 7 below. (Signature of Debtor required on all amendments.)

F. ☐ OTHER

7.

8.

(Date)_____19____

By:_____
    SIGNATURE(S) OF DEBTOR(S)   (TITLE)

By:_____
    SIGNATURE(S) OF SECURED PARTY(IES)   (TITLE)

10.   **Return Copy to**

NAME
ADDRESS
CITY, STATE
AND ZIP

(1) **FILING OFFICER COPY**

STANDARD FORM - FILING FEE $4.00
APPROVED BY THE SECRETARY OF STATE

UNIFORM COMMERCIAL CODE- FORM UCC-2

REDIFORM 5S802 Poly Pak (50 sets) 5P802

CODE
1
2
3
4
5
6
7
8
9

9. This Space for Use of Filing Officer
(Date, Time, Filing Office)

FIG. 4-7.

UNIFORM COMMERCIAL CODE FILINGS - CURRENT/CLOSED

Name and Location	Filing Date	City, State Where Filed	Acknowledgment Copy in File	Renewal Date	Date Financing Statement Terminated

FIG. 4-8.

Services are available whose business it is to prepare UCC filings for clients who do not have the time or prefer to have their filings handled by specialists. Before you hire one of these service companies to do a first filing, get references—and check them. Have the company advise you in writing—on the company's letterhead and over the signature of a company officer—the amount of the performance bond carried by the company. Have the company attach a photocopy of the bonding agreement to the above-mentioned letter, which should also include at least three current customer references. If the customer references indicate a high level of satisfaction with the service, and the bonding company verifies the status of the agreement, you might want to try the service. (See FIG. 4-9.)

MECHANIC'S LIEN LAWS

Just as the Uniform Commercial Code is not uniform in what the 50 state legislatures adopted vs. the original concept, so Mechanic's and Materialmen's Lien Laws vary from one state to another.

Most states accept the premise that any person who furnishes material or does work on a property can file a lien. An individual, a partnership, or a corporation can file a lien, and no regulation states that a person or entity must be a resident of the state in which they wish to file the lien. Labor or material is the basis for a Mechanic's or Materialmen's Lien. To qualify, both must have become part of the property or added value to it.

Two different concepts govern the filing of liens by subcontractors and materialmen. A filing is made not because one concept or the other is the choice of the person or company filing, but based on whether the state in which you are filing the lien follows the New York or Pennsylvania requirements for a given situation qualifying as eligible for exercising lien rights. The New York concept sets the allowable lien limit at the amount owed by the owner to the general contractor. If the amount owed to the general contractor doesn't cover the subcontractor's claim, the burden of proving that the owner owes the greater amount rests with the subcontractor. Pennsylvania and the states that follow its concept do not limit the amount of the subcontractor's allowable lien to the amount owed by the owner to the general contractor. Pennsylvania and its' followers give the subcontractor a direct lien regardless of whether there is proof that the owner has made payments to the general contractor.

The same warning applies here as with a UCC filing. Do not try to file a Mechanic's or Materialmen's Lien unless you are familiar with the procedural requirements in the jurisdiction where you are filing. Filing requirements do differ from state to state; the schedules of filing fees are not consistent; the duration of liens might vary; and the requirements for what must be included in the lien notice itself are often complex. Until you have gone through the filing process enough times and in enough jurisdictions to know how and where to look for the guidelines, let your company's attorney guide you through the process. And as you listen to him, also become familiar with the Credit Manual of Commercial Laws.

(Company Name And Logo)
SUPPLIER INFORMATION SHEET

To aid Form-File Services in the filing of financing statements, please provide the following information and return to Form-File.

1. EXACT ENTITY AND NAME _____

2. PRINCIPAL BUSINESS ADDRESS _____

    _____

3. CONTACT: _____   PHONE: _____
              _____   PHONE: _____
              _____   PHONE: _____

4. STATE OF INCORPORATION (IF INCORPORATED) _____

5. Please list *any* and *all* TRADE NAMES used by your company:

6. Please provide a description of the TYPE OF MERCHANDISE that will be covered under various security agreements, i.e. "Skis, bindings, poles and boots with the brand name 'BREAK-A-LEG'; Down coats and vests under the brand name 'FREEZ-A-LITTLE'."

7. Please circle which SECURITY AGREEMENT you have chosen: (a) Form-File's P.M.Z.B (copy attached); (b) an altered version of Form-File's form; or (c) your own agreement form.

NOTE: Form-File Services will prepare and process the necessary documents to provide you with a security interest by following the dictates of the Uniform Commercial Code in the jurisdiction of your debtor. We guarantee our information to be as accurate as REASONABLE CARE can make it. However, the ultimate responsibility for maintaining files rests with the filing officer and we will accept NO LIABILITY beyond the exercise of REASONABLE CARE.

                                    By: _____

                    (Business Address)

FIG. 4-9.

Chapter 5

Useful Tools for Gathering Necessary Information

THE QUALITY OF THE INFORMATION THAT GOES INTO THE EVALUATION OF A CREDIT AP-plication is vital to the quality of the credit decision. Your ability to evaluate data received from the applicant's suppliers and bank, plus currently applicable financial statements, might be quite good, but if the data is incomplete, inaccurate, or otherwise flawed, your credit decision will be equally flawed. In a small company, the owner's judgment of what is acceptable risk is the only judgment. In a bigger company, the decisions of a credit manager are subject to review and challenge by the sales manager, finance director, and chief-operating officer. Their common interest is to sell products to customers at volume levels that can help to achieve projected sales goals. These goals are the same goals as the person who is owner, sales manager, and credit manager in a small company.

Owners of small companies must be competent do-it-yourselfers in every area of company decision making. They have no choice. Senior executives are not available to question them regarding specific decisions—questioning that might force the credit manager at the bigger company to take another look at the data that went into a decision. The small company owner also does not have to sell other executives on the validity of any decision. This positive fact is enviable, but it is not totally free from the potential for danger. The positives are diminished by the fact that the owner has no seasoned executive against whom to bounce data regarding a puzzling situation. He has no strident, in-company voice that can push his momentarily nonfocused mind back onto the clear path. This totally unique position gives the owner one more special privilege—make that a "special responsibility." It enables the owner of a small business—YOU, Mr. or Ms. Entrepreneur—to constantly glance over both shoulders to catch errors in judgment before they can mushroom into costly mistakes.

If there is a single, nonnegotiable item in the steps leading to the granting or declin-ing of a credit line that stands above all others, it is good information—good credit expe-rience information. It is the basis for the subsequent evaluation of the risk factors in any sale on credit terms, and it is totally nonnegotiable! Never settle for less information than you need to make an informed account decision. Forget pressure from the appli-cant. Forget your own entrepreneurial sense of urgency and the thought that just this once you can waive getting the financial statement from the applicant, or getting a meaningful disclosure from the applicant's bank. Don't do it. Don't allow yourself to accept the absence of any document or information from a bank or supplier sources in the step-by-step gathering of "the tools."

Costly mistakes often are related to, but not always the result of, incomplete information or limited data evaluation skills. Some applicants will give you ambiguous statements, managed data, and slanted facts. During the evaluation of a prospective new account, you might encounter one or all of these toxic ingredients in the broad base of material that you must use. Your money is always on the line when you release an order, but it is never more at risk than when you release a first order before you have checked all pertinent reference data and found it to be satisfactory. Take a long look at names, locations, and data from all sources to assure yourself that the offered reference(s) is not a family member, a silent partner, or one who in some other way is much less than a disinterested party.

No statistic is available to cover the number of people who will say or do whatever is necessary to get your company to give them a line of credit. Also, no statistic is available to cover the number of accounts whose performance will fail to measure up to the quality of the experience reported by some other suppliers. When an increasingly slow account balance finally forces your company to put the customer on C.O.D. terms, this action ensures the safety and liquidity of those sales—right? Not really. Take the following as an example:

Your truck driver delivers an order for $1000 worth of products. He has been given instructions not to leave the order with the customer unless he receives a check for $1500—the extra $500 applicable to past-due balances. (You obviously will have made these arrangements with the customer in advance, including the type of check acceptable to you—bank money order, cashier's check, etc.). Someone in the customer's office tells the driver that the owner or authorized signature is away from the office until late in the day—but not to worry. They will mail the check that evening without fail! Does your truck driver call your office for a decision on whether to leave the order or bring it back? Too often the driver is swayed by the "in the mail" promise of someone he has had contact with before. He leaves the product and instead of reducing the accounts receivable balance by $500, the account goes up another $1500—and no "in the mail" check is received! Some customers are masters at working such angles. One of the oldest and most successful angle is the "away from the office, failed to sign the check" ploy. NEVER believe it unless you have security that few suppliers in such a situation are able to control.

Would you have any type of similar problem if the information that you gathered from the new account applicant, and from the applicant's bank and supplier references, had been complete and totally straightforward? Your first and basic strength is to properly evaluate good information before you formalize the relationship by assigning a credit line, but there is never a guarantee that at some point in your relationship with an account, a serious problem with receivables payments will not occur. Most commercial credit applicants are interested in the same things that you are—a solid business foundation plus the kind of good planning and hard work that leads to gradual increases in the levels of success. Most of your credit applicants are no more interested in taking advantage of your company than you are in bilking your own suppliers. Errors in judgment or downturns in the regional or national economy are some of the factors that can cause a successful company to experience serious problems.

Experience alone is not enough. You might be one of the most experienced credit managers in the business but your credit decisions still will be influenced heavily by the quality of "the tools"—the bank and credit references you receive from the applicant and the data upon which you base your decision(s). Experience is a great help, but it is not a good tradeoff for the integrity of an applicant or reliable financial and supplier data. You can make good credit decisions more frequently when the base of information is equally good.

THE CREDIT APPLICATION

The credit application (or the New Account Information Sheet) is usually the first paper a credit manager reaches for when the name of a prospective new account reaches his or her desk. It could be the second thing if the manager subscribes to Dun & Bradstreet's Service, in which case the manager first will check D & B's Reference Guide to get an early reading on the account—how it handles supplier obligations, what its estimated financial strength is, and how many years the company has been in business.

In the introduction to this chapter, I said there is no substitute for a good supply of reliable account information. The credit application is the window that provides you with the opportunity to get the quantity and variety of information so essential for a quality decision-making process. If a company offers you a window so smudged with incomplete or ambiguous responses that its value is almost negligible, insist that the applicant do a job on the smudged windowpane with the business equivalent of Windex—full, complete, and truthful answers to each question on the credit application. You not only are not obligated to accept an incomplete credit application, but you owe it to your company to reject the application until you have added all missing data. Call the company, ask for the authorized person who signed the application, and expedite getting the missing information. If you are unable to reach the person who signed the application, leave a message for that person to return your call. If you do not receive a return call by the end of the business day in which you placed the call, return the application with an appropriate cover letter.

Every line of the requested information is relevant to your evaluation of the account and to your subsequent relationship with it. Your applicant's receivables and payables departments often are located at different addresses—sometimes within the same city and sometimes a city or state apart. Your invoices should not wander in company limbo because information on the credit application failed to clearly state that each of the two functions—receiving and payables—has its own address. You also must know whether your company is dealing with a corporation, a partnership, or a sole proprietorship. You also need to know whether the customer is a company, a division, or a subsidiary of another company. Bank and trade references are vital to your pool of preevaluation information. You should not assign any applicant a credit line if you are not totally satisfied on the applicant's relations with its' bank and suppliers.

Don't be surprised if occasionally one of your major competitors surfaces on a list of references. Some of the responses from competitors will be complete, others less than candid (not untruthful, but responses that leave much unsaid in the area of experience data). When it happens, don't fight it. Get what you can from the reference and expand your base from information given to you by other references. A fact of credit management life is that most applicant's do what you and I would do in the same situation—they list bank and creditor names with which they've had the best relationships. But candor isn't limited to relationships that have not been handled properly. Most credit people will deal honestly with your inquiry within the context of their account experience. Statements that come from what might have been a good or a head-knocking experience is welcome information—information that is not available from other sources.

FIGURES 5-1, 5-2, 5-3 are samples of three credit applications. The format for each sample is basically the same with the exception of an obligations agreement. Two of the

ACCOUNT INFORMATION SHEET

Date_____

COMPANY NAME _____

BILLING ADDRESS _____

SHIPPING ADDRESS _____

PHONE NUMBER _____

PERSON TO CONTACT
REGARDING PAYMENT _____
(Name & Title)

TYPE OF BUSINESS _____ ANNUAL SALES _____

CORPORATION   PARTNERSHIP   SOLE PARTNERSHIP   RESALE #_____

YEAR BUSINESS ESTABLISHED _____ PRESENT OWNER(S) SINCE _____

IS THERE A PARENT COMPANY? _____

_____ IS THIS A DIVISION?   IS IT A SUBSIDIARY?

DOES COMPANY PLEDGE OR BORROW AGAINST RECEIVABLES? ____ AGAINST INVENTORY? _____

BANK REFERENCE(S):

BANK NAME _____ CITY/STATE _____

PERSON TO CONTACT _____ TELEPHONE _____
(Name & Title)

BANK NAME _____ CITY/STATE _____

PERSON TO CONTACT _____ TELEPHONE _____
(Name & Title)

TRADE REFERENCES:

COMPANY NAME _____ CITY/STATE _____

PERSON TO CONTACT _____ TELEPHONE _____

COMPANY NAME _____ CITY/STATE _____

PERSON TO CONTACT _____ TELEPHONE _____

COMPANY NAME _____ CITY/STATE _____

PERSON TO CONTACT _____ TELEPHONE _____

Information Furnished By:

_____ on _____
(Name and Title)   (Date)

(Please return completed form to:

FIG. 5-1.

EAGLE COMPUTER

983 University Avenue, Los Gatos, CA 95030
(408) 395-5005

CREDIT APPLICATION
CONFIDENTIAL INFORMATION FOR CREDIT VERIFICATION

DATE _____   DUN AND BRADSTREET NO._____

COMPANY NAME _____   PHONE ( ) _____

BILLING ADDRESS _____
(STREET P.O. BOX)   (CITY)   (STATE)   (ZIP)

SHIPPING ADDRESS _____
(STREET)   (CITY)   (STATE)   (ZIP)

NAMES OF PRINCIPALS OF FIRM   FEDERAL TAX I.D. # _____

President _____   Vice President _____
STREET ADDRESS   STREET ADDRESS

CITY, STATE, ZIP   CITY, STATE, ZIP

Corporation	☐
Partnership	☐
Single Ownership	☐

HOME PHONE   HOME PHONE
( )   ( )

Controller _____   Treasurer _____

Division of ☐
          Parent Company _____
Subsidiary of ☐

ADDRESS _____
(STREET P.O. BOX)   (CITY)   (STATE)   (ZIP)

TYPE of Business _____   Number of Employees _____

Credit Line desired per Month $ _____   How Long in Business? _____

Do you use Purchase Orders? _____   Purchasing Agent _____

Is Merchandise for Resale? _____

If an updated credit reference list is not supplied, please complete the reverse side.

Eagle Computer request for a copy of a recent financial is hereby   Complied with ☐   Refused ☐

If refused, please state reason: _____

We, the undersigned, agree to pay **Eagle Computer** within their terms. By affixing their signature below, the undersigned or if a corporation, the corporate officer (Agent) agrees that **Eagle Computer**, in the event of litigation arising out of the agreement, shall be entitled to their responsible costs and expenses incurred, including attorney fees.

AUTHORIZED SIGNATURE _____   TITLE _____

(OVER)

FIG. 5-2.

We, the undersigned, hereby authorize the following credit references to disclose all details necessary to enable **EAGLE COMPUTER** to establish an open account.

BANK REFERENCES (must have account numbers)

Checking: Name _____ Branch _____ Phone (___) _____

Address _____ Account No. _____

Loan: Name _____ Branch _____ Phone (___) _____

Address _____ Person to Contact _____

Assets Pledged?   Yes ☐   No ☐   With Whom? _____

TRADE CREDIT REFERENCES

(1)   Name _____ Phone (___) _____

Address _____

(CITY)   (STATE)   (ZIP)

(2)   Name _____ Phone (___) _____

Address _____

(CITY)   (STATE)   (ZIP)

(3)   Name _____ Phone (___) _____

Address _____

(CITY)   (STATE)   (ZIP)

Fig. 5-2. Continued.

forms include agreements that an authorized person must sign. These agreements state obligations that the customer company must fulfill under certain circumstances. The agreements also impose penalties in the event the customer defaults on payments, attests to the truth of false statements, hampers or tries to steer the investigation of his relationships with bank and trade references. One of the applications contains a paragraph that attempts to deal with every default/collection-related contingency; the second covers the responsibility for costs and expenses related to default of payment, collection, attorney fees, and other costs of litigation. The third application contains no statement(s) of liability, requesting only the signature of the person furnishing the information.

It is preferable to have the signature of a corporate officer (or an authorized signature) on the credit application. When an account reaches the point where some form of third-party collection action is necessary—and no Chapter XI filing has been made nor does it seem imminent—there is leverage to collect your receivables balance and also the costs of such a collection effort. An authorized signature on your credit application won't help a bit if the company has slid into a Chapter XI filing, or a bankruptcy liquidation. The signature will do nothing unless you can prove fraudulent intent. In itself, it will not lift you out of the pit where other unsecured creditors are mud wrestling for nickels and dimes that secured creditors have not already nailed down.

COVER LETTER

Unless you are dealing with a subject or problem that is not routine, you should generate most of your cover letters from form letters. You can save considerable time with form letters; you can alter them to deal more effectively with a specific situation; and you are usually better organized because they were carefully reviewed and edited before the final draft was added to the list of available letters. The purpose of form letters is simple. They serve as an explanation for an attached form which must be signed and returned.

PYRAMID CREDIT APPLICATION

NAME OF FIRM: _____   KIND OF BUSINESS: _____

ADDRESS: _____   DATE FIRM ESTABLISHED: _____

CITY: _____STATE: _____ZIP: _____   ANNUAL SALES: _____NO. OF EMPLOYEES_____

CONTACT REGARDING PAYMENT: _____   TYPE: _____CORPORATION_____INDIVIDUAL

PHONE NUMBER: _____-_____-_____   _____PARTNERSHIP_____SUBSIDIARY

FIRM LISTED IN DUN & BRADSTREET_____YES_____NO D&B NUMBER_____FED ID#_____

DOES FIRM PLEDGE OR BORROW AGAINST RECEIVABLES/INVENTORY?_____

(IF YES WITH WHOM_____)

IF SUBSIDIARY/DIVISION

NAME OF PARENT COMPANY:_____   DUN & BRADSTREET NUMBER_____

ADDRESS:_____   DOES PARENT GUARANTEE DEBTS?_____YES_____NO

CITY:_____STATE:_____ZIP:_____

BANKING INFORMATION:

1. NAME:_____ SAVINGS ACCOUNT #_____

   ADDRESS:_____ CHECKING ACCOUNT #_____

   CITY:_____STATE:_____ZIP:_____ LOAN NUMBER_____

   CONTACT:_____PHONE_____-_____-_____

FIG. 5-3.

2. NAME:_____   SAVINGS ACCOUNT #_____

   ADDRESS:_____   CHECKING ACCOUNT #_____

   CITY:_____STATE:_____ZIP:_____   LOAN NUMBER_____

   CONTACT:_____PHONE_____-_____-_____

TRADE REFERENCES:

NAME	ADDRESS	PHONE NUMBER	MONTHLY PURCHASE
1._____	_____	_____	_____
2._____	_____	_____	_____
3._____	_____	_____	_____

By affixing their signatures below, the undersigned (of if a Corporation, The Corporate authorized Officers/Agents) agree 1) That the information contained herewith is warranted to be true and correct, 2) to pay when due, all invoices from Pyramid Technology Corporation, 3) that in the event of default of payment when due all costs of collection, including Attorney's fees and Court costs, shall be paid by the Applicant, 4) to authorize Pyramid Technology Corporation to investigate any references herein listed or statement or any other data obtained from any person pertaining to the credit worthiness or financial responsibility of the applicant.

Signature_____Title_____Date_____
Signature_____Title_____Date_____

Please attach a copy of latest Financial Statements

Form 8/83

Fig. 5-3. Continued.

They are a cover for a photocopy of a missing invoice, a credit for an overpayment, or the authorized return of product(s). The variety of situations where a form cover letter is acceptable and economically mandatory is extensive. You should prepare form letters so that you need to add only a date, the name and the address of the addressee, and the name of the person to whom the cover letter is addressed. Type an envelope; attach whatever it is that your letter is covering and send it on its way.

Form cover letters are appropriate when sending application forms to customers, for sending the applicant's bank and supplier references a request for their experience, sending some credit memos (many require an explanatory letter), notifying an account that his account balance is past due, and many other purposes. Letters—even form letters—are expensive to prepare and mail. You should use form letters only when they are appropriate. Never use them as a substitute when a personalized letter of a phone call is the appropriate way to communicate.

Some credit managers fail to give themselves or their company the benefits that their unique position in the company/customer relationship makes available to them. They seem unable to accept the fact that from the beginning of the relationship, they can build a rapport with the customer that is separate from relationships between sales reps and the customers purchasing people. Too many overlook the fact that their relationship can be an invaluable asset in the effort to promote a long-lasting relationship between the two companies. Equally unfortunate is a credit manager/owner's failure to realize that good rapport with customers can be an invaluable asset in situations where the customer finds himself or herself in a temporary cash bind—often due to a receivables problem with one of its major accounts. Don't you make that mistake! When you share a first name relationship and an occasional lunch with the customer company's vice president of finance or controller, your good relationship with that person often enables him or her to promptly and candidly discuss details of the problem. When you have the facts, giving a customer of good faith and integrity the extra time necessary to pass through the cash crunch is no major decision.

Your first letter to the credit applicant/prospective customer probably will be the cover letter for the Credit Application and Resale Card (FIGS. 5-4, 5-5, 5-6, 5-7). Focus it on your need for information—bank and supplier references and financial statements—while including your company's appreciation of the order, a brief explanation of your company's requirement of C.O.D. terms for the first order or two (while you are processing reference data), and your request that the applicant return the Credit Application and Resale Form (with a copy of the customer's currently applicable financial statement) as promptly as possible in the enclosed, stamped, self-addressed envelope. This letter is a complete and straightforward request for the information and data that will enable you to promptly process the applicant's request.

A cordial cover letter will help to fix in the customer's mind the thought that your company offers good products and good service at competitive prices—and that you also seem to be good people. Your letter is an opportunity to expand the favorable impression of your company that must have brought the customer to you when he placed the order. It is true that some of the luster eventually might disappear from the relationship, and particularly if time brings payment problems or other problems. At day one or two of the relationship, however, you cannot know what direction the relationship eventually will take, so you mail a credit application, a resale card (if required in your state), and a cordial cover letter. You can do no more to get the relationship started in the right direction. If problems later cause the account situation to unravel, your experience will dictate your actions at that point, along with the nature of the problem(s), and the relationship between your company and the customer company at that point in time. Always do your best to project the best image for your company. Apply to all customer correspondence your clearest, cleanest thinking, and never downgrade the importance of those early "first impression" letters in determining the direction a relationship will take.

THE FINANCIAL STATEMENT

When the applicant returns the completed credit application, a copy of the currently applicable financial statement should accompany it. It is a key piece in the assortment of information that should be at your disposal when you make an evaluation of the total input as it relates to what your company can do. Don't let your earlier request for a financial statement disappear into the limbo of a nonresponse. Don't hesitate to ask a second time. At that point, you might find that the applicant is one of the individuals, partnerships, or close-held corporations that does not release financials—not to you, not to credit reporting agencies, not to anyone. But before your request draws the "we never release" response, tactfully pursue the subject until you are comfortable with the thought that it's a long-standing policy of this applicant to withhold financials, not a relatively recent change. What if this policy is a recent change? The reason might be quite valid, but accept it as your reason to be especially watchful during your evaluation

(Date)

Mr. Leonard Carter, Controller
The XYZ Company
1348 Sherman Way
San Francisco, CA   95114

Dear Mr. Carter:

Let me first thank you for the order your company has placed with us. We appreciate the confidence in our products that this order represents.

It is our policy to process the first order or two from a new customer on a C.O.D. basis. This is not a reflection on the credit worthiness of customers who are new to us. It is simply a recognition of the fact that we are new to each other and must be as prudent in our approach to open account terms as we feel sure you are.

Please complete the attached Account Information Sheet (also the Resale Form), attach a copy of your most recent financial statement, and return documents to this office in the enclosed stamped self-addressed envelope.

When reference data has been processed, we will hope to offer a mutually acceptable credit line on our standard terms of 2%/10 days, Net 30.

Sincerely,

Credit Manager

FIG. 5-4.

(Date)

Mr. Leonard Carter, Controller
The XYZ Company
1348 Sherman Way
San Francisco, CA   95114

RE: Credit Application and Financial Statements

Dear Mr. Carter:

We can expedite the processing of credit reference data if you
will complete the attached Account Information Sheet and return
it - with a copy of your most current financial statement - at
your earliest convenience.

We appreciate the confidence your company has expressed in our
products by giving us a first order. It is our hope that this
is the beginning of a long and a mutually satisfactory business
relationship.

Sincerely Yours,

Credit Manager

FIG. 5-5.

(Date)

Company Name
Street Address (or P.O. Box No.)
City, State and Zip Code

Attention: _____(Addressee's Name)_____

Dear Mr. (Ms.)_____:

A review of our files indicates that we do not have a completed Resale Card (Sales Tax Exemption Number) for your account.

To avoid having California Sales Tax charged to your invoices, please complete, sign and return the enclosed Resale Card.

We appreciate your prompt attention to this request.

Sincerely,

Credit Manager

FIG. 5-6.

RESALE CERTIFICATE - Sales And Use Tax

_____

_____

_____

THIS SIDE OF CARD IS FOR ADDRESS

STAMP
HERE

—

FIRM NAME _____

I HEREBY CERTIFY,
That I hold valid seller's permit No. _____
issued pursuant to the Sales and Use Tax Law; that I am engaged in the business of selling

_____
that the tangible personal property described herein which I shall purchase from:

_____
will be resold by me in the form of tangible personal property; PROVIDED, however, that in the event any of such property is used for any purpose other than retention, demonstration, or display while holding it for sale in the regular course of business, it is understood that I am required by the Sales and Use Tax Law to report and pay for the tax, measured by the purchase price of such property.

Description of property to be purchased: _____

_____

Dated: _____ 19_____   Signature _____

at _____   By and Title _____

Phone _____   Address _____

FIG. 5-7.

of input received from the bank and suppliers. Short of getting the financials, responses from these sources should give you a strong indication of what the financials would have shown.

When you do get financial statements from a customer, the quality of those statements becomes your primary concern. If they are internally prepared and/or they are statements prepared without audit, you must discount their credibility as input for account analysis or credit decisions. If you assign them value, assign them peripheral value only. Accept them only as an indicator of what the business or company's financial situation might have been at a given date or for a stated period. I raise the issue of credibility not because all internally prepared financials are inaccurate—either inadvertently or intentionally—but because too many financials are simply not a reliable reflection of the facts at a particular time or for a particular period. Too many accounts who have their own internally prepared financials slant them to favorably influence bankers and suppliers, particularly in businesses where there is instability or a downward trend—perhaps due directly to faulty management decisions or techniques. You must know everything about a new account—or a prospective new account—before you commit any of your company's dollars to it. If the account slants information you must presume the business ethics of the company slanting that information to be equally shoddy. Your company has a good reputation to uphold. Protect it in every area over which you have control.

When you find yourself in one of those positions where the unaudited financial statement of an applicant firm is signed by the owner, a partner, or a corporate officer, you have some potential legal leverage. You can convert the signature of an owner or a corporate officer attesting to the accuracy of the figures in a financial statement into a case of "misrepresentation with intent to defraud" if it later can be shown that the financial statement was persuasive in the granting of a credit line, or persuasive in a decision to increase an existing line. A realistic assessment of those facts tells you that you wouldn't want your hopes for a recovery of receivables dollars to be dangling from such a slender thread. The customer company probably would be out of business before your attorney could get a trial date.

Credibility obviously is increased greatly when a CPA or licensed public accountant has prepared the offered financial statements. Having said that, I must add that a CPA-prepared financial statement often is generated from unaudited general ledgers and other figures. Under those circumstances, it is essentially the product of information stemming from in-company practices, procedures, and controls. I need only cite the frequency of unexpected business failures, and media reviews of those failures, to remind you that there is never a guarantee. Even a CPA-prepared financial statement might not be the product of good figures. Accounts can conceal many serious problems if such is the intent of those who determine the quality of figures used in the preparation of financial statements. What is YOUR bottom line? You should not accept any set of financial statements as flawless, nor should you ever use a financial statement(s) as the sole indicator of financial strengths or weaknesses.

You don't have to be an accountant to get help from the financial statement of a customer or credit applicant. What you're looking for is ratios, and how to interpret and use them. You should know the meaning of current ratio, liquid ratio, and net worth ratio. You should know how to apply them to the financial statement of a customer or applicant. Following are some definitions and comments:

☐ *Current Ratio*—the current total of cash, securities, inventory, and accounts receivable (current assets) vs. all indebtedness due within one year (current liabilities).

You should not feel comfortable with a current ratio of 1.1. Under most conditions 2.1 is satisfactory.

☐ *Liquid Ratio*—cash and accounts receivable vs. current liabilities. If the ratio is less than 1.1, it is unsatisfactory. (1.1 means $1 in liquid assets to offset $1 in current liabilities. This figure is not strong enough).

☐ *Net Worth Ratio*—Owner's investment vs. creditor's investment. There is concern when the number of dollars (or total investment) of the owners (sole proprietor, partners, venture capitalists, and/or stockholders) is substantially less than the amount supplied by creditors (bank, suppliers, etc.).

Following are some other ratios relevant to the evaluation of an account or an applicant:

☐ Current Debt/Net Worth—Current debt should only be a small percentage of net worth. If it is heavy, there is a strong possibility that total debt will exceed net worth.

☐ Total Debt/Net Worth—When total debt exceeds net worth, there is a deficit net worth. When the deficit increases from year to year, or if it is not decreasing, beware!

☐ Inventory/Working Capital—Inventory levels should never be higher than necessary to properly service customers. Excess inventory levels tie up working capital and restrict liquidity.

☐ Long-Term Debt/Working Capital—Long-term debt should fit comfortably into the total financial picture. It should not take a disproportionate amount of working capital to service it.

☐ Net Profit/Net Worth—Net worth should increase from year to year. Is the account's net profit going back into the business or is it being absorbed in bonuses, etc., for owner, partners, or key executives? Unless the business is exceptionally strong, business worth should increase each year.

The Balance Sheet (Financial Spread Sheet) that is shown in FIG. 5-8 will accommodate as many as five annual financials. You will be lucky if you can obtain copies of the three most current ones, but that should not discourage you from trying for more copies. The subject form enables you to consolidate financial statement data onto the one form, making it relatively easy to spot favorable trends or abnormalities.

CONTACTING CREDIT REFERENCES

Your contact with credit references can be by telephone or letter (see FIG. 5-9). A few years back telephone calls were thought to be an extravagant use of the company's money, but that is not the case today. Sales people routinely use long distance service to call customers in-state or across the country: Credit managers do the same to expedite a credit clearance on an in-house order or to clear a credit line for a promising applicant. These latter years of the 20th Century have brought changes in all facets of business-related thinking. Perhaps the change that has occurred most rapidly is the realization that the telephone is faster and frequently more cost effective than the form letter. This statement isn't one that only a battery of accountants can prove. Anyone who tries to justify the extra time necessary to type and mail form letters (in volume) vs. the speed with which you can complete a telephone call is not destined for one of the higher rungs on the corporate ladder. This thought is a traditionalist mindset in a modern business environment. Today's business environment demands that you get and process information as fast and as accurately as possible. The telephone does it. It gives you immediate access to the appropriate information base, and it allows you to deal

BALANCE SHEET

FINANCIAL SPREADSHEET

Fill in financial data from recent balance sheets

ASSETS	1984	1985	1986	1987	1988
Cash	35,990	16,140	14,117	27,244	41,617
Accounts Receivable (Net)	52,148	67,184	121,414	138,797	140,816
Inventory	66,850	99,345	114,149	140,895	138,054
Prepaid & Other [1]	2,971	9,774	7,532	21,308	6,339
Total Current Assets	157,959	192,443	264,421	328,244	326,826
Net Fixed Assets	109,082	122,564	139,390	160,312	198,231
Other Non-Current Assets	-0-	7,564	5,300	4,218	4,478
TOTAL ASSETS	265,981	322,571	409,111	492,774	529,535

LIABILITIES	1984	1985	1986	1987	1988
Trade Accounts Payable [2]	57,992	62,742	51,101	72,360	63,025
Other Current Liabilities	-0-	-0-	-0-	21,596	23,108
Current Portion of Long-Term Debt	21,784	41,243	59,829	131,007	134,149
Total Current Debt	80,210	110,769	170,127	231,715	237,112
Long-Term Debt [3]	87,244	88,572	63,704	48,829	35,487
TOTAL LIABILITIES	167,454	199,341	233,831	280,544	272,599
NET WORTH [4]	98,527	123,230	175,280	212,230	256,936
TOTAL LIABILITIES & NET WORTH	265,981	322,571	409,111	492,774	529,535

Footnotes:
1. Include all prepaid expenses and other miscellaneous current assets.
2. Accounts payable to supplier only.
3. Debts not due for a year or more.
4. Owner's contributed capital and retained earnings (Assets minus Liabilities).

FIG. 5-8.

(Date)

TO: RE:

The above-named firm has given your name as a credit reference to assist them in establishing an account with us. We greatly appreciate your help and pledge that any information given to us by your company will be handled in strictest confidence.

SOLD FROM:_____   METHOD OF PAYMENT:

HIGHEST CREDIT:_____   Discounts_____

OWING:_____   Prompt_____

PAST DUE:_____   Slow_____

TERMS:_____   Pays by Note_____

                                                       Pays on Account_____
Remarks:_____
_____
_____
_____

Sincerely yours,

Credit Manager

Please complete and return to:

FIG. 5-9.

immediately with responses or statements that require clarification or elaboration. This fact doesn't mean that you throw out your forms and letters, or that you don't from time-to-time add new ones. Conditions and relationships exist where a letter—perhaps a form letter dealing with a routine request situation, or a negotiation requiring an exchange of form(s) and correspondence—is the only appropriate way to respond. Other forms and form letters continue to have a function as in the example of a bank or other reference who does not give information over the telephone; they also act as the repository for information you receive during a telephone conversation.

One of the situations where a telephone call is not always an acceptable alternative to a form inquiry is in your contact with the applicant's bank. Many banks will not give experience or account information over the telephone. One segment of the banking community slips into a near-catatonic state when faced with a caller who claims to be a prospective supplier. The request immediately bumps up against a response that asks the caller to submit a written request—on a letterhead that identifies the caller with his or her company. Some bankers will take your number, call their customer for authorization to give you the bank's experience, and follow through with a return call. Others will not get into any verbal transfer of information, falling back on an inflexible need for a written request. It might be annoying, but you must remember that you're asking the bank for help; the bank doesn't need you for a thing. So humor them. Play their game. Whether it comes to you verbally or in writing, get input from every available source because the last report that you receive, or the one you didn't get because you became impatient when you thought you were being jerked around, might be the key to whether you make the correct credit decision.

CREDIT INVESTIGATION FORM

The credit investigation form (FIG. 5-10) is a recap of the information your receive when—via telephone calls or letters of inquiry—you contact the applicant's suppliers. The form enables you to consolidate that information. You may then add financial statement data and the experience of the bank to complete the package.

All relevant bank information—checking accounts, savings accounts, equipment loans, land and building loans, or loans covering a revolving line of credit—is detailed in the top section of the form. Unsolicited comments from the banker can be very important, or they can be touched up with the rosy pink of self-interest (the bank has loaned more dollars to the applicant firm than the current trend seems to warrant, but the bank is trying to help the firm survive long enough to cut the bank's loan losses). Other bankers will not give you more than you can drag out of them. A perceptive credit manager might be able to make a proper judgment regarding information that smells of hype, but the closed-mouth reluctant banker who refuses to give you even a minimal amount of help is another matter. Ask the applicant to contact the banker and suggest to him that it is in their mutual interest to have their new supplier (your firm) approve a credit line. Your product line might be what the applicant needs to put some extra muscle in his performance and competitive strength—and that should be very good news to the banker.

The recap of information received from the applicant's three supplier references is important to your decision in the practical and psychological senses. Whether it comes from competitors or from suppliers in unrelated businesses or industries, supplier information is peer information. A credit manager can relate more readily to a supplier's experience with the applicant than to information from another source. Compare data received from suppliers for a pattern of consistency. If it is inconsistent, check supplier experience to see if the applicant has been taking better care of the principal supplier

CREDIT INVESTIGATION

Company Name:_____   Date Opened:_____

Financial Statement:_____   Credit Limit:_____

D & B Rating:_____   Limit Updated:_____

Bank:_____Comments:

Checking

Savings

Loans

Reference:_____Comments:

    Contact_____

    Years Sold_____

    Terms_____

    Recent High_____

    Current Bal._____

    Past Due Bal._____

    Prompt_____   Slow_____

Reference:_____Comments:

    Contact_____

    Years Sold_____

FIG. 5-10.

Terms_____

Recent High_____

Current Bal._____

Past Due Bal._____

Prompt_____ Slow_____

Reference:_____Comments:

Contact_____

Years Sold_____

Terms_____

Recent High_____

Current Bal._____

Past Due Bal._____

Prompt_____ Slow_____

Fig. 5-10. Continued.

than of the others. Is there supplier longevity? This longevity often is indicative of a relationship not tainted by collection problems or constant maneuvering for special treatment. It is also fair and relevant to mention that firms stop buying from suppliers for good reasons—better prices at a competitor, a more aggressive attitude toward business growth, inacceptable service and processing of paperwork, etc. As many valid reasons are available for a firm to stop buying from one supplier as there are reasons for a supplier to force the change by discontinuing open account terms. Don't unfairly penalize an applicant because the length of time with certain suppliers was the equivalent of a cup of coffee downed during a midnight stop on a coast-to-coast bus. The customer might have defected for good reason, so look for it.

Responses from reference inquiries can vary from three that put the prospective customer in a category only slightly below sainthood to another applicant whose name triggers experience data comparable to in-cadence retching. Accounts whose references report a good level of purchases over several years, and a payments record which is consistently discount/prompt to slow 10 or 15 days, should be a good account prospect if experience data is current. Returns from references of another account might be a mixed bag—one reference might report a good payment experience (prompt to slow 15) at a high credit of $7000 over three years; the second reference submits a less-glowing report with payments consistently 20 to 40 days slow at a high credit of $2300; and the third reference reports that the experience had become unsatisfactory with payments originally prompt to 15 days slow and, three years later, slow 45 to 70 days, and getting slower. The third respondent also might give you some written details. "This account paid 5 to 10 days slow at a high of $1100 for the first year. For the past year and a half sales have continued at the previous level, but payments have slowed to 45 to 70 days slow. The account is now on a two-for-one payment plan until they have cleared all open balances, then they will be C.O.D. customers.''

From this pattern of supplier responses, you easily can establish that the first respondent (prompt to slow 15 days at a high credit of $7000 over three years) is the primary supplier, the supplier whose nationally- or regionally-advertised product or products is the cornerstone of the customer's business. If the customer suddenly doesn't have those products, he is out of business. Respondents two and three are not in such a favored position. Respondent number two is selling at the next highest level, but obviously he is not a primary supplier. Supplier number three has been selling at the lowest level. He probably has a product line or lines not essential to the customer's business. Consequently, he is getting the shabbiest treatment.

When you don't know what lines certain suppliers carry, you should be able to get the information from your company's sales manager or territory salesman. He or she probably has known the account for a period of time, or if you are working with a new contact, he or she will know what lines the business carries from talking with the purchasing agent. Don't shade your evaluation of an account because of what the salesman tells you, but also, do not hesitate to get his or her impressions of the account: a single-story office and warehouse building in a good industrial area, a clean, well-organized warehouse area, an adequate stock of the principle product lines; clean and well-maintained delivery vehicles, and knowledgable, helpful, and busy personnel. You cannot translate any of the above into an assurance that the applicant will pay within an acceptable time frame, but it is helpful information in the context of fleshing out the total picture of a well-run business—or, at its worst, a business that is run in a haphazard manner.

''Too new to rate'' is what you frequently will hear when a firm has been in business less than six months. When you get that response, go back to the applicant for the name(s) of a supplier or bank with whom the applicant—either as an individual or in another business—has had more than six months experience. The bank reference must be one that can give you helpful information. This criteria also is applicable to supplier references. When a business is new, no bank or supplier has meaningful data regarding it. At that point, you can key on what the banker is doing with the account (or if it is a sole proprietorship or partnership, what the bank's experience has been with the sole proprietor or partners as individuals. Also get information on what experience business people in other business ventures have had with the individual(s). When a business is so new that it has no payables record, you must take whatever help the bank's relationship with the applicant gives you. Combine this help with financial statement(s) of the proprietor or partners (or an opening financial statement for the business itself), antecedent data on partners, proprietor, corporate officers, etc., product line(s), and other data relating to the business or company. It's the best you can do with what is little better than a start-up firm. When a company has been in business six months or more, you must have current business data. A banker and suppliers are available, and they have done business with the new firm long enough to have helpful information. You need to know what their experience has been, what their opinions are now, and what they see as the future trend.

If telephone calls and form-letter inquiries have been effective, your credit investigation is approaching the point where you soon will be ready to evaluate the consolidated input and assign, or decline, a credit line. Never exceed prudent limits in your effort to move the applicant inside your company's parameters for an acceptable credit account if the data you have accumulated doesn't warrant it. *Never* go beyond prudent reason in your efforts to interpret borderline data in a favorable light, and *Never* allow yourself to be pressured into selling an account that doesn't even qualify as a "maybe". You'll select many good accounts for your company, and now and again you'll pick one that becomes a loser. Ideally, the time to lose one is before you have extended a dimes worth of credit, and at the point where your evaluation of the account tells you to let some other supplier assume the risk.

A CREDIT RATING AND REPORT SERVICE

The service with the most recognizable image, and the one that offers its customers the most comprehensive variety of options, is Dun and Bradstreet. This firm provides a service of variable scope tied to an annual contract. The customer can put together almost any level of service from a minimum base of 100 reports per year to an unlimited number on the high end. The *subscriber* (D & B's term for those who use the service) also can select Reference Guides for regions of interest (Pacific Coast, Rocky Mountain States, East Coast, etc.), for a combination of regions, or for the entire United States and Canada. Reference Guides (available on a semiannual, quarterly, or bimonthly basis) list nonretail businesses and companies by state, county, and nearest town. An Industrial Classification Code Number identifies the company's primary type of business, a single digit identifies the year in which the business was established or incorporated (if less than ten years), and Dun & Bradstreet includes a rating for the account. The Reference Guide will show no rating (a "blank rating") if sufficient current data is not available to rate the account.

If your company is active in many geographic areas of the country, or if it is selling in the international marketplace, you may subscribe as I have outlined above. You may obtain base reports and supplementary reports from one or more regions of the United States plus Reference Guides for the same regions. Other contract services include PAR and one for an international report service. Other special service options include accessing the Dun & Bradstreet data bank via computer link between the two units—yours and D & B's. You should explore details regarding specialized options directly with Dun & Bradstreet and not through these pages.

The type of business, geographic scope, age, and financial condition of the potential subscriber company, and the need for access to information as customer relationships progress should be primary influences on the timing for deciding whether to subscribe. An annual contract for Dun & Bradstreet's Basic Service will involve a memorable number of dollars, and the more you tack onto the contract, the more indelible the imprint on your memory and the company's checkbook. The cost should not, however, be the only consideration. If this service or any other service enables you to avoid one or more sizeable receivables losses, the one experience can save your company more than the annual cost of the service.

Information Provided in a D & B Report

A Dun & Bradstreet subscriber who orders Base Reports on various firms also may order Continuous Service on certain accounts. Continuous Service means that whenever D & B gets new information relating to a firm—an updated financial statement, a change in key management personnel, any new acquisitions, a pending merger—they will forward an updated report to the subscriber. Base Reports contain a rating for the account. The ratings range from Blank (not enough information to rate) through AAAA1 (Over $10 million net worth and a "High" credit rating, which is synonymous with Excellent). The report will state whether the company is a sole proprietorship, partnership, company, or corporation, a division or a subsidiary, and the name of the parent company. It also includes the date of the report, the number of employees on that date, the supplier payments experience data, and the bank's comments regarding the firm.

Antecedent data that these reports contain is usually not readily available from other sources. Data regarding the founders of the company, their successors, current active founders and the backgrounds of the founder's successors—purchasers of the company or key management people also is available. D & B lists Chapter XI or general bankruptcy problems in the immediate backgrounds of any partner or managing owner. They also list suits or liens filed against the company by the IRS, a State Board of Equalization, or a civil proceeding involving the company's product(s).

As individual pieces of information, I cannot categorize these items as earth shaking. When thrown into a text context of "what is a meaningful contribution to the body of an individual account's information," their variety of root areas makes a contribution that is significant to the whole. Once again, we're talking basics. The more we know about an account, and about the people who own and/or manage it, the better and more diversified our pool of information, and the better our judgments and decisions.

Should your company subscribe to Dun & Bradstreet's service? I can't give you an answer. I do suggest that if your business is growing at a steady rate, if it currently has 200 or more accounts whose levels of purchases run from "no impact if lost" thru "a BIG impact if lost" (and of which several are slow pay or increasingly slow pay), you are a candidate for the service. Probably the majority of credit professionals feel that the report data—base, continuous service updates, and information pertaining to personnel or internal/external changes—makes it a worthwhile service for many companies below, at, or above the activity range just described. You cannot obtain the information, or some facets of it, from other sources unless you're willing to take time-consuming detours. You should weigh the thought carefully of whether the annual cost is currently beyond your company's financial capability vs. the benefits of the service. If you decide to try the service, the basic service for your geographic area of business interest is usually enough. You always can increase the number of services in your present contract or add them to the next contract.

The National Association of Credit Management

NACM offers an alternative to the service provided by Dun & Bradstreet but they offer it in a different format. The Association's National Business Credit Report does not attempt to assign credit ratings. The Payment History section of the report draws ledger experience form NACM's member companies on a regular basis and includes member number, business category, opening year of business, month and year of report information, last purchase activity with each respondent supplier, high credit with each supplier, amount owed to each supplier, aging of account balances in all categories of aging, payment terms, and any member comments. Sections are available that summarize totals of reported trade experience in both dollars and percentages, an inquiry record lists previous inquiries on the subject business during the previous 90 days, bank data lists credit history and loan information on commercial accounts, historical information is available on all aspects of the business—including principals, information is listed pertaining to suits, SBA loans, attachments, bankruptcies, etc. Much of the information that Dun & Bradstreet's Basic Credit Report furnishes is available also on NACM's National Business Credit reports. Reports are available by telephone, mail, or via a link between your computer terminal and the central National Automated Database Center in Houston. You must, of course, join the National Association of Credit Management.

One of the Association's major benefits is the availability of membership in a broad range of credit groups. CMA's credit groups meet for a business lunch on a monthly, semimonthly or quarterly schedule. Members submit discussion information. The Association compiles it, distributes it at the start of the meeting and discusses it with members under the monitoring eyes of an Association representative. This representative is present to avoid any possibility of discussions getting into the mine field of antitrust regulations. Group members discuss old accounts, new accounts, recurring and new-problem accounts, the bold or peripheral return of a notorious industry jackal, any sudden negative change in the payment pattern of an established account, etc. The number of participating members is important to the volume and scope of the information they exchange, but it does not negate the possibility of an important exchange between as few as three or four members.

The worth of NACM and D & B reports hinges on the number of firms who furnish experience data on a regular and timely basis (for an effective update of reports), the quality of the skills of field and in-office reporters and analysts, and the depth and reliability of information received on suits, bulk transfers, attachments, tax liens, SBA loans, bankruptcies and other recorded data. D & B's ratings come down to the net worth of a company (a high of AAAA through a low of E) and the way a company handles its' bank and supplier obligations (1 is high—4 is definitely not good). NACM lists all of the data it can gather but makes no attempt to assign a credit rating. The judgment of risk is left to member managers.

Let me urge you not to back away from a reporting service because you have limited credit management experience and don't know if the service is for you. It is for you if your company's activity volume warrants it. Never allow yourself to slip into a ''no professional growth'' cop-out. Reports are easy to read and interpret. Guideline instructions are a part of your subscriber kit and should help you to phase them into the evaluation process quickly and effectively.

CREDIT GROUPS AND ASSOCIATIONS

For the regional or area business who is unable to stretch its limited budget to accommodate the cost of membership in a national credit organization, there is the option of a local small-business group. These meetings often are sponsored by the local chamber of commerce and although they are not directed exclusively toward credit management problems, they offer a helpful alternative to the industry meetings sponsored by national credit organizations. Locally organized and locally directed meetings usually address the general business needs and problems of the community of small businesses, and that's fine. If you are a credit manager and your community is not large enough to have an industry credit group, the next best thing is a group that includes a mix of businesses and industries. You have credit problems with some of your accounts? So do they. You solve your problems with one technique or another—and so do they. Wouldn't it be interesting, and of mutual benefit, to find out how these other people who are not professional credit managers handle some of their credit problems? You can be a pro with years of experience behind you or a neophyte who still faces a career load of decisions, but you still can learn something from the way others handle their problems. Of course, what you sometimes learn is that you NEVER want to make a credit decision of such poor judgmental quality as the one you just heard described. That fact in itself is worth the price of admission to almost any group meeting!

Whether the group is large or small, whether it is affiliated with a local or national organization, or whether it resembles a pickup group, *confidentiality* is the key admonition. At all levels of such meetings, the universal admonition should be that whatever you hear or discuss during the meeting—or at any time between credit management people—you should never repeat to a customer. A violation of this need for confidentiality cannot only have legal implications, but it is the most effective way imaginable to destroy the willingness of group members to freely discuss account experiences. You can destroy years spent nurturing a group to the point where there is complete candor among members with one careless comment.

Owners who double as credit managers are not generally accepted in industry credit groups. When a credit group does accept an owner/manager as a provisional or probationary member, he/she must prove by words and actions that his or her primary interest in group membership is the exchange of credit information and account experiences for credit management purposes and not information he/she will convert into a sales tool. With an owner who also makes the credit decisions, there is always reasonable doubt regarding motivation—so much doubt that many groups and associations will not allow a firm to join a credit group if the firm doesn't have a full-time employee credit manager. Putting aside the question of conflict of interest when an owner also is attending credit group meetings, professional credit managers feel that if a company doesn't have enough accounts to employ a full-time credit manager, it doesn't have a broad enough account base to provide experience data equal to that which other group members offer.

The free exchange of credit information among members of a specific industry is extremely helpful. No one manager can be aware of every potential or emerging trouble spot in the company's business area. If your company isn't a member of a local, regional, or national credit group—one whose primary focus is in your industry or area of business—make arrangements to join the group. When the problem is one of several similar businesses in your region but no credit management group, take the initiative. Contact other industry credit managers and try to bring them into a formal, bylaws type of group or organization. You—and they—need the help of such a group.

Thousands of businesses in all geographic areas of the United States find it advantageous to sort themselves into groups of similar interest for the purpose of exchanging credit information and credit experiences. When you first come together, there will be some doubts as to whether it will work. Fortunately, for all members, the great majority of groups develop into a long and mutually successful experience. With the initial realization that it takes time to build confidence in the integrity of your peers, your group can be a success too.

ACCOUNT PROSPECT LIST

If you have determined that your company can benefit from a Dun & Bradstreet services contract, your D & B Reference Guide offers a dimension beyond its obvious use when screening and evaluating the background of a credit applicant. You can use it to provide your sales department with lists of prospective new customers whose credit ratings, and years in business, indicate that there would be no credit problem at a credit line compatible with the financial and credit strength of the business. This information would not be conclusive—certainly not a promise to sales people that you could grant credit—but it is a good indication of an acceptable account.

Remember that the use of Dun & Bradstreet's Reference Guides, or the reports and services data from this or other commercial reporting companies, is confidential. Under no circumstances should you repeat the contents of a report, or any segment of information from that report, to the person or company about whom the report was prepared. An entrepreneur (or credit manager) may, however, use the D & B Reference Guide to prepare a list of prospective customers in selected areas or over a rather broad area. The determining factor will be whether your company is interested in getting the most out of its present sales area before considering expanding into adjacent territories, or is the company first interested in moving into new territories and later closing gaps in the territory or territories they already service.

The Prospect List shown in FIG. 5-11 offers the format for compiling information taken from the Reference Book. Select a section of a county, state, or region that your sales (or senior management) people indicate is where they would like to see growth. Go to that section of the Reference Guide. Determine from the front of the Guide which of the Standard Industrial Classification Code Numbers cover the types of firms who are and who should be interested in your company's products or services. Go down the columns of listings and pick out the applicable ones. List them on the Prospect List form (even those firms whose rating does not appear to. qualify them for credit). Indicate which of the listed firms seem to offer the best financial and longevity credentials, and let your company's sales manager take it from there.

This method is an excellent way to prescreen the pool of potential customers in a given area. It can be an important assist in any company—small or larger—where sales people must cover a territory too large for one person but not large enough for two people. The ratio of unknown diamonds to known jewels (and duds) is in the category of the longshot, but the potential for picking up good journeyman prospects is very high. Unlike most cold calls where the sales person has no clue as to the financial strength of a company, accounts on this Prospect List offer one form of first-step prescreening, and that's an enormous plus.

The sample Prospect List shown in FIG. 5-11 is set up to illustrate how a manufacturer or distributor of grocery items or alcoholic beverages would use the form. The SIC Code lists virtually every type of business. Select those who would be interested in your goods or services, then apply the same procedure.

PARTNERSHIPS

It is important to the security of your accounts receivable that you know the type of business entity that your company is selling. Is it a sole proprietorship? Is it a partnership? If it is a partnership, is there also a silent partner who might have liability in the event of a business failure? Is it a general partnership or a limited partnership? If it is a limited partnership, are the claimed limitations the same as those that are allowed by the statutes of your state? If the business uses a "trade style" (also commonly known as a "fictitious name"), how do you penetrate the trade style to get partnership or company information? Is your customer a division or a subsidiary of a parent company? If it is one of these two, what should you know and/or be doing about your customers in these various business formats? What are the variables between the various types of partnerships and company structures that you must be aware of to give your company's receivables assets appropriate levels of protection?

If you have survived this flurry of questions, be relieved to know that we will answer them in the pages that follow. You must know the who, what, and where of a credit applicant or a customer who already has a receivables balance on your aging report. Available protective devices are not uniformly applicable. This information is an important area of credit and credit management—one too frequently overlooked in the push to ship merchandise or to move too quickly to other areas of credit.

General Partnerships

You should not attempt to spend a lot of time memorizing major and secondary points relating to partnerships. It is enough that you remember certain major differences

PROSPECT LIST

SIC (Standard Industrial
Classification) Code Numbers
51-41 Groceries, Gen'l Lines
51-49 Groceries & Related
Products
51-82 Wines & Distilled
Alcoholic Beverages
51-81 Beer And Ale

Date Of List __8/17/85__

Date of Reference Books __Fall '88__

SIC Code	Name of Business	Location (City/County)	Business Estab.	D & B Rating
51-41	Waterside Markets, Inc.	Alameda, Alameda	1982	FF3 FAIR 10/20,000
51-41	Carson's Groceries, Inc.	Berkeley, Alameda	1979	CC2 Good 75/125,000
51-49	Dempster's Distributing, Inc	Bakersfield, Kern	Over 10	DD2 Good 35/50,000
51-49	Webster's Distributing	Belmont, San Mateo	1980	CB2 Good 125/200,000
51-81	Bentley's Distributing Co.	Chico, Butte	1983	CC3 FAIR 75/125,000
51-81	Simpson's Distributing Inc.	Campbell, Santa Clara	1981	BB2 Good 200/300,000
51-82	Wine World, Inc.	Santa Clara, Santa Clara	1979	1R2 Good 125,000+over

FIG. 5-11.

and guidelines and know where to go to get answers to the others. Credit people have neither the time nor the legal training to give answers to questions that the company attorney can best resolve or as you become familiar with it, the National Association of Credit Managements's CREDIT MANUAL OF COMMERCIAL LAWS can resolve. The manual is not a substitute for your company attorney, but as you become more experienced in the credit management process, it should enable you to extract and apply various types of useful guideline material. Using this book, an appropriate level of experience, and the sources mentioned previously, you should have no difficulty gathering enough data regarding partnerships to make responsible decisions for your company.

The Uniform Partnership Act provides statutory guidelines for the various states, defining the rights, powers, and liabilities that accrue to the general partners in a business or firm. A general partnership can involve two or more people and is the most common form of partnership. It is a relationship of interlocking restraints, obligations, and ramifications, only some of which you have the time or need to know. The Act is specific in its statement that a partnership is not valid unless it includes everything that is in the definition of a partnership. It isn't a partnership—and there isn't partnership liability—if one or more of the ingredients is missing.

Probably the most important single item is the matter of liability. General partners usually have unlimited liability for the firm's obligations. A general partner who elects to withdraw from a partnership cannot terminate his or her liability to creditors (either past or future) until he has notified all people, companies, and businesses with whom the firm does business. The withdrawing general partner cannot simply clean out his or her desk and walk away from the liability of a general partnership without giving appropriate notification to all interested parties. If the withdrawal isn't done within applicable legal guidelines, the general partner's liability will continue whether there is or is not any further active participation in the business by that individual. Creditors are entitled to know—must in fact know—when such a major change occurs in the security base of a customer firm. What responsibility do silent partners have? They are very much a part of this category too. In terms of the law, they are "silent" only in the context of not identifying themselves with the firm or the general partners. As for the silent partner's relationship to the firm's obligations, the silent one(s) has the same unlimited liability for the firm's obligations as the general partners.

A general partnership requires a great deal of faith in their mutual integrity because the responsibilities and acts of one general partner are the responsibilities and acts of all general partners. They share equally in the profits (unless otherwise stated in their business agreement), and unless the agreement states otherwise, they share equally in liability for expenses and losses incurred by the firm. Most states require the filing of a partnership certificate, and also a fictitious name certificate if the firm name doesn't include one or more names of the general partners. Individual assets of the general partners are not exempt from creditor action if creditors have proceeded against the firm's property to satisfy liens and judgments, and after such proceedings there are still unpaid balances and obligations.

The death of a general partner means that the partnership is at an end, although it is not cut off immediately because the surviving partner or partners need to settle the affairs of the partnership. There is usually a prior agreement between the partners—one in which a value has been set on the share of each partner with perhaps an insurance policy on the life of each partner as the source of buy-out funding for the surviving partner(s). A prior agreement also allows the surviving partner or partners to buy the deceased partner's interest in the firm at a previously-determined price (or one tied to a current valuation of the firm's assets and liabilities). The agreement puts no constraints on cash flow as it would if the surviving partner was using company money to partially fund the buy out. The business is able to continue, but without the deceased partner's contribution of particular business, sales, or technical expertise. This loss could prove to be a problem and something that the surviving partners, and the company's creditors, will want to monitor. Meanwhile, the deceased partner's estate receives the benefit of a full-value buy out of his or her share in the firm.

Limited Partnerships

A limited partnership is exactly what the name implies—no active role in the business a contribution to the partnership capital, and no personal liability for its debts. The limited partner's liability is confined to the amount he or she invests in the partnership, and on the same plane with all partnership property, it is subject to creditor claims.

It isn't always easy to determine whether general partners also have one or more limited partners. Most states require the filing of a limited-partnership certificate signed by all parties and containing the firm name, principal place of business, type of business the partners will engage in, names and addresses of partners (which are general partners and which are limited partners), the amount of capital put up by each, and the period of the partnership. Other requirements and nuances exist, all of which you can get from your company's attorney, or you can find them in NACM's Credit Manual of Commercial Laws.

You should also know that a limited partnership (unlike the liability of general partners) continues only for the period stated in the limited-partnership certificate. Limited partners also do not usually participate in the management of the business. Their pay is interest on money invested and a percentage of the profits. If the firm turns out to be a loser, the limited partner's liability is the amount of his or her capital investment. Contrary to what can happen when a general partner dies and there has been no buy-out agreement, the death of a silent partner usually does not terminate the partnership.

How do you know whether a general partnership also has one or more limited or silent partners? It would be wise to include a question regarding that issue on the New Account Information Sheet. It is important to a decision whether you should or should not sell a general partnership, and the amount of credit you might be willing to extend. Protect yourself also with a question regarding the existence of a buy-out agreement in the event of the death or incapacity of a general partner, and how the agreement is funded: life insurance, treasury certificates, company stock, etc. These questions are important and could be very important to the future security of your receivables account when a partnership faces forced dissolution because of a partners death, or if a partnership is able to continue because of sound advanced planning.

PARENT FIRMS/DIVISIONS/SUBSIDIARIES

Do you ever pause in your preliminary appraisal of an account to determine whether you're selling a company that is a parent firm, a division or a subsidiary? If the question wanders through your mind, you should put a hold on it long enough to get an answer. It's important that you know the type of business entity your company is examining. Unless you consciously make the effort to get and use that information during the credit evaluation, your company could eventually face an entirely different sales and collection situation from the one you think you're getting into.

A *parent firm* is a company that stands alone—entirely on its own. It is solely responsible for all of its actions and decisions. No ''deep pockets'' are standing behind it from which it can get money to support it when business declines. If the company has financial problems and the banker turns away—in many cases the bank is the only deep pocket to which the firm can turn—then the problem can prove critical for the parent, the divisions, and the subsidiaries. If the parent company fails, or makes a Chapter XI filing to attempt a reorganization of the business, the assets of divisions and subsidiaries become hostage to creditor claims along with assets of the parent firm.

A *division* is a part of a company—not a company in its own right. It is a specific part of the whole. It might be the ball-bearing division of an automobile manufacturer, or it might be the dairy products division of a food-marketing chain. Regardless of its relative importance as one part of the whole, selling to a division gives the supplier the added comfort of billing to the company's payables section (one payables section frequently handles payments for all divisions of a small company), or billing to the payables section of the division itself.

When a division handles its own payables but becomes increasingly slow in processing payments, the supplier should look for indications that the parent systematically is syphoning money out of the division. You must do your homework on the company's relationship with its suppliers before you begin to sell one of the divisions. When goods are sold to a division and you try to collect the money from the head office of a company that is gradually running itself into the ground, your efforts are about as effective as a flash flood warning received after the town is already under six feet of water. It is an after-the-fact situation that can only do damage to your company's bad-debt reserve.

When you sell the subsidiary of a parent company, it can be an excellent piece of business, or it can be a tricky and a dangerous relationship. A well-prepared report from a commercial reporting firm should alert you to the fact that your potential customer company is a subsidiary. The report also should include the parent company's name, headquarters location, and principal type(s) of business. What does it do for you if the company is a subsidiary? An early negative is that it might not be possible for you to get financial information (bank, financial statements, etc.) on the subsidiary company. Many parent companies incorporate figures from their subsidiaries into the parent's financial statement. The parent company also might have a policy of not divulging financial information on the subsidiary companies.

Unless you pick up a rumor from peer credit managers, or subscribe to a reporting service, being unable to get financial information could be your first indication that the prospective customer is not a ''stand alone'' company. It could be your first indication that the incorporated company is still a part of a larger company. You also might be unaware that the prospective customer company is quite profitable but that each month (quarterly or semiannually) the parent firm skims off large sums or varying percentages of the revenues. The parent company might have instructed your prospective customer as a matter of parent company policy to drag its feet in the processing and releasing of payments. It happens to many good, aggressive, successful companies who allow other companies to acquire them for reasons that seem so right at the time of acquisition. Many learn too late that the reasons for allowing other companies to acquire them were the right ones, however, they should have chosen another company to acquire them.

When you have determined that a company is a subsidiary of a financially strong company, you must remember that this financially strong parent could turn its back on the subsidiary in its time of financial need. A parent company usually is not legally obligated to perform mouth-to-mouth financial resuscitation on a subsidiary, nor must they provide intravenous feedings of cash. Some parent companies accept responsibility for the debts of their subsidiaries, others do not. Whenever there is a question regarding

(Company Letterhead)

CORPORATE GUARANTEE

The XYZ Company_____(address)_____
agrees to guarantee payment for purchases made by its' subsidiary, _____(name and address)_____, from
the _____(creditor/supplier company's name and address)_____,
during the period from _____ thru _____
inclusive.

Should the _____(subsidiary company)_____ fail to
make payment or payments within the Net 30 Days sales/credit
terms of the _____(creditor/supplier company)_____, the
___(parent/guarantor company)_____ will upon notification
received in writing from the _(creditor/supplier company)_,
and upon receipt of invoices for which the payment claim is
made, promptly pay the submitted past due invoices as covered
by this agreement.

It is understood that payments for invoices is subject
to verification of the quantities ordered and received, the
prices quoted and billed, and such other obligations and
requirements as may be a part of the agreement between the
___(subsidiary/purchaser company)___ and the ___(creditor-_____
_____supplier company)_____.

Dated _____   by _____
                                          Treasurer
                                       The XYZ Company

FIG. 5-12.

the financial stability of a subsidiary, inform the subsidiary that your company cannot offer credit terms unless the financial officer of the parent company (VP of Finance or Treasurer) furnishes a letter to your company stating that the parent company accepts payment responsibility for all obligations incurred with your firm by the subsidiary—or accepts such obligations to a specific dollar limit and termination date. If you're satisfied that the parent company has no serious financial problems, such a letter will give "deep pockets" protection to your receivables interest in the subsidiary company. A parent company should have no corporate or legal problem with your request for the letter of guarantee. When a parent company gives such letters in support of a subsidiary's customary business activity, rulings on the legality of such letters have been uniformly positive. Such letters normally qualify as being "in support of the subsidiary's customary business activity."

A letter such as the one described doesn't give your company the same level of protection from other claimants as does a Uniform Commercial Code Filing, but this letter is a different type of protection for a different type of problem. The letter from a parent firm is intended to ensure that a financially strong parent firm will accept responsibility for monies owed by a subsidiary. In the event of the subsidiary's failure, the parent company will dig into its deep pockets and pay your company.

ASSUMED OR FICTITIOUS NAMES

When I discussed partnerships, I mentioned the subject of assumed or fictitious names (trade styles). Credit managers need to know how they can get information regarding a partnership operating under a "trade style." The people who operate under a trade style (an assumed or fictitious name) should know that they have specific legal obligations to those individuals, partnerships, or business firms with whom they do business or might do business. Following is a look at the more important aspects of dealing with "assumed or fictitious" names.

State legislatures have dealt with the subject of assumed or ficitious names by enacting statutes that require people who transact business under partnership or assumed names (trade styles, etc.) to file a certificate detailing that information. Prior to the enactment of such legislation, it was often almost impossible for suppliers and other interested parties to determine who had financial responsibility for obligations incurred under the assumed or fictitious name. After the various states enacted legislation, credit grantors and others who previously had hesitated to do business with a fictitious or assumed name entity were able to learn—without difficulty—with whom they would be dealing.

The statutes of most states provide for fines and/or imprisonment for failure to comply to this legislation; this is obviously not an area of responsibility to be taken lightly. A few states impose no penalty for failure to comply with the filing requirement, but that latitude from one state to another is not an acceptable reasons for failing to make a proper filing.

Where is the filing done? In some states you file the certificate in the office of the Clerk of the county in which the company has its principal place of business. Other states require you to make the filing with the County Recorder, Office of the Town Clerk, Clerk of the Circuit Court, or a variety of other designations.

Statutes governing this matter run the gamut of what each of 50 state legislative bodies decided was appropriate for their state. I suggest that, if you are also a partner in a business operating under an assumed or fictitious name, you should check for information regarding filing requirements with the County Clerk or the County Recorder of the county in which the headquarters of your business or firm is located. If another agency has filing jurisdiction in your state, either of the above-mentioned county agencies should be able to give you the information.

Compliance is a simple matter of completing and filing the appropriate form. Failure to comply is not something that you should rationalize into an area of unimportance if your state is one that can impose a fine, a prison sentence, or both. I don't know how you decide your priorities, but the possibility of becoming attached to one of those penalties would be more than enough incentive for me to get it done—immediately!

Chapter 6

Consolidating and Evaluating Credit Information

IF GATHERING GOOD INFORMATION (WHICH IS THE TOOLS) IS THE BASIC STEP IN THE sequence leading to a solid credit decision, then knowing how to use it is of equal importance. You can be a world-class collector of information and data but if you cannot interpret and apply it, then collecting it is pointless. Unless you are capable of taking data from various sources and systematically assembling it into a helpful bank of quality reference data, it will not be useful to you.

The wonderful part of this gather, evaluate, and decide process is the absence of any insurmountable complexity. It's true that you must have some experience before you begin to offer four- and five-figure credit lines, but that's only common sense. No person should expect to walk untrained into a decision-making situation and begin immediately to grind out decisions of high or professional quality. Some owners of small companies might be pushed into making decisions—including bigger dollar decisions—than an inexperienced employee at a bigger company. Other owners of small companies have a chance to grow into credit decisions in step with company growth. You shouldn't expect to always have the answers to your daily credit management problems. Not all of the pros do either! Facing new and complex situations, and getting the right answers from a combination of experience and reliable sources, is part of an owner's business and professional growth. Gradually increase your knowledge about credit to the point where you are prepared to handle more complex credit problems, but don't jump ahead of your present decision-making capabilities. You'll feel more at ease making credit decisions as your experiences take you into new applications of your analytical and judgmental skills.

The title of this chapter (Consolidating and Evaluating Credit Information) goes to the core of what you must do with the information you gathered in Chapter 5. It gives you the sequence of forms and guidelines to consolidate information and to make sound credit decisions. You might have limited credit management experience, but your interest in knowing enough about the process to make good credit decisions for your company is mutually understood, and it certainly isn't too much to expect of yourself. This chapter will provide you with the framework for putting together good and practical credit decisions—a plateau of decision making from which your company's eventual growth might gradually lead you into more complex and less-clearly defined areas. When that happens, you already will have the foundation necessary to build the additional skills you will need to deal with the more complex areas of credit.

ACCOUNT INFORMATION ANALYSIS SHEET

This form brings together all of the bits-and-pieces of information that you gathered from the banker, suppliers, and the applicant (financial statement). It consolidates the data in such a way that you are able to make side-by-side comparisons of the experience of three suppliers; you are able to observe the bank's experience and comments; you are able to note the strengths and weaknesses of the applicant firm as indicated by the financial statement, and if you have access to reports prepared by credit reporting agencies (Dun & Bradstreet, The National Association of Credit Management, etc.), you are able to compare them. Everything is in front of you on the one form. Having brought all of your information to this point, you are in the equivalent of baseball's catbird seat.

When you have good supplier data on every line of an Account Information Analysis Sheet (FIG. 6-1), you are ready to challenge the decision-making process. Unless information in one or more of the key areas is misinterpreted, you should not have a problem making a sound decision. If references one, two, and three on the Account Information Sheet have each sold the account successfully for one or more years, and high credit, open balances and past-due figures are in line with sales terms, you have good reason to be pleased. When you can add a good bank relationship and a financial statement to those pluses that help to confirm the good supplier and bank reports, your pleasure should be allowed to become a smile.

The smile disappears when the facts change, and you find yourself looking at experience data that indicates the applicant is 25 to 50 days past due with one or more of the three supplier references. You can say goodbye to the catbird seat if the bank's report reflects chronic, past-due loan payments. Substituting this new set of experience data for the first one, you are faced with an account that only might be good enough for a small first order and credit line, or no credit line at all. Be wary. Don't add your company's name to the list of suppliers who have become increasingly disenchanted with the direction this customer is taking.

Assigning a credit line involves a long sequence of items and utilizes an important section of credit procedures. Everything relevant to the procedure of gathering, consolidating, and evaluating information is important. Almost every segment of the account-evaluation process is equal to the others in its importance. Your first step after you have consolidated the reference data is to look for a payment pattern in the responses you received from the applicant's suppliers. Each supplier sells a customer to a credit high that might be higher or lower than others, but the customer should pay all suppliers, whether they are large or small, on a reasonably equitable basis. If one or two suppliers are the majors and they have reported account payments as "prompt to slow 30 days," your question is to determine whether the prospective customer pays other suppliers within a similar time frame as it relates to their sales terms. When you find that there is no consistency in payment treatment from major suppliers to other suppliers, it usually means that your applicant keeps major suppliers happy by paying them within their terms (or past due a very few days) while paying other suppliers much more slowly. If sales to this prospective customer would put your company in the "slow pay" group, it could be a major point in the direction of your credit decision. It isn't unusual for a customer who is experiencing tight cash flow to first take care of the major supplier(s), but he should not abuse the accounts of other suppliers to support this policy.

ACCOUNT INFORMATION ANALYSIS SHEET

Company Name:_____　Credit Limit:_____

Mail/Billing Address:_____　Date Assigned:_____

_____

Supplier References:	No.1	No.2	No.3
Years Sold			
Recent High Credit			
Current Balance			
Past Due Balance			
Terms			
Disc/Ppt/Slow to _____			
Supplier Comments			

Bank Reference:

Savings (Date opened & average balance)_____

Checking (Date opened & average balance)_____

Loans (Equipment, land, buildings, revolving, etc.)_____

Credit Line (Including loans)_____

Comments_____

Financial Statement:

Date(s)_____

Audited or Unaudited_____

If audited, auditor's comments_____

_____

_____

Dun & Bradstreet, NACM or other credit report:

Name of reporting company_____

Date of report_____If D&B, what rating?_____

Additional comments_____

FIG. 6-1.

The bank's experience with your credit applicant might not reflect the payment pattern reported by most suppliers. It should come as no surprise that some suppliers report a pattern of slow payments while the bank reports that the customer pays within the terms of loan agreements. Any business that faces a monthly or periodic *cash-flow shortfall* (not enough cash generated from accounts receivable to handle the monthly cash requirement) has no alternative but to take good care of its banking relationship. Without ongoing bank support, the cash shortfall could trigger problems that might quickly deteriorate into a crisis of survival. It follows that the endorsement the bank gives this customer should be as strong or stronger than those of supplier respondents.

Should you be concerned that a banker might endorse a relationship with the customer beyond a level than the facts of their relationship could support? Bankers might respond to your questions with enthusiasm, sarcasm, or dismay, but almost never do they respond with information that is a deliberate intent to mislead. Where you should exercise conservative judgment is in the weight given to the bank's position as the supplier of your credit applicant's primary raw material—money. What more obvious incentive could there be for a firm to properly handle the relationship with its bank than the chilling thought that they could jeopardize or terminate a vital business relationship if they do not meet the company's loan repayment agreements. Supplying money to a customer is a privileged position. It is one not equalled by a major supplier. That position should cause you to assign a little less weight to the bank's experience than you do to supplier relationships, a good Dun & Bradstreet rating, or a respectable financial statement.

To bolster an applicant's case for a credit line, CPA-prepared financial statements (preferably audited statements) should show an acceptable level of profit from sales. You should always ask a credit applicant for the ''currently applicable financial statement'' and if available, the next two most recent ones to help you track whether the business is experiencing good growth, or is on a downward trend. You should not evaluate internally-prepared financial statements in the same context as statements an outside accounting firm prepares. If your applicant gives you internally prepared financial statements, consider them as general information only.

Whether you do or do not have access to Dun & Bradstreet reports and ratings (or the reports of other credit reporting and rating agencies), you eventually might find it helpful to use one of these services in your own company. Reports and ratings are valuable not only for the broad scope of their content but for the interpretation given data by Dun & Bradstreet's credit analysts. An experienced credit manager at times will question whether an assigned rating is justified by the report data. You might not have the experience of a professional credit manager but your knowledge of an applicant company might give you reason to disagree with a rating. The offset to this question regarding accuracy of a rating is that you should give weight to your own knowledge. Mentally deduct something from the higher rating and add something if your personal knowledge of the account tells you the rating is a bit low. These reports are usually the work of an experienced analyst, but if the information available to that analyst is not as complete as it should be—and we have discussed that several times in these pages—the quality of his or her decision and rating will be impacted adversely. Such reports can be helpful yardsticks in arriving at your own decision and/or a yardstick against which to measure your decision. If you know the companies to whom you sell—their backgrounds, the history of their owners, and their reputation in the trade—and your decision does not agree with Dun & Bradstreet's rating, you are not automatically wrong. Evaluation of data is a matter of interpretation, experience, and judgment. Two people could use the same reservoir of information and still arrive at surprisingly different ratings. There should, however, be no major difference in the decisions unless one of the people evaluating the data has more or less experience, overlooks something, or makes a judgmental error.

You should have a high level of interest in accounts that show a supplier payment's record within or near terms over a period of one year or longer. These accounts should get and hold your attention. When you are convinced from the information you have received that supplier accounts are handled in a satisfactory manner, be careful to check whether the average high credit experience of the reporting suppliers is within the range of the applicant's requested credit line from your company. If the figure is comparable and there is nothing derogatory in the input from bank, suppliers, credit reporting agency, or the financial statements, you should offer the applicant a credit line somewhat below the high credit figures reported by other suppliers. Why below those figures? Because you try to avoid beginning a credit relationship by offering a new account, a credit line/limit that your best judgment tells you is close to your company's allowable maximum for the account. Try to open the account with a credit line that is below the highs being sold by other suppliers, unless the first order is going to immediately push the limit to, or above, your "best judgment" maximum. To increase the first limit even slightly beyond the earlier maximum, the account must be good to excellent in every area of sales, supplier, and bank experience. Only when the first order represents a unique opportunity to develop what you hope will become a very solid account should you consider giving the applicant a credit limit as high or higher than the highs reported by other suppliers. Remember too, that you are not, and probably will not be, a major supplier of the applicant firm. Unless your product(s) fill more than a support gap in the product lines carried by the applicant, there should be no valid reason for the credit line you give the applicant to approach those of the major suppliers. If the requested credit line is unusually high, let the applicant know that you are pleased to have the opportunity to process the credit application, but you are surprised at the size of the requested credit line since your product line is a support product (if of course this is correct) rather than one of the major product lines. Why, you might ask, do you need an opening line that seems more suited to what fits your needs from a major supplier? The answer probably will be acceptable, but why do they request a credit line that is out of synch with usual requirements for a business of the applicant's size, area, and activity? Press diplomatically, but firmly, for a satisfactory answer. You want to sell product(s) but any major variation from what you can immediately or easily understand should not be allowed to pass without some questions.

THE "RIGHT TO KNOW"

Never extend credit terms—or more than a token amount of credit—to a customer who is unwilling to give you the information necessary to properly evaluate the account. Any company or business that claims exemption from the necessity to cooperate with a prospective supplier by not furnishing credit reference data is taking an unacceptable position. The applicant firm might seem to be doing very well and the image of stability and long-term success might seem very tempting, but unless the expected level of purchases is so low or so infrequent as to make the normal credit evaluation procedure a mutual embarrassment, you must reject the application.

Example: The focus of this hypothetical example is on a person who has had three, high-volume, floor-covering dealerships in various parts of a state or region over a period of ten or twelve years. He is notorious for impacting each market area with prices so low that he made a competitive shambles of regional or area marketplaces for legitimate members of the floor-covering industry. He buys large quantities of carpeting, gradually builds up large past-due balances, strings his supplier accounts to unacceptable aging limits, liquidates heavy warehouse inventories for cash, files for bankruptcy under Chapter XI of the Bankruptcy Act (see Chapter 11) and ultimately is discharged as bankrupt, then disappears for a year or more.

Nearly two years after the last bankruptcy, a new floor-covering distributor surfaces in another section of the same region or area. The front man for the company is not the person previously mentioned, but he has experience; he has been associated with companies both successful and unsuccessful; he has been known to engage in some borderline practices; and he offers an aggressive style of merchandising that contrasts with the slower pace of others in the area. One major manufacturer has been looking for an aggressive outlet in the dealers area and accepts the account with a minimum of background checking and risk evaluation. (A major manufacturer in an industry can occasionally take this risk. The small company cannot).

About this time, you are approached for a credit line. You know the business is new, but you send a copy of the New Account Information form and ask for a copy of the company's opening financial statement—the company now being in business about two months. You have an in-house order for what would be a substantial dollar amount for one of your established accounts, and there is pressure from the applicant for you to release the order. You are not swayed by dealer assurances that "We've got plenty of money to handle our accounts. There's no problem." You don't release the order on that type of self-serving assurance. Urge the applicant's spokesman to complete the application and return it to you.

The next day a friend in the trade calls and mentions that his salesman called on the account. As he was leaving the office he saw "the person" drive around to the back of the warehouse. He immediately asked the man who had represented himself as the owner if "the person" was involved in the company. The reply was to the effect that "he's a friend and he's helping set up some things, but has no interest in the company." You contact the agency in your state that handles the approval and monitoring of corporations, find that "the person" is not listed as a partner or company officer, and wait for the New Account Information form.

The form finally arrives with a copy of the opening financial statement. Supplier references are the previously mentioned major supplier and one other (both sold for less than two months) with the major's account already 10 days past due and the other 15 days past due. You contact the bank and are told that the company's opening-and-average balance has fluctuated between "a high 4 and low 5 figures" (something between a low side of eight-to-ten thousand and ten-to-twenty thousand on the high side). The bank has extended no line(s) of credit and the account has leased all vehicles, warehouse equipment and office fixtures. The internally prepared opening financial statement indicates that the company started the business with a net investment of $22,000.

You do not bite. Trade talk becomes increasingly persistent that "the person" is spending more time at the store and, though there is nothing to link him directly with the company, his involvement is evident. Three times "this person" engineered a planned bankruptcy that bilked his suppliers of hundreds of thousands of dollars, but he was clever enough to provide no hard evidence upon which a district attorney could build a case. When will the fourth bankruptcy occur? The account probably will file at some point down the road, after "the person" assembles all of the pieces necessary for a near-fraudulent bankruptcy—one that cannot be proven. Don't let your company be victimized by a seasoned scam operator such as "the person." Your company might make a few dollars in the early stages of his game but if you allow receivables totals to gradually become bigger and older, your ultimate loss will be "the person's" gain.

It seems incongruous to say that selling one or more of the biggest companies in the country could present problems, but problems are quite possible when the subject is a level of sales that would represent a substantial percentage of your company's total annual sales. It isn't a question of whether the giant companies will pay, the question is "when will they." Your small company would be justified in welcoming one of the huge corporations to your aging report; you could not, however, afford to allow that corporation to be casual with payments for your product(s). Forty-five or fifty days from invoice date might not be a problem for the major supplier who has no cash-flow problem, but your company might have a serious cash-flow problem if payments from your casual giant did not arrive until 15, 20, or even 30 days after the due date. Take a close look at the promptness record of the giant company before you commit the liquidity of your company to it.

I also would like to mention that doing business with many of the branches of federal, state, and local governments can be very profitable—also frustrating, exasperating, and a potential hazard to your cash flow. It is another of those supplier/customer relationships to which the small company should devote a little precommitment thought and investigation. Payments can range from prompt to sporadic to very slow, and the flow of bureaucratic questions, delays, and red tape can be very testing. Unless your company's product(s) or service has the potential for nothing more than a minimal problem situation, locking a large percentage of your business into a relationship with an agency of the government could lead to some new and potentially unwelcome business and financial experiences.

Can any kind of a case be made for taking on a relatively high percentage of government business? Of course. The ideal scenario would be the combination of a small company with a strong cash flow and a product/profit margin that would not be unfavorably impacted if receivables payments were to extend 15 to 30 days beyond normal payment expectations. There is no question that in such a situation, and with other factors also in balance, that you could make a very strong case for taking on some government business or some business with one of the giant companies.

THE "HE'S ALRIGHT" SYNDROME

It is always startling to learn that the charismatic man or woman who was so successful at getting investors to hand over large sums of money was totally dishonest. The personal and business vulnerability can be even more serious when we're talking about relationships with people who are much closer to us than strangers.

Is the new account an acquaintance, a friend, a good buddy? These words are not synonyms for the term "good customer." Any time you lull yourself into thinking you can bypass the procedures—checking bank and supplier references, etc.—because you're dealing with a friend or acquaintance, the painful fact is that these people have the potential for being very hazardous to the health of your accounts receivable. When you ship that big one-time order, or when you set the account up on a continuing credit line that allows it to get several smaller orders before individual balances begin to become past due—the story has already taken a familiar turn. Acquaintance, friend, good buddy? Perhaps. An opportunist who is using your personal relationship to his or her advantage? It isn't nice to contemplate, but it happens frequently enough to warrant a warning.

Don't skip any of the procedural steps. Check the credit references of friends or acquaintances as thoroughly as you would the references of that out-of-the-blue stranger. The one time that you fail to follow your procedures could be the time you set your company up for a serious collection problem, or loss. The only way you can have presale knowledge of how a business or company handles supplier relationships is from supplier information, credit reports, and the banker's comments. If good old "he's alright" or "she's alright" is indeed a solid article—a good friend in every sense of the term—then asking him or her for some preshipment reference data will be applauded as good business practice. If your request prompts seemingly uncharacteristic grumbling and testy asides, a look at your friend's relationships with suppliers could make you very happy that you did not exclude any of the customary steps from your account evaluation.

ASSIGNING A CREDIT LINE

At this point, you have a cross section of input from those who have been or are currently dealing with the credit applicant. You have consolidated that input on the Account Information Analysis Sheet and the final step in the evaluation process is to reject the applicant or write a figure in the Credit Limit box in the upper right-hand corner of the Analysis Sheet.

Before you write that figure, and as a part of your future pattern for analyzing and assigning credit lines, turn to the end of this chapter to the Checklist Form (A "Credit-Worthy" Customer—The Ingredients). Check the information on your Analysis Sheet against the checklist guideline questions. From that recap of what you should be looking for vs. what the applicant has to offer, a credit decision should not be difficult.

NOTIFYING THE CUSTOMER

Customers are indispensable. They make it possible for your company to have its chance to succeed. If you have no customers, or you don't have enough customers, the fact that your company would have been brilliantly managed is irrelevant. If customers aren't there in adequate numbers, no level of management skill can do more than sustain a struggling firm for any longer than an average length of time.

The treatment a credit customer receives from the person who handles credit decisions has great impact on how he or she perceives your company. Every company anywhere can use all of the good customer relations input they can get. You or your designated employee can help your company's image in the way you handle problems and by your cooperation and helpful spirit in other areas where there is a problem that could adversely effect your company's relationship with the customer. Prompt, courteous correspondence (FIGS. 6-2 and 6-3) is also important—whether in answer to a customer's letter or to put something in writing as a means of ensuring mutual understanding. The use of correspondence plus telephone calls to clarify, discuss, or expedite, should become an important customer relations extension of your approach to credit management.

RECORDING AND REVIEWING CREDIT LINES

Use the Credit Lines Form (FIG. 6-4) to keep a current list of the credit lines/limits that you have assigned, the date and amount you assigned, and the date you should review the account. If the account is new, the prudent procedure is to review the credit line three months after the date you assigned the original credit line. Unless the monitoring of accounts receivable gives you reason to review the credit lines of certain accounts more frequently (a pattern of less-prompt payments, reports of payment or other problems from other companies, etc.), put your review of credit lines on an interval of six months. When combined with your normal daily monitoring of aged trial balance reports (aging reports), it should be frequent enough to enable you to pick up early signs of an account problem before it becomes a matter of serious concern.

CREDIT FILE CONTROL SHEET

There is similarity between the Credit File Control Sheet (FIG. 6-5) and the Account Information Analysis Sheet (FIG. 6-1). Much of the data is the same and your first

(Date)

Company Name
Street Address (or P.O. Box No.)
City, State and Zip Code

Dear Mr. (Ms.) _____:

Thank you for your prompt response to our request for credit references and credit reference data.

We have assigned your account a temporary credit line of _____
on our standard sales terms of 2%/10 days, Net 30. The account
experience will be reviewed at the end of 90 days, and if our
experience and your product requirements indicate the need for
an increase, we will hope to do it at that time.

Your interest in our products is greatly appreciated. We anticipate a long and mutually rewarding relationship.

Sincerely,

Credit Manager

FIG. 6-2.

(Date)

Name of Account
Street Address (or P.O. Box)
City, State and Zip Code

Dear Mr. (Ms.) _____ :

It is my pleasure to advise you that we have set an opening
credit line of $5,000.00 for your account. This should not be
construed as a maximum figure for use over the long term but
rather an opportunity for our two firms to become better business acquaintances before we consider increasing the line.

Please call if I can assist you in any way. We greatly appreciate your interest in our product(s) and anticipate a mutually successful long-term association.

Sincerely,

Credit Manager

FIG. 6-3.

CREDIT LINES

Account Number	Name And Location	Date Originally Assigned	Amount Originally Assigned	Date Reviewed	Current Credit Line

FIG. 6-4.

CREDIT FILE CONTROL SHEET

IDENTIFICATION

Name (and/or trade style):_____

Billing/Payments Address:_____

DOCUMENTS IN FILE

Credit App.(Date)_____App. Rec'd_____References
Contacted_____

Security Documents_____UCC Filing: Date_____

Location_____

Credit Reports: (Report Date)   (Update Requested)   (Update Rec'd)

D & B_____

NACM_____

OTHER_____

Bank Reference(s)_____

_____

Trade Reference(s)_____

_____

Financials, Business Plan, etc._____

_____

Comments (Territory Rep)_____

_____

FIG. 6-5.

AUTHORIZATION

Credit Requested:

First Order_____

Anticipated High Credit_____

Credit Line:

Amount_____ Special Instructions_____

_____

_____

by_____ date_____

Experience Analysis @_____ : _____

_____

_____

Experience Analysis @_____ : _____

_____

_____

Fig. 6-5. Continued.

reaction might be that the only benefit from the similarity is that you can transfer much of what is needed on the File Control Sheet directly from the Analysis Sheet. That is true in one sense—not true in the other.

Any duplication of work occurs because the two forms have different purposes. The Analysis Sheet is an important evaluation tool—one you will use when examining an applicant's request for a credit line. When you have completed the account evaluation and you have assigned or declined a credit line, the part played by the Analysis Sheet is over and it becomes a support document—a very important one—in the customer file. When you have assigned or declined a credit line, the Credit File Control Sheet becomes the top document in the file folder directly under the Letter Notifying Customer of Credit Line, Incoming/Outgoing Letters (re: discounts, missing invoices, past-due balances, etc.), and the Customer Call Sheet. You use it as the base reference document when you review a credit line, when you increase a credit line, or when you need a total input of information because of an account problem. The File Control Sheet is a recap of the other documents in the file folder—the ones that went into the original credit evaluation plus changes in bank or supplier data you received subsequent to that evaluation. Unless there is a need to recall in greater depth some specific bit of information or reference data, documents filed under the Credit File Control Sheet become a very lonesome group.

NEW ACCOUNT SITUATION—EXAMPLE #1

Your company is a small supplier and your maximum credit line to customers is $2500. The credit applicant has been in business for three years and releases no financial information.

First Reference: Sold two years to a high credit (HIC) of $1500. The customer consistently pays 30/40 days slow with recent slowness to 45/50 days. $980 is open with $390 current and $590 slow to 48 days.

Second Reference: Sold two and one-half years to H/C of $850. The customer, until recently, paid 20/30 days slow—now 30/45 days slow. $720 is open with $340 current and $380 past due to 42 days.

Third Reference: Supplier of primary product line. Sold three years to H/C of $2300. $2300 is open with $640 current and $1660 past due 30/46 days.

The Banker: Speaks somewhat guardedly regarding the account and its prospects. Has a medium, five-figure credit line secured by accounts receivable, merchandise, and capital equipment. Facilities (land and buildings) are leased. Says the account has had sales and management problems that to date do not seem to have been solved. The banker has been working with the account (restructuring loan agreements, etc.) to ease the considerable strain on the cash flow.)

The Questions: You are asked to approve an order for $380 with additional orders to follow over a period of the next two weeks. The requested credit line is $1500 based upon projected product requirements.

☐ Do you approve the $380 order on credit terms?

☐ How do you evaluate the request for a $1500 credit line given the input of suppliers and banker?

☐ If you decide not to sell the account on open terms—or at a credit limit below the requested $1500—under what conditions might you sell the account? If you do sell the account on open terms, what is your rationale?

The Answers:

☐ You do not approve a $380 credit sale.

☐ Each supplier reference reports slow-to-slower pay and a deteriorating account situation. The banker's report strongly supports the experiences of the suppliers and offers nothing to encourage thoughts of a turnaround. No incentive is strong enough to involve your company at a credit level of $1500. This account would be a collection problem from the moment your products left your warehouse.

☐ If the order would involve special purchases of materials or ingredients, special packaging and labeling, etc., get an advance payment large enough to cover your costs of manufacturing the special product; perhaps the alternative of 50 percent of the dollar amount of the order if that percentage of the total order will cover your manufacturing costs. The balance? Instruct the freight company or your driver to get the balance still due (cashier's check or money order if there has been any report of a problem with company or personal checks—and be sure to notify the customer to have payment ready in the amount and form you specified) when you make the delivery. Payment later that afternoon, the next day, or the next week? No way! The driver (yours or the freight company's) is to get the customer's payment in the form and amount you have specified when the delivery is made, or they are to return the order to your company.

Uppermost in your mind should be the thought that this is not a customer situation that you can develop into something good, profitable, or meaningful. If a prospective customer who has these types of problems is not favorably inclined to play your game by your rules, don't touch the account.

To convert Example #1 into an acceptable credit situation would necessitate changes in the input of suppliers and banker. If the past-due figures submitted by the three suppliers were to each lose 20 days, the resulting past-due average of 10 to 20 days per account (down from 30 to 48 days past due) would be acceptable. Changing the bankers input to indicate that the account handled loan obligations as agreed—and with no apparent sales, financial, or management problems—would effectively eliminate that problem area.

With no derogatory reports from the suppliers or the banker, your decision on the $380 credit sale would change to a ''yes,'' and you would give your approval to the applicant's request for a $1500 credit line.

NEW ACCOUNT SITUATION—EXAMPLE #2

Example #2 directs your attention to a credit application from a two-man partnership. It is a close-held corporation with each partner owning 50 percent of the stock. Because it is not a publicly held company, they do not release financial information. The applicant firm is well-known in the trade and has been in business for approximately nine years.

Your firm is not the same small one profiled in Example #1. It is larger, offers sales terms of Net 30, and extends credit to several accounts in the $5000 to $6000 area.

First Reference: Sold for years to a H/C of $3600. The customer usually pays within terms, and never more than 10 days slow. $950 is open and nothing is past due.

Second Reference: Sold for about a year to a H/C of $5200. Customers pays within terms. There is an open balance of $2840, and nothing is past due.

Third Reference: Sold for approximately four years to a H/C of $4480. Supplier states that here have been a couple of slow pay situations due to some problems with the merchandise. The account pays within terms to a maximum of 10/15 days slow. $2100 is open and nothing is past due.

The Banker: States that he helped the account with a capital-equipment loan of $150,000 when the account started the business 9 years ago. Payments have been as agreed and subsequently he has provided the company with a standby ''cash flow'' credit line of $50,000 (not currently being used). The banker is very satisfied with the relationship and expresses a high regard for the two partners.

Additional Information: One partner is the company president, handles administrative matters, financial and corporate planning. He is 46 years old, married, spent 15 years as general manager of a large regional company in the same business. Personal record is clear.

The second partner is the company's vice president/sales. He is 41 years old, also married, and had 12 years of related experience (division sales manager/same business) before they formed the partnership. Personal record is clear.

Questions: The first order is $1480. The customer expects to buy between $2000 and $2500 worth of product(s) each month.

- ☐ Will you approve the $1480 order on credit terms?
- ☐ How do you evaluate the request for a $2500 credit line?
- ☐ If you decide to assign the account a credit line of $2500, what is your rationale?

Answers:

☐ You will approve the $1480 order on credit terms.

☐ An evaluation of the supplier reference data and the banker's statements make it clear that you will approve the $2500 opening credit line.

☐ The application is obviously a solid, well-managed firm. In addition to the excellent supplier and bank reports, your $2500 credit line is well within the maximums offered by other suppliers.

NEW ACCOUNT SITUATION—EXAMPLE #3

Example #3 uses the same set of facts as those outlined in Example #2. The two partners and their close-held company are unchanged—unchanged until a major problem occurs that periodically confronts managers in the real world of credit situations.

The facts as they relate to your company are exactly the same as stated in Example #2. Your challenge is how to deal with a radical change in the internal structure of the customer company.

The Facts: Health reasons make it mandatory that the company president (one of the two partners) sell his 50 percent of the business. The other partner agrees, with the bank's support, to buy his partner's share of the business for $200,000—$75,000 to be paid immediately from bank-advanced funds and the other $125,000 in the form of a secured note (UCC filing) against the business. Payments are to be $2500 per month for a period of approximately five years (including interest charges, etc.).

The Questions:

☐ What, if anything, will this do to the business?

☐ What are some of the potential dangers that did not exist prior to the dissolution of this partnership?

☐ What is the major danger? Is it financial, or is it in the balance of experience and skills, now greatly diminished via the loss of one partner?

☐ The business has been netting between $35,000 and $40,000 a year for the past three years. Will a payment of $2500 a month ($30,000 a year) put too severe a strain on it?

☐ How would this change (these changes) influence your thinking regarding your credit line for this firm?

☐ Would you immediately downgrade the credit line? Would you continue the same credit line but monitor the account more closely? Would you decide that the succeeding partner must know what he's doing, so you assign the account no more attention than you previously gave it? Would you panic, leave your company and take a job in a distant state under an assumed name? (If the latter, please consider another line of work.)

☐ If account balances slowly begin to stretch out on your aged trial balance report (aging sheet), what do you do to protect the interest of your company? Do you do any of the options mentioned in the above paragraph? What other suggestions or options do you have?

The Answers:

☐ Obviously, the banker does not think that the combination of the above problems poses a major danger to continuity of the business or he would not advance $75,000 to enable the surviving partner to gain control of the business.

☐ If the business has been experiencing steady annual growth, and the projection for continued growth is good, the question of whether one partner can continue to successfully operate the business has been partially answered.

☐ The second part of the answer is not as obvious as the first. There will be no replacement for the partner who was the company's president—it's financial and business planner. How will the purchasing partner deal with the absence of these very necessary strengths as he attempts to project financial needs and plan steps and plateaus of growth consistent with the capabilities of what is now a different company? How will he avoid the dangers that could result from stretching beyond the capabilities of the business to handle these situations?

☐ You would probably not downgrade the credit line, but you would monitor it carefully for at least a year after the departure of the one partner (the company's president). You would definitely not increase the credit line until the company's performance under the surviving partner's management indicates a level of continuity that spells survival first—growth second.

☐ If the account begins to lose ground and balances begin to slip into new and unacceptable aging areas, you will want to contact the account (before it has slipped more than a few days), discuss the transitional problems with the surviving partner, check with peer supplier credit managers for their input, and decide whether to reduce the credit line. Also decide whether you should go to some formula for account balance reduction (your driver picks up a check for one and one half times the value of each new order when he delivers them, or hold orders until the account pays the oldest open balance(s), etc.

Do not make a premature, panic-induced decision. Unless account balances begin almost immediately to stretch into new past-due aging, take no precipitous action. First, do a rapid evaluation of what might be only a temporary situation. If your discussions with peer credit managers indicate the beginning of a downward trend, that is the time to reduce your credit line and move for faster collection of past-due balances, What do you do if the decline becomes more rapid? You must then go to a program that requires lump-sum payments at short intervals plus C.O.D. payment for current deliveries of product.

(CHECKLIST)

A "Credit-worthy" Customer—The Ingredients

It is not essential that all of the positives be present to have a "credit-worthy" customer. Conversely, one or more negatives or questionables should not be grounds for summarily rejecting an applicant. Look for good, strong balance. A minor weakness here or there that is offset by one or more strengths should balance out into an acceptable credit risk if the requested credit line is appropriate to the total worth of your input from all reference and reporting sources.

☐ Is the business well established?
☐ Is it a growth, static, or declining situation?
☐ Is new technology, or technological improvement, a threat to the product line(s), services, etc.?
☐ If technology is important to the continuing success of the business, is there an ongoing and effective program of R & D?

☐ Does the customer operate in a growth-oriented area, an area of limited growth potential, or an area in economic decline?

☐ Is the business well-managed? Are management and support people experienced and competent?

☐ Is cash flow adequate for the level of business?

☐ Is there strong short- and long-term bank support?

☐ If the business extends credit to its customers, does the credit management person have the experience for his or her level of responsibility? (Remember that your receivables are probably only as good as theirs.)

☐ If there is a heavy investment in inventory, is it justified by geographic, market, or other conditions?

☐ Is receivables aging in line with sales, sales terms, and the company's need for internally-generated cash flow?

☐ Is internally-generated cash (receivables collections) adequate for normal business requirements or is an abnormal level of bank support used to supplement cash flow needs?

☐ Is there a good balance of management, financial, manufacturing, and marketing skills?

☐ Is there enough depth in the various areas of management so that the loss of one person would not adversely impact management's strength?

☐ If the business is a sole proprietorship—or a partnership, the age or ages of the owners, their health and probable (if older) retirement are important factors. If the death of one partner removed his or her area of expertise from the business, would it run as effectively? Could the surviving partner afford to buy the level of expertise or skill provided by the late partner?

☐ Is there a surviving partner buy-out arrangement, funded usually by life insurance or a combination of life policy and a form of deferred-payment program to the widow or estate?

☐ Is there supplier continuity, and do suppliers generally express satisfaction with the relationship?

☐ What does the banker say about the customer? If the banker has granted loans for capital equipment and operating funds, is he or she satisfied with the agreement and the customer's performance?

Take a close look at any negative or questionable responses before you assign a credit line, but accept the fact that an overwhelming majority of favorable answers to the above questions is about as good as most credit accounts will get.

Chapter 7

Living with
Your Credit Decisions

IF SOMEONE TELLS YOU THAT RISK IS NOT A BUILT-IN PART OF CREDIT DECISIONS YOU should not believe them. People like yourself or people who spend their entire working day in the imprecise world of judgments make credit decisions, and Risk—hopefully reasonable and manageable but still spelled with a capital R—is the ever-present challenge to the success of all credit judgments/decisions. Even in a work environment where the full scope of decision-making tools is available—data such as supplier references, the banker's references, commercial credit agency reports, peer information within a trade group, and an experienced professional to analyze and evaluate the data—the resulting decisions will be imprecise judgments that include varying elements of Risk.

Too many unknowns and intangibles exist for the credit manager or owner/credit manager, regardless of his or her experience level, to expect them to make only infallible judgments. How can you know that an applicant or a current customer is not concealing personal, health, or business problems? How can you be sure that an apparently successful business partnership is not being bent and twisted from within to the point where it is no longer very stable? Do you like what you've seen of the small company that is asking you for a sizeable credit line? Is the founder going to tell you that he is about to retire, or that he is quietly reducing his interest and activity in the company, and that future management control, and decisions, will be in the relatively inexperienced hands of his son-in-law? No. You probably will not hear a word of warning from any of the above in any of the given situations. Is there Risk? You'd better believe it!

What does the owner of a small company do to be sure that his or her company has the strongest level of protection from bad-debt losses? One of the best things you can do for yourself and for your company is to load the evaluation and decision-making processes of the credit function with procedural uniformity. It has a nice ring, but the truth is nobody cares how it sounds if it doesn't contribute something. Fortunately, it does. It can help you minimize the number and potential effects of the risk-prompting variables while improving the effectiveness of the credit-management process. It can be one of your strongest and most effective allies in helping you to make a higher percentage of good credit decisions. Do everything in sequence. Make the sequential approach your guideline for dealing with applicants from the first contact thru all the years of your association with a company that becomes a customer. You will take your accounts through other sequences in the credit management process but nothing will make your work easier, your hours of credit management more productive, or your credit department more effective than adopting as your everyday guideline the one phrase—procedural uniformity.

Follow the lead of experienced credit managers and look constantly for the hedge against the unknowns, the intangibles, and the imprecise. Experienced credit managers look also for evidence of stability in a company's financial depth and the quality of its personnel. They look also for well-planned growth and the potential for trouble-free longevity. Their hedge against Risk should be a combination of the depth and experience of a company's management, the high-profile recognition factors of the product line(s), the company's financial stability, and the unique geographic nature of the market area (a semi-protected market with little or no competition). You must follow their lead and try to hedge your *Risks*—those unknowns, intangibles, and the imprecise. You will try to assemble the greatest number of pluses and the smallest number of minuses before making a judgment that puts your company's money at Risk.

You can live with your credit decisions—even the occasional one that turns sour—if you never allow yourself to forget that all decisions are sprinkled liberally with ingredients and factors about which you have no knowledge and over which you have no control. This fact doesn't mean that when you sit down to make credit decisions, you are putting your hands on the throttle of a runaway train. You must always be in control of your decisions and of the decision-making process. You are the one who controls the approval of orders and credit lines. The hand on the throttle is yours, but absolutely no reason exists for it to be a runaway train. When your decisions are the result of a good input of information, sound evaluation and judgment, and procedural uniformity, your hand which is on the always-in-motion affairs of your credit department, will ensure as steady a ride as most credit professionals could give your company. As an owner, and a conscientious mover for your company, you always will regret the loss of a receivable's balance, but you will not waste time faulting yourself for the loss. If you did a solid job with the account, save the self-chastisement for a situation where you really should have seen the emerging problem before it was too late.

PAYING YOUR DUES

Avoiding the losers always has been the name of the credit-management process, but no person who manages credit for any period of time succeeds in avoiding every loser. Rid yourself of any preconceived notions regarding the infallability of a professional—in his or her own credit environment or sitting where you make the decisions for your company. The professional will lose one now and again just as the less-experienced person does. The difference between the professional and inexperienced manager is that if a professional is good, he or she will seldom, if ever, make the same mistake in judgment a second time. You must do the same thing. Take each negative experience and turn it into a learning one—one that you can sucessfully in your future efforts to reduce the toll taken by the intangibles and by Risk. You have an incentive for doing a good job that even exceeds the motivation of a professional. Pride in a job well done isn't the only thing that should motivate you. You have to be very interested in what happens to the "bottom line" because if you are the owner, it's yours! How much additional incentive does a man or woman need? Probably none.

Large and small companies find themselves doing scenes from the same scenario. The premise is the same for both categories of companies. If, each year, credit managers for a small and a large company routinely handle relative numbers of new, and existing, accounts, and to these account situations bring a level of competence and experience appropriate for the level of his or her decisions, each manager will have an occasional bad-debt loss. It is not possible to be infallible, and it is unrealistic to expect it. An account relationship begins with as many verified facts as possible, and those facts are constantly updated; yet certain intangibles, when combined with the normal flow of business problems, make it impossible for any credit manager to always come up with winners.

How can you maximize your chances of picking a high percentage of winners for your company? In addition to self-restraints which we already discussed, let me suggest that you do not give away the store. Who would do such a foolish thing? When you develop a friendship with some customers, you must never let that relationship influence your business judgment as it relates to the amount of credit or the credit terms that you should offer them. You don't want the personal relationship to interfere with the business relationship. Never let the personal relationship inhibit you from insisting that the customer make his/her account payments within the parameters of good credit management and of your company's credit policy. Always avoid letting your customer maneuver you into an involvement that is not a good credit risk—not just a borderline account, but one that is clearly not a good risk. The only acceptable credit philosophy is the one that cautions to sell only to accounts that can, and will, pay—and pay in a manner compatible with your credit terms and policy. An account that becomes a bad-debt loss because of poor judgment is as damaging to your company's financial statement as the common theft of money or merchandise. You must face the fact that the customer is not always right and not always honest. The customer's abuse of the credit privilege is the same as that customer having a hand in your till. You don't need that kind of help or that kind of business. You can count—and keep—your own cash.

Some owners of small companies find that they are not able to deal effectively with credit problems that are different or unusual. The daily prayer seems to be less Biblical than hopeful, being something on the order of, "Oh Lord, deliver me from evil—and please don't send me any credit applicants who need special terms!" Some owner/credit managers will shy away from an account or an order simply because they cannot handle it within their regular credit terms. Example: One of your customers is stretching to break into a new market area and needs more of your product(s) to meet the requirements of several new customers. After hearing the customer's plans, your best judgment confirms that the new area should deliver some good business. Let the customer know that you want to help, but tell the customer that carrying several hundred (or thousand) dollars of new credit on extended terms would unfavorably impact your own cash flow. Guided by the nature of the order and the quality of the customer, ask for a payment of 25 percent or 50 percent of the dollar total when you accept the order. With the major portion of your manufacturing or production costs covered, you then will be in a position to offer mutually-acceptable terms on the balance. Another extended-terms option is a one-third payment with the order (when the order is delivered or 30 days after delivery), a second one-third payment 60 days after delivery, and the final one-third payment 90 days after delivery. Credit on extended terms is not for everyday use or you'll be looking at an aging sheet that has too many special, slow-pay deals. Relate "extended" to "special," but do not overwork either term by too frequently linking them with another word in common credit management usage—and that word is "terms." With *special dating* (extended terms) to help the customer put more of your product(s) into the new sales area, the additional business should more than offset the costs to you of the longer terms.

ACCOUNTS RECEIVABLE AGED TRIAL BALANCE REPORT

No single document is more important to the effective management of your accounts receivable than a properly prepared Aged Trial Balance Report. Special or extenuating circumstances might be applicable to certain balances on the report sheets, but an Accounts Receivable Aged Trial Balance Report (an Aging Report) should put you on top of what is or is not happening to your accounts receivable. Each report should give you data in detail for each account through the date of the report. If that data is not in a format that you can handle easily and effectively, you must take the necessary steps to make changes immediately.

FIGURE 7-1 is an example taken from a computer-prepared Accounts Receivable Report. Variations occur between computer programs, but this example is a satisfactory product from an acceptable program. A keypunch operator inputs certain information for each account (invoice data, credit information, payments, etc.) which subsequently is brought together when you run a receivables printout. The operator who puts data into your receivables accounts must be experienced to handle the responsibility. Receivables aging reports that are loaded with errors create problems that become long-lasting headaches.

Note the column of three-digit numbers on the left side of the sample report. These digits are account numbers that you assign to identify the various accounts—numbers that you can increase to four or five digits if your company's active accounts number is in the thousands. List all branch locations that have their own payables section below the home office location and assign them a subaccount number. A home office account number 2655 would have branch listings of 2655.1, 2655.2, etc. You can generate and post invoices for each location, thereby respecting the autonomy of the various branch and subsidiary locations.

Customer names, invoice dates, invoice numbers, and invoice amounts extend across the report to, and through, the Total Amount column at midsheet. The Date is the point from which you begin individual invoice aging, issue credit memos, identify invoices to which credit memos apply, and post the dollar amount of each invoice or credit memo. List individual open account totals as of the report date directly below individual invoice and credit memo totals in the Total Amount column.

The sample Accounts Receivable Aged Trial Balance Report reflects aging of accounts on credit terms of Net 30 Days. The comments that follow are applicable to other sales and credit terms as well.

0-to 30-Day Accounts

This account column is either the "not to worry" or the "too early to worry" column. The totals in this column represent current invoices—all still within your terms—and, at this point, probably warrant your attention only if older balances are behind them. The assigned credit line/limit is the primary thing to watch at this point. If your company has a separate order desk, you can simplify interfacing with your department for credit clearances when you key the program for storage of individual accounts receivables data to refuse any order that would push the open credit total beyond the assigned credit line. Order-desk personnel will not be able to process the order unless you or a member of your department allow the order to bypass the credit limit. This simple and automatic safeguard eliminates unpleasant surprises, testy confrontations, and bruised egos. You should watch for signs that a 0 to 30 days account is slipping—or slipping more frequently—into the 31 to 60 days column. A developing pattern of late payments can be a potentially dangerous sign.

Date: 26-NOV-86

ACCOUNTS RECEIVABLE AGED TRIAL BALANCE

AS OF 11/26/86

DOCUMENT TYPES: 1 = INVOICE 2 = PAYMENT 3 = CR MEMO 4 = FINANCE CHARGE 5 = DEBIT MEMO 6 =

WARRANTY OVER CREDIT = *

11/26 Called. Check for $936.00 mailed today.   * Call 12/1 if no check

---------CUSTOMER---------	SM# ----------DOCUMENT ----------	APPLY	CREDIT	TOTAL	---------------------------AGING---------------------------			
NUM NAME	TYPE DATE NUMBER TO-DOC		LIMIT	AMOUNT	0-030 DAYS	031-060 DAYS	061-090 DAYS	091- OVER DAYS
406 Gladings Co.	405-632-1098							
DEBIT MEMO	5 08/28/86 12345			1,140.00			1,140.00	
DEBIT MEMO	5 09/24/86 12418			936.00			936.00	
INVOICE	1 10/31/86 12522			1,488.00	1,488.00			
PAYMENT	2 11/04/86 4499 12345			1,140.00-			1,140.00-	
				1488.00	1,488.00	0.00	0.00	0.00
414 Gladstone Co.	88 213-564-1053		3,500.00					
INVOICE	1 10/30/86 12508			748.10	748.10			
PAYMENT	2 11/14/86 19217 12508			748.10-	748.10-			
				0.00	0.00	0.00	0.00	0.00
415 Gold Star Ind.	99 916-145-3902		500.00					
DEBIT MEMO	5 09/30/86 12438			108.00		108.00		
INVOICE	1 10/10/86 12463			112.00		112.00		
INVOICE	1 11/10/86 12541			135.00	135.00			
PAYMENT	2 11/21/86 12100 12438			108.00-		108.00-		
				247.00	135.00	112.00	0.00	0.00
421 Gopher's	88 415-173-2956		3,500.00					
DEBIT MEMO	5 09/24/86 12420			180.00			180.00	
PAYMENT	2 11/18/86 20684 12420			180.00-			180.00-	
				0.00	0.00	0.00	0.00	0.00
425 Graystone, Inc.	99 800-429-3618		1,000.00					
INVOICE	1 10/27/86 12493			46.50	46.50			
PAYMENT	2 11/07/86 1942 12493			46.50-	46.50-			
				0.00	0.00	0.00	0.00	0.00

FIG. 7-1.

427 Gregorio's	88 213-196-5827	1,500.00						
INVOICE	1 10/30/86 12515		292.50	292.50				
			292.50	292.50	0.00		0.00	0.00
428 Green & Co.	88 508-491-3875	5,000.00						
INVOICE	1 10/30/86 12516		1,277.00	1,277.00				
PAYMENT	2 11/11/86 2929 12516		1,277.00-	1,277.00-				
INVOICE	1 11/14/86 12558		2,016.00	2,016.00				
PAYMENT	2 11/25/86 2954 12558		2,016.00-	2,016.00-				
INVOICE	1 11/26/86 12587		1,392.00	1,392.00				

Fig. 7-1. Continued.

31-to 60-Day Accounts

Don't underestimate the potential for trouble in this aging category. It is quite possible that an account item or balance is only a few days removed from joining the black sheep in 61 to 90 days. Accounts which are just past 30 days might not represent a problem, particularly if balances are frequently in that area. Balances that are stretching to, and through, 50 and 55 days are another matter. It is never good news when accounts begin to lean against aging of 61 to 90 days.

A telephone call to the customer who has an unpaid 40- or 50-days balance is a must. If the balance is several days beyond the usual payment pattern, push the payables person into giving a reason(s) for the delay. If something is happening, externally or internally, to impact cash flow for more than a temporary period, you want to know it NOW. When a couple of telephone calls bring no promises—or promises but no check—and the aging has stretched to an uncomfortable 50 or 55 days, you might want to consider holding orders until the account pays all (or the oldest) past-due balances. Again, your past experience with the customer will have considerable bearing on the action you take.

61-to 90-Day Accounts

A balance in this category means that the account is between 30 and 60 days past due, and that is unacceptable. Unless you have made arrangements in advance to allow one-time aging of 61 to 90 days—perhaps because of some temporary cash-flow drain, the reasons for which are very clear—you would not sell additional product on ANY terms until you have received a satisfactory lump sum payment or a C.O.D. payment of $2.00 or $3.00 for every $1.00 of product you release. If the customer needs your product(s) and you have good reason to assume serious problems exist, insist that you receive regularly-scheduled, lump-sum payments PLUS C.O.D. payments as described previously. When it becomes obvious that payments to all suppliers are slowing, a long-term customer relationship is no longer your primary concern. Your primary concern—once you determine that the customer's downhill slide is irreversible—is to collect your company's money as rapidly as possible.

91-Day and Over Accounts

When you are not receiving regular payments on any balance in this aging column, don't delay. Send out your final payment demand letter, if you haven't already done so. If you do not receive payment by the deadline date specified in your letter, assign the account to your collection agency. You should not continue your own collection effort at this time. These accounts need aggressive collection attention, including the possibility of having an attorney obtain a judgment. Your work with other accounts would demand that you devote a disproportionate amount of your time to an account in this type of trouble.

Should you sell to an account that you have assigned to a collection agency? Not a dimes worth of anything until they have paid the assigned balance, they have paid all other balances, and they have reimbursed your company for any suit and/or collection fees. Perhaps at that point, there might be a strong reason to consider selling the account, but only on a C.O.D. basis. Once you have gone the collection, or suit-and-collection route with an account, there should be no incentive for you to tempt fate again with open-account sales. You still could be in a vulnerable position if you accept company or personal checks in payment of C.O.D. purchases. Should there be any indication that suppliers are experiencing NSF check problems with this customer, tell the customer you will only accept cashier's checks and bank or postal money orders.

Minimize the number and dollar value of the accounts that slide into this column. The odds of a collection assignment or a bad-debt loss increase dramatically as accounts travel across your receivables aging report. By the time they are in the 91 days and over column, the percentage of loss is very high.

Unless there is a high level of activity in your business, one Accounts Receivable Aged Trial Balance Report each week should be enough. Don't try to get by with less than one new report each week. If yours is a high-volume company, two or more reports a week is appropriate.

When properly prepared and used, the "aging report" is your most important information-and-control tool. Each new report should include all billing and payment activity through the report date, providing the credit administrator with a complete report of all open items on each account. It's easy to forget the handwritten notes and reminders that you added to the preceding report. Although you don't want to clutter a new report with an excessive number of notations, you should transfer items that are still applicable to the new report.

If you have been concerned about the problems that attach to converting to a data processing system, don't fight it. We are decades past the early IBM era when credit managers raised their voices in anguished protest as they called the roll of benefits and information that most certainly would be lost forever in the transition from bookkeeping machines to a card-punched IBM system. Were they right? Did we lose much in the transition from old to new? A few things were lost, but in the final analysis, the change has been enormously beneficial to credit people everywhere.

And about those "anguished voices"—I know all about them. I had laryngitis for weeks.

CREDIT LIMIT UPDATE

When an account is new to your company, you should monitor more closely than one with which you have had some experience. The first update of your experience with the account should be 90 days after you assign the original credit line. Subsequent reviews should be at intervals of six months. This check up isn't based on an inflexible time frame because there might be one or more reasons for you to monitor certain accounts more frequently. One of the best reasons for a review or update is when an account wants to increase purchases of your product(s) to the point where the original credit line would be too low. Your company always must be receptive to new business—or more business from good, current customers—so bring out the customer's file, update it with your own experience, add other updated report and experience data, and make your decision.

The one thing you must never do is step back from the legitimate needs of an account on the upswing when every indication points to a well-managed growth cycle. These accounts offer the best chance for safe, solid growth for your company and theirs. To abandon a promising new account relationship at such a point would be foolish unless the current update indicates that your company is the only supplier whose account is being handled properly. If the business is experiencing a problem but there is no indication that it has slipped into a serious downtrend, you still might successfully sell the account. You should monitor gradual loss of business over a few months with the emphasis on maintaining close payment control of all open balances, including the balances of other suppliers.

The Credit Limit Update Form (FIG. 7-2) is designed to recap data currently applicable to the account. It deals with the aging of account balances during the three or six months of your experience with the account, the most current D & B rating, and the date of the most recent financial statement. Base your comments on aging and payment experience described previously, then add the credit limit requested and the reason for the increase. The core for any consideration of a credit line increase is the reason. A properly-managed firm will not use a frivolous reason. If the reason is not allied with growth, a special customer order, an expansion into a new territory, or some equally good reason, then you must question seriously the motivation for an increase in the credit line. If account balances are beginning to string out across the aging sheet and most of the original or current credit line is already represented in current and past-due balances, you do not want to increase a credit line for the sole benefit of the customer, and you especially do not want to add new dollars to those already extending deep into the past-due columns of your aging report. Never allow your company to be put in the position of becoming a secondary source of financing for any customer unless it is a prearranged, short-time or one-time agreement. Should you give an account a credit line or a credit increase for a good reason? Absolutely. Should you give the account a credit line increase for much less than a good reason? It's not a good idea.

Later in this chapter you will see a sample account review situation for a credit line increase. The example offers a step-by-step hypothetical situation for an account review at 90 days after you assigned the opening credit line. The same procedure is applicable to accounts with which you have had a longer period of experience. In any evaluation or analysis of an account, that "longer period of experience" is an important plus.

UNFAVORABLE CHANGES IN PAYMENT PATTERNS

The reasons for unfavorable changes in payment patterns are many and diverse. In addition to cash flow or other business problems, they can range from a missing invoice to a difference in goods received vs. quantity billed, a pricing problem, unauthorized quantity and price deductions, and discounts taken after the maximum allowable date. These problems are the easy ones, or the ones that should be the easiest to correct.

A missing invoice can become a problem because you do not know that the customer doesn't have a copy—not until the invoice begins to move across the accounts receivable aging report. It isn't a problem if the account pays within terms. You'll pick it up almost as soon as the balance slips into the past-due column. But what are you looking at if the account frequently has balances that extend from 30 to 60 days past due? Until you receive a check for other invoices issued during the same time period, or unless you verify with the customer which invoices the customer lists as unpaid, you won't know

CREDIT LIMIT UP-DATE

Customer Name_____ Acct. #_____

Present Limit $_____   Aging as of _____

Date Approved   _____   Current $_____

Approved by   _____   30 - 60 $_____

                                              60 - 90 $_____

                                              90 plus $_____

D & B Rating   _____   Balance $_____

Date of last Financial_____   Last 6 months sales $_____

Terms, Aging and Pay History:_____

_____

_____

New Limit Requested $_____ By date _____ By whom_____

Reason for Requested Change:_____

_____

_____

Recommendation:_____

_____

_____

AMOUNT   APPROVAL

_____   By:_____   Date:_____

_____   _____   _____

NEXT REVIEW DATE: _____

IN-PUT TO SYSTEM BY:_____ DATE:_____

FIG. 7-2.

whether the customer's list of open invoices agrees with those listed on your aging sheet.

Customers sometimes will pay an invoice that differs in the quantity received from the quantity billed, computing the value of the goods not received, deducting that amount from the invoice, and sending a check for the quantity received. Prompt payment is never out of season but handling it in this manner could be the first horror in an escalating chain of horrors. What you want your customer to do is call your office when there's a difference—in the unit price or quantity delivered—so you can issue a credit memo. Not only does this solve the problem of an incorrect payment from the customer, it also enables you and the customer to clear up any difference in a conventional, tidy manner. Customers are not looking to create extra work for you or for themselves. A mailing to your credit customers of the form letter shown in FIG. 7-3 should be a giant step in your effort to eliminate dangling balances when a customer computes his or her own credit allowance.

ACCOUNT REVIEW—CREDIT LINE INCREASE

You have been doing business with the account for three months. When you assigned an opening credit line of $1000, it allegedly represented a line that would take care of this customer's needs for the next six to twelve months. You were relatively comfortable with that credit line and time projection because your evaluation of the account told you that a $1000 credit line was about as high as you should go.

After selling the account for three months, receivables aging has slipped to 36 days past due for purchases the customer made during the first 30 days and 15 days past due for purchases made during the second 30 days. The oldest past-due balance (36 days) is $540; the total open balance is $1150; an in-house order is for $360; and the customer is pressuring you to double the credit line.

How will you answer the questions that follow? Try to answer them without first reading the answers that follow each of the questions. Remember, there are correct answers other than the ones given.

Question: What are your options?

Answer: Your options are few based upon your brief and increasingly unsatisfactory experience with the account. No obvious justification exists for you to increase the present credit line. You are justified to tell the customer that past-due balances must be received within the next 10 days. If you do not receive payment, you will have no alternative but to hold orders until account balances are current.

Question: How will you handle the pending order for $360 and the customer's pressure to increase the credit line?

Answer: If the customer needs the $360 order as desperately as he or she states, you can release it on C.O.D. terms. Why not release it on open account? You don't want to convert your $1150 problem (current open total) into a $1510 one.

Question: Can you justify continuing the current credit line?

Answer: You only can justify continuing the $1000 current credit line if the customer pays the past-due balance(s) within 10 days from the date of your phone call.

Question: Do you assume that the customer will pay closer to terms if he or she is given the $2000 credit line?

Answer: You should *never* assume that a customer who does not properly handle a $1000 credit line will turn into a big receivables winner if you increase the credit line. If the account doesn't do a good job of paying at the lower credit line, your experience will be worse at the higher credit line.

August 25, 1988

To Our Customers:

We have no desire to project the image of a whining, complaining or ungrateful supplier. Our customers are much too important for us to slide into any of those unpleasant behavioral attitudes. This is meant only to be a mutual self-help, and if it works for you it will automatically work for us.

When you receive an invoice that lists a quantity of product that does not agree with the quantity you received, please do not change the invoice and pay what you calculate to be correct. It may be correct, but call us with the information so we can promptly issue a credit, mail it to you, and protect your discount on the specific invoice for 10 days beyond the normal discount period. Issuing the credit simplifies our bookeeping and should also simplify yours if for one reason or another we calculate two different amounts for the goods billed but not received.

Errors or questions regarding the price quoted to you and the price billed? Please contact this department as soon as you notice the discrepancy - and before the invoice is input for payment. We'll either promptly correct the problem with a credit for the difference or have our sales representative call you to discuss or clarify any misunderstanding that may have occurred.

We can do our best job for you when your telephone call puts the matter of correcting our mistake or problem exactly where it belongs - in our lap.

Many thanks for your cooperation.

Sincerely,

Cecil Bond
Credit Manager

CB:ac

FIG. 7-3.

Question: What information could the customer furnish that might enable you to live with all, or part, of the past-due balance, pending order, and request for credit line increase?

Answer: If the customer tells you that he or she has negotiated a new credit line with the bank, that it becomes effective on a specific date, and you are able to verify this information with the banker, you would probably release the $360 in-house order and delay increasing the credit limit to $2000 until the customer has paid past-due balances and (per your telephone conversation) the banker notifies you that the new credit line has become effective. You might also favorably consider the situation of a sole proprietorship (or a partnership) that has a comparably slow payment record, in-house order, and a request for a credit line increase to $2000 *if* a new partner is about to pump money into the firm. This information too is verifiable. You will check the financial qualifications of the new partner. If he or she is reluctant to give out information, make it clear that you cannot release more product(s) or consider an increase in the open line until reasonable data is available to you. When you are satisfied that the new money has gone into the business, again review the request for a credit line increase.

The hypothetical situation states that your original evaluation of the account told you that a $1000 credit line was as high as you should go. To justify an increase to $2000—even if you delete the past-due balances from the hypothetical situation and you give the account an on-time payments performance—something new and positive would have to come into your review to warrant doubling a credit line that 90 days before was set at $1000—which was the allowable high. Certainly your short-term experience with the account is not a plus. A plus could be that the account has improved their marketing approach, or the account has taken on an excellent new product line and is successfully expanding its territory. Try to come up with new data while reviewing the original bank, supplier, and report data to see if your evaluation of the account was incorrect. You must have some good, new data if you are to give the account an increase to $2000.

PAST-DUE DISCOUNTS

Discounts taken after the allowable period has passed is a problem that continues to be a hang-up of a hard core of almost every supplier's customers. Disallowing the discounts and notifying the customer by telephone or letter that they must pay the disallowed discount(s) as part of the next receivables payment is never totally effective. Some accounts will stop the practice for a while than revert to their game of pushing for a few extra days. Others will stop taking the discount but will disregard invoices or letters detailing the amounts of the disallowed discounts. If you push for payment of the unearned discounts, stating perhaps that you will not ship any product(s) until they pay the unearned discount total, some accounts will stop paying their invoices. At this point, it becomes a nasty and complex standoff—a game of waiting for the other to back down—and too often it is the supplier who caves in to the customer who abuses the system. The supplier gives in to the customer with a mild admonition that "it is not to happen again" because there is supplier fear of losing the account. How can you reconcile that attitude with those customers who pay by the rules? Why should the "pay by the rules" customers be penalized by paying within discount terms to get their discount when the abuser does not? Frequently the two firms are competing in the same market area

A discount should be available to all customers, and you should deny discounts to those customers who consistently and flagrantly use discount terms to their monetary and competitive advantage. Curing it is not easy. The options are few, but the integrity of one of your company's key sales and customer relations policies is at stake. When telephone and letter payment requests have been unsuccessful, you should notify the customer that you will not ship any products or perform any services until they have paid the disallowed discount balances. You might also point out to the abuser that the discount becomes an unfair and legally-questionable competitive tool if you do not administer it fairly, and you are certain that he or she would not want the policy to be inequitably administered. Candidly, the abuser probably doesn't care if you equitably administer the discount policy as long as they can take advantage of a weak policy of enforcement. You should be equally uncaring about how the offending company feels about taking unearned discounts. It is your company's policy and your company's reputation for integrity and equitable treatment of its customers that is at stake, and it is your job to get the abuser company back on track. Abusers have a tendency to flaunt the successes of any bullying tactics to other trade members, and that can be a real embarrassment for any company whose other customers view the unearned discount as the preferential discount it really is.

We have touched upon other reasons for unfavorable payment changes in earlier chapters. To mention some of them again: internal problems caused by the death of a partner or the dissolution of a partnership with the resulting loss of expertise in one or more key management areas; the use of bank borrowings or other funds to buy out the interest of a partner; expanding the business too rapidly for the available financial resources, and often without an appropriate level of management experience to direct it; and in conjunction with the too-rapid expansion, pushing into a new sales and marketing area before properly researching it for negative economic and competitive factors. Remember also that owners sometimes lose their drive when the business attains a certain level of success, with one or both partners taking more time away from the business for family and personal considerations. At times, this stepping back from the previous level of involvement in the business seems to work very well. Too many times, however, it does not. When an owner or owners become so detached that the business slides onto a plateau of no growth, a serious problem already has settled over the business. A status of "no growth" also almost inevitably leads to the failure to replace customers who leave as part of the normal process of customer loss. Given such an unfavorable environment for continued business success, the alternative is a gradual-to-rapid decline.

These reasons are some of the more obvious reasons for a firm whose payment pattern has been satisfactory for months or years to slide into a mode of increasingly slow payments. To turn such a situation around demands the earliest possible action by a strong and competent management—and a strong and competent management rarely allows a company to find this level of trouble. What is your response to signs of a problem(s) in one of your customers? No blanket answer will cover all problems and conditions. Monitor the account's actions closely. Deal with the account from a position of caution, and continue to sell the account only when, and as, your judgment and available information indicate that you can do it safely. You will want to hold past-due balances to a minimum number of days, applying payment pressure to the account as you feel the necessity to protect your company's receivables interest. Your criteria for what you must do in any situation is always the same. You are sympathetic to the legitimate problems of a customer, but you must ultimately do what is in your company's best interest.

THE SLOW-PAY ACCOUNT—GAMBLE OR PRUDENT RISK?

Owners who make credit decisions have enough other problems in their daily lives without an unreasonable number of slow-pay accounts. On the other hand, carefully selected slow-pay accounts—if they are a fit with your company's credit policy and cash-flow requirements—can be profitable businesses. You might categorize slow-pay accounts in one of three ways—occasionally slow, chronically slow, and terminally slow. Avoid the latter group, but if your credit policy is a middle-of-the-road (moderate) policy, take on the well-established account that always pays a few days beyond terms. If you select them carefully, there should be no more danger of a receivables loss than with your other accounts. When an account has been in business for years, continues to be profitable, and is known for a policy of putting some weight on its suppliers (chronically 15 to 25 or 30 days slow), this account is not involved in a budding bankruptcy, it is their way of business life. This account doesn't care what the credit ratings say, it has the money to pay closer to terms, but exercises a combination of arrogance and purchasing clout to exploit a position of strength, and persists in releasing supplier payments many days beyond terms.

You must avoid any account that represents an unacceptable level of risk. Watch for companies that have been in business for two or more years, have made little or no progress, and are reported by their suppliers to pay 30 to 45 days slow—and getting slower. When current suppliers report such unsatisfactory payments experience, you should avoid the account and the inevitable collection problems that your company would soon face. Consider how the loss of a key customer would impact a firm already struggling to survive. The loss of that key customer almost certainly would push the business into a Chapter XI filing.

Manufacturers, distributors, and service companies can make money from a relationship with a customer who virtually ignores sales terms *if* the percentage of profit for the goods or services is high enough to compensate for chronic slow pay—for the loss of the contribution to cash flow that the receivables dollars would have made if the account paid closer to terms. Be very wary of the area into which you would be moving some of your company's receivables before you take on any of these accounts. You must be satisfied completely that the potential customer who does not pay within terms—who apparently rarely has paid any supplier within terms—offers a potential for profitable business that your credit policy can accommodate *and* poses no threat to your annual provision for bad-debt loss.

CREDIT MEMORANDUMS

Living successfully with your credit decisions involves many factors that are unrelated to the ability of an account to pay for what it buys from you. An entire spectrum of reasons exists for why an invoice problem—something that you should have been able to settle quickly and amicably—will result in the customer refusing to pay even the dollar amount that is *not* being challenged! To extend this totally irrational reasoning, the customer might subsequently refuse to make *any* account payment until you have resolved the one problem. That attitude does not create a problem if the customer repeatedly has attempted to get the supplier to address a problem long enough to issue a credit, but without results. It is a frustrating experience and one the customer should not tolerate. For no other reason or rationale, however, should your company allow the customer to trash the rules of the game. If you become involved in a situation where the customer is unjustifiably withholding payment because it is alleged that an invoice-adjusting credit memo is due, respond promptly and courteously to the legitimate concern of your customer. Beyond that point of reason, you should not allow any customer to dictate the ongoing terms and tone of your relationship.

You can put an end to one of the chief sources of customer frustration and anger by promptly issuing credit memorandums. Not only does prompt attention to the issuing of credit memos minimize the negative effect of pricing errors and product(s) shortages, prompt action can add some goodwill to a negative situation. If not handled promptly and tactfully, these incidents can drag on until there is mounting confusion, too many telephone calls and correspondence, and a level of customer anger that you can diminish only over a long period of time. The possibility that a seemingly simple invoice adjustment could become your longest-running project of the year is more than enough incentive for you to see that you issue a credit memo as soon as the need surfaces. The sample copy of a credit memo in FIG. 7-4 uses the invoice form for that purpose.

PAST-DUE BALANCES

Unless your credit responsibility never exceeds a dozen accounts, it is difficult to visualize a time when you will not have past-due accounts on your aging reports. The form shown in FIG. 7-5 should enable you to consolidate problem accounts—minor accounts and others—into an effective recap of what is taking place on the Aged Trial Balance Report. Whether the report is just for your information or goes also to a partner, the form is an effective weekly, semimonthly, or monthly tool for relating the number and status of accounts in the various past-due categories. A bracketed line or two under each listed account will remind you (or indicate to the person to whom you give a copy) of the status of the action you are taking to collect these balances.

You always will have accounts that regularly appear on a past-due list because their cash flow is not strong enough for them to do better. Careful monitoring on your part should pick off most serious problems, but whether the account is a regular or a first-timer on the past-due list, move quickly when you see signs of trouble.

NFS CHECKS—THE END OF A RELATIONSHIP

It is appropriate to close this chapter with a look at the effect "bad checks" have on a credit relationship. You may substitute any euphemism you choose (NSF, Insufficient Funds, Refer to Maker, etc.) but if the check doesn't clear the drawer's bank, the relationship between the two parties has been damaged. If you can show that the problem is with the bank and not your customer, a full measure of understanding is in order. When the problem is not the bank's and there is the suspicion that the customer released the check knowing there would not be enough money in the account for the bank to pay it, it is the beginning of a major break in the relationship between supplier and customer. What happens if you receive a second "bad check" within a short period of time? The relationship is at great risk of being strained beyond the point where a policy of credit sales—or accepting company checks for C.O.D. sales—can or should be continued.

People who make credit decisions often have compartmentalized minds which enable them to meet new or recurring problems by tapping into an accumulation of past experiences. This repository of credit experiences is not open to customer surveillance and enables an owner/credit manager to deal quickly and firmly with those customers who begin to slide into a pattern of multiple bad checks. The customer who commits two, or more, of these acts within a period of a few weeks is severely damaging the company's reputation. Legal implications also are attached when a person or company flirts with a formal charge of *passing bad checks* (offering a check in payment for merchandise when they know that their funds are not in the bank to cover the check and probably will not be, intent to defraud, etc.). The charge has a much stronger chance of prevailing if the person or company offers the check as payment (or C.O.D. payment) for goods or services to be received. The key word is "intent," and it is usually so difficult to prove that companies have neither the time or personnel to spend building a case that fits that parameters of "intent" or "knowledge of insufficient funds" when they offered the check as payment. A firm or an individual might be sending checks of this type to

CITRUS FRUIT SALES, INC.

CUSTOM & CONTRACT
PACKAGING

FOOD PRODUCT DEVELOPMENT

QUALITY — SINCE 1933 — PRODUCTS

1631 Almaden Road
P.O. Box 6274
San Jose, CA 95150
(408) 287-6290

	INVOICE NO.	PAGE
CREDIT	15963	

INVOICE DATE
3-14-87

COCKTAIL MIXES	•	PUNCH CONCENTRATES	•	SNO CONE SYRUPS	•	SAUCES	•	SYRUPS	•	FOOD PRODUCTS

SOLD TO	Lester's Products 1746 Indiana Blv'd San Jose, CA 95123	SHIP TO	

OUR ORDER NO.	ORDER DATE	ACCOUNT NO.	SLSM. NO.	YOUR PURCHASE ORDER NO.	SHIP VIA	FREIGHT COL./PPD	DATE SHIPPED	TERMS
					Returned via Customer's Truck			

QTY. ORDERED	QTY. SHIPPED	QTY. B./O.	ITEM NO.	UNIT	DESCRIPTION	UNIT PRICE	EXTENDED PRICE
				36 cases	Bloody Mary Mix	$21.50	$774.00
					(To credit customer with 36 cases of Bloody Mary Mix purchased 2-17-87 on Invoice 15641.)		
						TOTAL ▶	$774.00

SERVICE CHARGE: 2% per month on accounts over 30 DAYS

FIG. 7-4.

PAST-DUE BALANCES

Report Date _____

Account Name	Acct. No.	Current 0 - 30	31 - 60	61-90	91 & Over	Total

FIG. 7-5.

most of his or her suppliers, but seldom is there a provable case if checks eventually are made good.

A legitimate possibility always exists that your customer who has never written a "bad"check before, did not receive a promised check from his or her customer—a customer who had never failed to keep that promise. On the basis of that promise, he had released your check and the checks of several other suppliers. Let's look at the same premise in another direction. The check from the customer's customer was received and deposited in plenty of time to cover your check and the others but *it* bounced! Some credit managers would scoff at the story, but it isn't an uncommon predicament for a small company or business. Customers can issue checks in good faith against a check they received from a third party—particularly a company whose checks have always been good. Consider your own embarrassment if your company released checks to your suppliers and the big check from your customer failed to clear the bank. In such a chain of events, it's quite possible for any company or business to be the inadvertent victim. You always should give your customer the benefit of a reasonable explanation for something that has never happened before. If it happens a second time, within a time frame relatively close to the first, accepting the credibility of anything less than a rock-solid explanation is probably not wise.

Don't hesitate to view incidents of NSF checks, and an explanation that is weaker than the NSF check itself, as an indication that "cash trickle" has replaced cash flow. At this point, your knowledge of the account and the account's paying habits, and the candor with which the customer states and discusses his or her company's problems, is crucial to your future course with the account. Don't let yourself be blindsided! The receivables dollars of your company might be at serious risk unless the customer gives you full disclosure of the problem, says what is being done to correct it, and offers a reasonable time frame for correcting it. If your experience with the customer is such that you have no reason to question the explanation, the corrective measures, or the time frame, your decision probably will be to carefully monitor the customer's actions while working with them to overcome the problem(s).

Customers whose NSF checks cause suppliers to give them the option of buying on C.O.D. terms (cash, cashier's check, bank money order) or not at all, rarely agree with that decision.The customer might, as a major confidence, admit to what is described as a "minor short-term cash-flow pinch." With another account, it could be true. Unfortunately, this customer's attorney could at that very moment be drawing up the papers for a *Chapter XI filing* (reorganization of the business under the protection of the bankruptcy court—see chapter 10). Need I add that your first notice from the Bankruptcy Court—a notice in which the Referee In Bankruptcy will advise of the filing and state the date for the first meeting of creditors—will be your first and an after-the-fact notice. At that point, you already will be on the hook.

Can all of the above occur from an NSF check or two? It is quite possible because an NSF check or two to your company almost certainly means that other suppliers are having the same experience. Once the pattern starts, it is very difficult for a company to reverse a deep-seated cause that has led to this effect. Do not prematurely abandon an account, and certainly don't abandon them if you can determine that the company has the capabilities to overcome the problem. Do not, however, try to hang on to an increasingly difficult and dangerous customer—one whose problems might have started with a couple of NSF checks but have increased dramatically in the weeks since your customer's bank returned those first NSF checks unpaid. Your company can build something new and meaningful with a replacement customer, or you can at least avoid becoming one of the creditors of record when the NSF'er goes feet first into the waters of Chapter XI.

Chapter 8

Credit Decisions— The Good, the Fair, and the Ugly

IF EVERY ONE OF YOUR CREDIT DECISIONS WERE TO SUDDENLY AND INEXPLICABLY FIND their niche in the category of good or fair, and you could somehow know that all future decisions would automatically home in one of those categories, books such as this one would have no validity. A small manual would offer enough space in which to communicate the essential guidelines for the purely administrative facets of credit management. Because this world is less than a utopian world, we always shall have with us that third and smallest category—the ugly.

The credit decisions you made yesterday and the yesterdays before that ultimately will settle into one of these three categories—the good, the fair, and the ugly. Unless you change the guidelines for a particular account, your experience with the account probably will continue to reflect no measurable change. From that earliest point when you relied solely upon the experience of others, your experience with the account gradually will become the experience of primary importance. What your peer credit managers are doing and experiencing always will be relevant to your own decisions, but it will be secondary to your own experience. Your evaluation will become the determining factor in any decision to continue selling on the terms and dollar lever you first assigned or whether your company's account experience indicates that you should make an upward or downward adjustment.

Watch for signs. Any account that requires you to call them two or three times each month for collection, particularly after a long period of an acceptable payments pattern, warrants careful monitoring. When such a customer begins to slip, dig for answers. You don't need a medical degree to know when the vital signs are faltering. Are changes occurring in the way an account makes its payments? Get some answers!

Occasionally you will have an account whose response to your strongest in-house collection effort is verbal abuse. Hold your temper, but take that response as your cue not to drag out your in-house collection effort. Assign the account to a collection agency—one that specializes in collecting commercial accounts. For a variety of reasons, (particularly to avoid having a formal collection assignment picked up by a credit reporting service, or a suit become a matter of public record), the first notice from a collection agency occasionally will cause the delinquent account to send all or part of the money. When that happens and your collection service agreement specifies "10 days free demand," the usual collection fee of 18 percent to 35 percent (percentages vary from one agency to another and according to the dollar amount of the assignment) is not applicable. What happens if the demand letter sent to your customer by the collection agency draws a "payment in full" response within 10 days of the collection agency's letter? With the "10 days free demand" provision, there is no collection charge. Remember, however, that when one of your customers is sliding, whatever the collection service gets for you is that much more than your own efforts generated. If they collect your money, they earn their fee.

Any account that slips into the category of the ugly, which is 90 days and over past due, dulls the luster of what might be an otherwise well-managed receivables aging report. The in-house collection guides and procedures that follow should be helpful in stopping most potential candidates for the ugly category from marching nonstop from "current" to "90 days and over."

COLLECTIONS—KEEP IT LEGAL

Some tactics are unethical and illegal regardless of the circumstances. It is illegal to threaten or harass a debtor. You must be very careful that what you consider to be nothing more than a good, aggressive collection effort does not stray from that corridor into the sometimes grey areas of harassment or threats. Ambiguity is in any area where you cannot clearly draw lines but it is particularly frustrating to walk a tightrope of ethical collection conduct when you know that the person or company with whom you are dealing is addicted to devious thinking and behavior. When the situation is extreme, the benefits of the law definitely tip in favor of the unscrupulous. The law is meant to be equitable for all parties, and it is legally and morally correct to protect against threats and harassment, but the law does sometimes lose sight of where justice begins and ends. The obvious becomes blatant when the one allegedly needing protection is busily engaged in trying to take advantage of its creditors. At that point, the law's protective umbrella can be somewhat less than equitable.

Never stray from a totally ethical and legal collection procedure or your debtor might counter your efforts with a suit alleging that your actions have been detrimental to his or her business and reputation, and also injurious to his or her mental health. In that same context, never use the services of a commercial collection agency whose reputation for ethical practices is not well-known. You could incur liability because of the actions of an authorized representative. Problems of this nature can get very complicated and suddenly quite expensive if a suit becomes a jury trial and the jury is persuaded that your actions have heaped wrongs upon the head of your former customer. Some collection actions are so heavy-handed as to provide a legitimate basis for a suit alleging damages. Such reprehensible behavior has no place in credit management. Many legal options are available for attempting to collect your money—your own efforts, the efforts of a commercial collection agency, and the use of an attorney. If you've tried them all, including obtaining a judgment against assets that cannot be found or do not exist, then you have confirmed that this is a bad-debt account. Put it in the category of a learning experience. Charge the account balance against the Bad-Debt Reserve, and get on with managing your other accounts.

WHY DOESN'T THE CUSTOMER PAY?

People who have limited credit management experience learn rather quickly that some customers do not have the cash flow necessary to pay invoices within sales terms. This fact should be no problem if everything else is within acceptable parameters. Depending upon your company's credit plan, you usually can sell such accounts on credit terms knowing that you probably will have to wait an additional 20 or 30 days for your money. It's the other category of credit customers—the ones who rarely fail to pay within terms—who cause concern when an invoice or a balance slips into the past due-column. You aren't accustomed to seeing a past-due balance on accounts of this type, and the first reaction is to wonder what is going wrong. This reaction usually is tempered promptly by the more reasonable realization that one past-due invoice does not indicate a disaster in the making.

Money is not the only reason a customer doesn't pay an invoice. Would you be in a hurry to pay an invoice if you were shipped defective or out-of-spec products? Would you rush to pay if you received goods that had been damaged in transit? How quickly would you authorize payment for a shipment that had one-or-more of the wrong quantity, size, color, or formula? If that sampler of bad news is not enough to hold up a check, how thrilled would you be to find that the invoice price is substantially more than the price quoted when you placed the order? When there is more than one of the previous items on the same invoice, the customer will not pay that flawed document until you have corrected it. You would not rush to clear such an invoice, and your customer will not rush to clear yours.

The items listed previously are a few of the legitimate reasons for a customer who always pays within, or near, terms to withhold payment for an invoice or statement items. The trick is for you, the supplier, to take the initiative. Do not wait for the customer to do something about it. When you see that an item has become past due, call the customer's payables person or department and ask the question not covered in the above paragraphs: Does payables have a copy of the invoice? If not, revive the payment process by putting a copy in the mail. If the problem isn't one of a missing invoice, the information you receive from payables regarding the reason(s) for holding up payment should put you in a position to move toward doing whatever is necessary to eliminate the problem.

The owner who makes company credit decisions should be as familiar with customer accounts as any professional would be in a similar situation. The levels of skill that come into play when making credit decisions might not be comparable, but in the area of knowledge of accounts, you should have few problems. Your experience with an account is the best source of information for determining the reasoning behind a customer's request. A quick way to determine whether a customer likes to use "buy time" ploys is to check the file folder. Does the customer wait until you call to ask about a past-due invoice before requesting an invoice copy? Has the customer recently requested one or more invoice copies. Have those requests come within a short period of time? Have you been experiencing unauthorized deductions from payments which then required telephone calls and/or letters before you resolved each incident? Is the customer attempting to take discounts when it is obvious that the discount was taken days past what would be a more than generous one-time extension of the discount period?

The reason for these questions is to help you find an explanation for deviations from a normal industry or customer processing and payments pattern. Under normal circumstances, there is nothing unreasonable about a request for an invoice copy. You might not have mailed a copy. It might have slipped into the limbo of lost mail, or it could have disappeared after it reached the customer. Unauthorized payment deductions usually are isolated incidents caused by specific but nonrecurring facts or assumptions. When you find that a customer has developed a fondness for taking payment deductions to which the company is not entitled, stop it before the customer can claim a string of unchallenged deductions as precedent for continuing the practice. How do you handle disallowed discounts? Game players will hammer you with the tactic if you let them get away with it. If one customer succeeds in establishing a pattern that puts a hole in the integrity of your discount terms, your company is discriminating against every customer who does play by your rules. Every customer who takes the discount within your terms, or does not take it at all, is paying more for your product(s) or services than the customer who takes your discount policy and bends it into a mockery of fair, competitive practices and solid business integrity. It is important that you do not allow any customer to compromise the competitive position of your other customers through the abuse of your discount policy. Protect your company's good reputation. Your company's chances for continued success hinge as much on its good reputation as on any other single factor. (FIGURES 8-1, 8-2, and 8-3 show samples of letters covering disallowed discounts, unauthorized payment deductions, and missing invoices.)

IT'S YOUR MONEY

When an account begins to show you one or more of the following symptoms, move quickly to update your information. Review your recent payments experience with that of other suppliers, add any additional relevant pieces of information you might have culled from conversations with other owners—at an industry meeting, from a commercial credit report, or some other source—and prepare to take a firmer hold on the credit reins. It might be only a momentary problem before the account settles back into a normal pattern, but as I have said at various points throughout this book, you don't want or need any surprises that could become costly.

The "much less than worst" scenario? The scenario is that your customer files for protection under a chapter of the Bankruptcy Act (Chapter XI, business reorganization/continuation) within two, three, or four months after you have collected your money. Other companies will be unhappy when they learn that you are no longer involved. Some unpaid creditors will voice the opinion that you received "preferential treatment." The burden of proof is theirs. Never voluntarily surrender your money to a Trustee who has been elected by the creditors so he can take it and throw it back into the "general assets" pot. The court might order you later to do just that, but if it is the Trustee who wants you to return the money, he might have very little leverage to force it. Most bankruptcy cases have few assets, and there is usually not enough available money—or money involved in your alleged "preference"—to justify spending some of it on a possible extended in-court effort to prove that you knew the debtor's precarious situation when you got the alleged "preferential payment(s)." If the amount is large, the Trustee might consider making the effort to take it from you. If the amount is not large, probably there will be nothing more threatening than bluster.

Remember that *you* were the one who saw the problem developing and had the good judgment to get all, or most, of your company's money before there was a bankruptcy filing. You did your job. Unless you arranged something with the debtor that was truly preferential, there should be no successful claim against your money. The problem with those who complain of a preference is that they didn't do as good a job as you did. It's always possible for one creditor to get a piece of information through legitimate channels and, on the basis of that information, decide to accelerate the collection of an account balance. What will probably happen the next time there is a similar Chapter XI filing? Another creditor probably will get information that will enable his or her company to get out of an account before you and other creditors. Of course, you won't be pleased, but if your information indicates that the one creditor got out of the account as the result of information he or she legitimately obtained, you should have no problem with it.

(Date)

Customer Name
Street Address (or P.O. Box No.)
City, State and Zip Code

Dear Mr. (Ms.) _____:

We have applied your check No. _____ to the invoice (invoices) listed on the remittance section of the check. Unfortunately, the deductions(s) taken on invoice _____ (invoices numbered _____ and _____) is/are not allowable on the basis of information in our files.

If you can provide us with information that will substantiate the deduction (these deductions), we will be happy to adjust our records. If that is not possible, please forward your check in the amount of _____ to cover the unauthorized deductions.

Sincerely,

Credit Manager

FIG. 8-1.

(Date)

Customer Name
Street Address (or P.O. Box)
City, State and Zip Code

Gentlemen:

We are unable to allow the discount(s) taken on your check
#_____ and applicable to invoices _____.

The deduction was taken after the discount period had expired,
so we must ask that you include the disallowed amount of
$_____ as a part of your next account payment.

Sincerely,

Credit Manager

FIG. 8-2.

(Date)

Customer Name
Street Address (or P.O. Box No.)
City, State and Zip Code

Dear Mr. (Ms.)_____

Thank you for letting us know that you did not receive a copy
of ____(Invoice date and number)_____ in the amount of _____.

If the attached copy leaves anything unanswered, please contact
me at your early convenience.

Sincerely,

Credit Manager

FIG. 8-3.

You always should investigate rumors—particularly persistent rumors. When you hear that an owner or partner is spending too much time away from the business, is driving a new and expensive car, and is getting into a lifestyle that is not reconcilable with the size and quality of the business, do some investigating. Any significant change in lifestyle or a change in a long-term pattern of responsible, effective management is an indicator of some potentially serious problems for the business. Any serious business problem is a threat to the safety of your receivables dollars.

The following line is redundant because it has been said in so many different ways, but it is so important to the success of your company: Never, *never* lose sight of the fact that customers are important people, but never forget that it is *your* money.

CUSTOMER CALL SHEET

The Customer Call Sheet is an important part of the ongoing record keeping for each account. It is particularly important since you will use it to record the facts of calls regarding payments. If you properly maintain your Call Sheet, you won't have to go back over six months of receivables aging reports to know how a certain account has been handling its obligations. Your Call Sheet record will show no collection calls, an occasional call, or a number of calls. It might not tell you whether the account pays on a discount or prompt basis, but it will tell you at a glance whether the account has been a problem.

The Call Sheet is a key record in the systematic accumulation of verbal and written customer contacts. When an account is doing well, you might have almost nothing on your Call Sheet and only an occasional letter relating not to a payment problem but to a missing invoice or a pricing error. When an account consistently requires telephone calls to get your money released, it is a problem that eventually might lead to a bankruptcy filing. If that occurs and your company eventually must qualify the failed account as an allowable bad-debt deduction (for IRS purposes), a record of good continuity between collection calls and collection letters should ensure that a writeoff of the balance will not be challenged successfully. Your records will substantiate the quality and consistency of your in-house collection effort—an effort which might or might not have included assignment to a third party. Whether you did or did not assign the account would depend upon the circumstances of the business failure and would not be relevant to qualifying the writeoff if your records of telephone calls and letters indicates a consistent and an appropriately aggressive approach to the account.

Make your comments on the call sheet (FIG. 8-4) brief, but complete, as to what you said, what the customer said, and what was promised as a result of the call. In the "Follow" column you should note the date for the next call if what was promised during the conversation—and by a specific date—is not done. You consistently might contact one person, but be sure to note any change from the name shown at the top of the sheet. In some of the larger companies, it is not unusual for the "contact name" to change once or twice a year. Names are important. You might remember the person's name if you had to call again but in your absence, your designated employee wouldn't know who in payables had made the payment commitment.

COLLECTION CALLS

The purpose of these examples is to give you some idea of how you can structure the various types of collection calls. It is not my intention to provide you with scripts for these calls, only some guideline material. Unless you give the calls your own flavor and style, they won't be effective. Deliver your company's message in a way that is comfortable for you, being careful to control the content and flow of the conversations

CUSTOMER CALL SHEET

Owner _____   Company Name _____

Contact _____   Phone _____

Date	Contact	Subject/Comments	Follow

FIG. 8-4.

from the moment you place the call. You want the customer to know what your company expects, and it wouldn't be necessary for you to make a collection call if the customer's payment performance met those expectations.

You might feel a certain amount of hostility toward a customer who has evidenced a callous disregard for honesty and integrity in his or her relationship with your company. If you have such feelings, don't let them surface in conversations with the principal or other people at the account. When you call the firm, tell them what you expect them to do, the time frame within which you expect them to do it, and what you can and cannot do for them during the period of time it takes to eliminate the receivables problem. The absence of hostility in your voice and demeanor will allow you to concentrate on your message and deliver it in a straightforward, nonacrimonious manner. It is your telephone call, and you should be in control of it; but before you can be in control of the call, you must be in control of yourself.

Example #1

The following is an example of a collection call to a customer who owes $1288 for products covered by an invoice that is now 20 days past due. This customer has done business with your company for years; he usually pays within 10 days of Net 30 terms, and is rarely past due more than 10 or 15 days. Of course you want to generate payment but your primary concern with this account is the possibility that he did not receive the invoice.

(Your call goes through to Accounts Payable)

"This is Marcie in payables."

"Marcie, this is Frank Martin (you) at the Turnkey Company in Seattle, Washington."

"I didn't hear the company name."

"Turnkey, Marcie—the Turnkey Company."

"Oh, yes. We don't have a very good connection."

"Marcie, our records don't indicate that we've received your payment for an invoice that's 20 days past due. I'm wondering if you received it and if you did, when you expect to release payment."

"Let me check it for you. What's the invoice date and number?"

"The number is 592, dated 5/15, amount of $1288."

"Number 592 dated 5/15. Just a minute, please."

"Thank you."

(A minute or two of silence, then Marcie returns)

"I'm glad you called. Someone filed that invoice in the paid folder."

"I thought it must be something unusual because you almost always pay closer to terms. When should you have the payment processed and released?"

"It's early enough so I can input the data today. The check will go out this Friday."

"Great! Thanks for your help, Marcie."

"You're welcome. Goodbye."

"Goodbye, Marcie."

Example #2

Now let's change the scenario to reflect less cooperation on the part of your customer or your customer's payables person. Remember that when you're dealing with a person in accounts payable, or dealing with a person who *is* accounts payable, if that person isn't the owner or a management person, he or she is usually not authorized to process or release your check unless instructed to do so by the owner, controller, or financial officer. Accounts Payable employees get as fed up with the hassles that result from stall tactics and broken promises as you do. When there's a payment problem that obviously is beyond the control of the payables person to whom your account is assigned (as in a several-person department), go right on up the line to the payables supervisor, the controller, or the financial officer. If your product(s) is one that the customer must have and the account is more frequently allowing balances to become borderline unacceptable before paying, use your sales and credit manager hats. Call the customer's purchasing manager and tell him or her that you are going to hold product shipments if they do not make account payments closer to terms. The customer's purchasing manager will involve the company's financial people and manufacturing manager to ensure that there is no interruption in the flow of product from your company, and that the flow of payment checks is more timely.

You place a call to the controller of this firm—a firm whose payment record and promises of payment have been inconsistent. The firm has made payment promises but rarely kept them. It frequently takes two or three collection calls before you receive a promised check, and then it is probably two weeks or more after the first call and payment promise before you receive it.

(Your call is taken by the controller)

"Frank—how are you?"

"My health is fine, Carter. It's your account that's my problem. What happened to the $1862 check you agreed to mail not later than last Friday?"

"The money just didn't come in, Frank. I would have called you but right up until Friday afternoon I thought we could release your check."

"You did get some money? You were able to release some checks?"

"Oh, sure. A few that I simply had to let go."

"Good. Now as of this moment, Carter, I want you to consider that my $1862 check is among those that you must release on Friday of this week."

"I'll try, Frank, but when the money doesn't come in, I can only do so much."

"I understand, but I've waited longer than a reasonable length of time. Do what you have to do, but we're at the point where the check arrives in my office by next Tuesday or I don't release any more product until it does."

"Hey! We need those shipments! Our manufacturing people will be all over me if you hold orders!"

"That isn't my problem, Carter. If you want an uninterrupted flow of product(s), I want an uninterrupted flow of payments. Don't tell me you'll send a check by a specific date and then not do it."

"You don't believe in making it easy for a person, do you?"

"I can't make it easy for you when we're dealing with a past-due balance the size and age of this one. We sell to customers who pay within terms or close to terms, and I expect your company to do the same. You'll get the check out by this Friday?"

"I'll see that it's released."

"I appreciate it, Carter. Goodbye."

"Goodbye."

The following example is the only one that I shall personalize. I developed this relationship while I was a corporate credit manager in the floor-coverings industry and it spanned the 14 years I was in that industry. It is an excellent example of rapport at its finest between a corporate credit manager (myself) and an owner whose integrity was as sustaining for me as my willingness to work with him was for his company—and for him. Remember that strong customer relationships are at least as important for the small company as they are for credit management people in the bigger companies. Develop good relationships with key people in your key customer companies. Many relationships will be confined to telephone conversations or an occasional meeting at an industry function. Others will involve a lunch now and then—not only because you have business to discuss, but because there is genuine pleasure in getting together. It couldn't be better for you or your company!

Example #3

I receive a telephone call from the president and owner of a twenty-six year old firm (floor-covering contractor and retailer) with whom my company has done an ever-increasing level of business. At this point in the relationship, our annual sales to this company are about $400,000. The conversation is as follows:

"This is Cecil Bond."

"Cec, this is Charlie Webster. How are you?"

The call came in on my direct outside line. Charlie usually did not use that line.

"I'm fine, Charlie. This call is a surprise. What's doing?"

"I've got a problem, Cec, and it could be a big one."

"Oh? What is it?"

"One of my major customers has filed a Chapter XI, and I don't think they can come up with a reorganization plan that the creditors will buy."

"Are you secured, Charlie?" (referring to accounts receivable balances protected by a Uniform Commercial Code filing).

"Probably 40 percent of our account is in with the general creditors. I've done business with these people for 16 years. I never thought their account would be a problem."

"If you think that highly of them, probably most of their other creditors do too. It's possible that you can work out a plan that's acceptable to them."

"I suppose there's a chance. Meanwhile, we won't be getting the $82,000 check that they were going to mail this week. The absence of that check puts our cash flow in a real vise."

"What about scaling back your payments to suppliers? Tell the others what you've just told me. Tell them you'll prorate payments on a percentage basis for two or three months, then you'll increase the payment amounts until you're back on a normal payment schedule."

"That schedule would give us some breathing room."

"What do you think, Charlie, can you work your way out of the cash bind in four to six months?"

"Oh, sure. The account is a major one, but we're in good long-term shape. We can close the gap within six months and move forward."

"Good. Charlie, use my name and our conversation if it'll help you with some of your other suppliers. If anybody hesitates, have them give me a call."

"I appreciate it, Cec. Are you going to be in the area later this month?"

"Yes, I think I'll be down there—here it is—on the 24th, 25th, and 26th."

"Pick a day and let me buy lunch."

"You're on. What about the 26th. I'll confirm with your office when I get in on the 24th?"

"Great! See you on the 26th—and thanks again, Cec."

"No problem, Charlie."

There is one priceless ingredient in a genuinely strong customer relationship—a relationship in which the years of your association with an owner or partner give you total confidence in the personal and business integrity of that person. Do your best to generate those same feelings of confidence and integrity in others by your actions and deeds. A relationship of that quality can return business and personal dividends beyond any expectations.

Not every collection call will fulfill your expectation of a resolution to the past-due payments problem. Customers exist whose credibility and use of time-buying ploys will test your patience to the maximum. Following a particularly unsatisfactory string of collection calls, you might lean toward the thought that your customer list has too many people who seem to want to trash the supplier/customer relationship. You will move that thought quickly out of your mind because the overwhelming majority of your customers—if you have selected them wisely—are people of integrity who will give your company the kind of treatment they expect for themselves. It is unpleasant, however, when you start to recap a conversation on your call sheet and find that the customer cast his or her commitment not in stone but in Silly Putty®.

You do not want your collection calls to become adversarial. When a customer whose account is totally out of phase with payment terms persists in trying to turn payment problems back onto your prices (too high, not competitive), your products (inconsistent quality, etc.) or your delivery time ("You don't deliver on time and that costs me money!"), do not say what you are justified in thinking. You must convince problem accounts such as the one just described that credit sales are unacceptable until account balances are close to payment terms, or you should put some constraints on the when and how of product releases. Is the account past due? *really* past due? Then don't release any product or perform any services until aging and balances are in line with your company's credit policy. Is the customer unhappy? You have been unhappy with the account's payment performance much longer than the customer has been unhappy. The only thing that should change this relationship is the customer's money—and in the amount requested.

LETTERS REQUESTING PAYMENT (INCLUDING FINAL DEMAND)

The letters that follow (FIGS. 8-5, 8-6, 8-7, 8-8, 8-9, and 8-10) are examples of collection letters that you should use in conjunction with telephone calls or as a followup when your calls have been ineffective. Customer attitudes will determine the timing for going from telephone calls to the more formal approach of a collection letter. The first letter should state the date(s) of telephone calls, the promises of payment made to you, the balance that is past-due, and the need for a prompt payment response. Do not mention in this letter about a collection effort other than an in-house effort if you do not receive payment by the date specified. This letter is the first collection letter of a series that should not exceed three before you assign the account to an outside collection service. Accelerate the urgency if the first letter doesn't get you a check. Go with a second letter that leaves no question in the customer's mind regarding the seriousness of the past-due problem, but do not mention a third-party collection assignment. If you still do not receive a check, send the Final Demand letter (FIGS. 8-11 and 8-12) via certified or registered mail to ensure that the intended recipient gets it, knows exactly what you are about to do, and is aware of the time frame available to him or her before you take the collection action stated in the Final Demand letter. No longer does any latitude or inclination to negotiate a payment program with this customer exist—not if you have done a thorough job of communicating your company's payment requirements in the telephone calls and letters that preceded the Final Demand.

At this point in the relationship, you probably have been given three or four payment promises (all broken), a few lies or distortions of truth when you pressed for an explanation of the customer's problems, and a rather well-documented feeling that you

(Date)

Company Name
Street Address (or P.O. Box No.)
City, State and Zip Code

Attention: _____(name)_____, ___(title)_____

Dear Mr. (or Ms.) _____(name)_____:

The attached copy (copies) of invoice (invoices) _____
(and _____) is/are being forwarded as you requested
during our telephone conversation on ___(date)_____.

This information should enable you to verify the accuracy of
these invoice balances and expedite the processing of payment.

Sincerely,

Credit Manager

FIG. 8-5.

(Date)

Company Name
Street Address/P.O. Box No.
City, State and Zip Code

Attention of (name)
          (title)

Dear Mr. (or Ms.)_____

The call sheet for your account indicates that telephone calls
to your office on (date) and (date) were not successful in
obtaining a payment commitment for past due balances. Copies
of the subject invoices were mailed almost two weeks ago, and
there has been no indication that the merchandise failed to
arrive on time and in good condition.

Customers are very important people but the continued success
of our company demands a solid reciprocal with our customers:
we give you good merchandise and good service at a fair price
and we expect payment within (or near) sales terms. Anything
less - on your part or ours - erodes the relationship to the
point where there no longer is mutual confidence.

Your check for $ _____ (Invoices _____ and _____) in our
offices by (date) is the confidence builder we need to consider future open account sales.

Sincerely,

Credit Manager

FIG. 8-6.

(Date)

Company Name
Street Address/P.O. Box No.
City, State and Zip Code

Attention: _____(name)_____, __(title)___

Dear Mr. (or Ms.) _____(name)_____:

Attached is a copy of invoice _____ dated _____
in the amount of _____. This invoice is _____ days past
due and is unfavorably impacting the aging of your account.

Please contact me if there is a problem with the merchandise. If
not, your payment response by _____ will be greatly
appreciated.

Sincerely,

Credit Manager

FIG. 8-7.

(Date)

Company Name
Street Address/P.O. Box No.
City, State and Zip Code

Attention of (name)
     (title)

Dear Mr. (or Ms.) _____

Our company takes great pride in developing good customer
relationships. Most of our customers have been with us for
a number of years, which I guess is one of the positive
results from what we try to do in support of our customers.

Not every customer can discount invoices, pay within terms,
or even pay a few days past terms. We accept that fact when
account data is evaluated and a credit line assigned to a
customer. From that point forward it becomes a matter of
developing a rapport with the customer - a rapport that
will enable both of us to address any problem that may
arise before it becomes a contentious issue.

We have slid to a point where there is an unanticipated problem - and no rapport. Your account is ___ days past due, we
need $_____ yesterday, and the promises made during tele-
phone conversations have brought no money.

I must now hold orders until we have your check for $_____,
which must arrive prior to (date). The hold also includes
any C.O.D. orders that have not been released.

Sincerely,

Credit Manager

FIG. 8-8.

(Date)

Customer Name
Street/P. O. Box No.
City, State and Zip Code

Dear Customer:

Our payment records do not show that we have received your check
for _____ and _____ invoices in the amounts
of _____ and _____.

If our records do not agree, please contact the undersigned so
that we may go over our respective records, locate the problem,
and make whatever adjustment (s) may be necessary. If you find
that our records do agree, prompt payment of the above-listed
balances will be appreciated.

Sincerely,

Credit Manager

FIG. 8-9.

(Date)

Customer Name
Street/P.O. Box No.
City, State and Zip Code

Dear Customer:

Our payment records do not show that we have received your check
for __(month and year)__ invoices in the amount of _____.

If our records do not agree, please contact the undersigned so
we may go over our respective records, locate the problem, and
make whatever adjustment(s) may be necessary. If our records do
agree, prompt payment of the above-listed balance will be appreciated.

Sincerely,

Credit Manager

FIG. 8-10.

(Date)

Company Name
Street Address (or P.O. Box No.)
City, State and Zip Code

Attention of (Name)
            (Title)

Dear Mr. (or Ms.) _____:

There has been no response to our telephone and letter
requests for payment of your account balance, currently _____
days past due.

We can devote no more in-house time to the collection effort.
I must now tell you that the account will be referred to our
collection agency on (date)   if we have not received
payment in the amount of $

Sincerely,

Credit Manager

FIG. 8-11.

(Date)

Company Name
Street Address (or P.O. Box No.)
City, State and Zip Code

Attention of (Name)
            (Title)

Dear Mr. (or Ms.) _____:

We have not been successful in our effort to collect past due
balances owed to this company by your firm. Because telephone
and letter requests for payment have not been successful, we
are unwilling to devote any more in-house time to the collection effort.

I must now tell you that the account will be forwarded to our
collection service on (date)   if payment in the amount
of $ has not been received in this office.

Sincerely,

Credit Manager

FIG. 8-12.

cannot believe anything these people tell you. You have spent more time and effort trying to salvage the account than the customer's attitude deserved, so let it go. Let the people who spend their work days trying to collect money from these types of accounts handle it now. You have many other accounts whose problems have been getting less than a reasonable share of your time. Get back to doing a total credit job with all of your company's accounts.

DAILY FOLLOW-UP SCHEDULE

A peer credit manager introduced me to the form shown in FIG. 8-13 several years ago. It fills the need of every credit person who has collection responsibility, serving as an effective reminder system to ensure that follow-up collection calls or letters receive attention when, and as, necessary. You can file the Daily Follow-Up Schedule, which covers a two-week work period, in an easy reference binder. It offers an alternative answer to the problem of failing to do a follow-up on the proper day or at the proper time. The columns are purposely narrow. They are not intended to be a substitute area for notes on yellow-ruled paper or for the recapping of telephone conversations on individual customer call sheets.

If you currently are using a large calendar pad or an appointment book to keep track of this information, and it works well for you, then you don't need this form. Use the form or method that gives you the appropriate level of day-to-day control over these follow-up obligations. Be consistent. When you say you are going to do something, be sure that the commitment does not get lost. A consistent—and a persistent—pattern of calls and letters is imperative if you are to achieve maximum success with your collection efforts.

SUING IN SMALL CLAIMS COURT

Creditors have known for a long time that it doesn't make any business sense to have an attorney represent their company when seeking a judgment against a debtor for an obligation of $1500 or less. Long before "do it yourself" became a popular attitude, Small Claims Court was the place where a business person could pick up a kit of forms, follow a set of instructions, and take the suit cycle from filing to, and thru, the court's decision.

I obtained the forms used to illustrate this section from the Municipal Court of California, Santa Clara County Judicial District, Small Claims Division, and plaintiffs filing in that judicial jurisdiction should be the only people using them. You must sue in the right court and in the right judicial district—a rule called *venue*. If you are to file your claim in another county or state, contact the Small Claims Division (or Court) of the judicial district in which you will file your claim. You will be told where to obtain the necessary forms and instructions.

You might encounter few, or many, variations in the filing procedure from one major jurisdiction to another, but what is included here should not be atypical of the basic process of filing-through-judgment (and appeal, if that option is exercised by the defendant). In the subject jurisdiction (Santa Clara County Judicial District), the number of forms is seven. If the defendant appeals to the Superior Court from a Small Claims Court ruling in favor of the plaintiff, the defendant would activate the eighth form—Notice of Filing Notice of Appeal.

Copies in sequential order follow a brief description of each form. Also included is a copy of the Fictitious Business Name Declaration (mentioned in an earlier chapter) and an explanation of its' importance and relevance in California, and in many other states too.

DAILY FOLLOW-UP SCHEDULE

Monday	Tuesday	Wednesday	Thursday	Friday	Monday	Tuesday	Wednesday	Thursday	Friday

FIG. 8-13.

MUNICIPAL COURT OF CALIFORNIA
SANTA CLARA COUNTY JUDICIAL DISTRICT
SMALL CLAIMS DIVISION

☐Santa Clara Annex
1675 Lincoln St., SC 95050
(408) 246-0510

☐Los Gatos Facility
14205 Capri Dr., LG 95030
(408) 866-8331

☐Gilroy Facility
7350 Rosanna St., GI 95020
(408) 842-6299

☐Palo Alto Facility
270 Grant Ave., PA 94306
(415) 324-0391

☐Sunnyvale Facility
605 W. El Camino, SV 94087
(408) 739-1502

CASE NO. S. C. _____

PLAINTIFF HAS DEMANDED THAT DEFENDANT PAY THE SUM AND IT HAS NOT BEEN PAID.

1. MY NAME (plaintiff) _____

2. MY ADDRESS _____ ZIP _____

3. MY TELEPHONE NUMBER _____ 4. AMOUNT OF CLAIM _____

5. NATURE OF CLAIM _____
_____

6. DATE AND PLACE WHERE DAMAGES OR INJURY OCCURRED, OR WHERE OBLIGATION WAS TO BE

   PERFORMED _____

   Claim for Automobile Damages: I am _____ the registered owner of the vehicle

7. THIS COURT IS THE PROPER COURT FOR HEARING YOUR CLAIM. SEE INFORMATION FOR PLANTIFF FORM FOR ASSISTANCE AND INDICATE PROPER LETTER IN BOX ☐. FOR F OR G ENTER PROPER NUMBER IN BOX ☐.

8. (a) If you are suing an individual, give his full name. (b) If you are suing a business firm, give the firm name and the name of the owner. (c) If you are suing a partnership, you must name the partners. (d) If you are suing a corporation, give its full name, and the name of a director of said corporation. (e) If your suit arises out of an automobile accident, you must name the driver and registered owner.

9. I UNDERSTAND I HAVE NO RIGHT OF APPEAL FROM A JUDGMENT ON MY CLAIM

10. MY CLAIM IS AGAINST (defendant)

NAME	ADDRESS	CITY	ZIP

DECLARATION OF NON-MILITARY STATUS

The declarant is the Plaintiff in the annexed and foregoing action, and/or he takes this declaration for said Plaintiff and declares the Defendant, and each of them, of more than one, is not now a person in the Military Service of the United States as defined in Sec. 101 of the Soldiers' and Sailors' Relief Act of 1940, and amendments thereto.
I declare under penalty of perjury that the foregoing is true and correct.

Excuted on _____   _____
                                              SIGNATURE
The declaration under penalty of perjury must be signed in California, or in a state that authorizes use of a declaration in place of an affidavit, otherwise an affidavit is required.

ORDER TO PLAINTIFF TO APPEAR

Your case will be tried on _____ at _____M., in Dept. _____ of said court.

YOU ARE HEREBY DIRECTED TO APPEAR on said date and to bring with you all books, papers and witnesses needed to prove your claim.

> **IMPORTANT Please check the Court Calendar in the lobby of the building for the Department of this Court that will hear this matter.**

REQUEST FOR DISMISSAL

If case is paid or settled before trial, sign below and mail this form to the above entitled court. THIS CASE MAY BE DISMISSED.

Dated: _____   _____
                                        Signature of Plaintiff

361 REV 11/86

FIG. 8-14.

☐ Suit Form—Plaintiff's name, defendant's name, nature of the claim, etc.

☐ Proof Of Service—States how, where, and by whom relevant papers were served on the defendant.

☐ Plaintiff's Claim—Describes the amount of debt, effort to collect, and rules of the court.

☐ Defendant's Claim—Counter-suit stating amount owed defendant, effort to collect, etc.

☐ Order to Appear For Examination—Issued against Judgment Debtor and/or Third Person because the Judgment Debtor claims the Third Person has possession or control of property which belongs to the Judgment Debtor, or concerning a debt owed the Judgment Debtor by a Third Person.

☐ Abstract of Judgment—Judgment Creditor or Assignee of Record applies to the court clerk for a certified copy of the Small Claims Court judgment.

☐ Memorandum Of Credits, Accrued Interest, And Costs After Judgment —Self-explanatory. All payments and charges pertaining to the case through the date executed.

☐ Notice of Filing Notice of Appeal—Judgment Debtor appeals to the Superior Court from the Small Claims Court judgment or denial of motion to vacate the judgment.

You will use an additional form in conjunction with a filing in Small Claims Court in California and many other states. It is the Fictitious Name Declaration. Failure to comply with California Law (and the law in other states) could cause the court to dismiss your claim. You file the Fictitious Name Declaration, to use the example of California, with the clerk of the county in which the principal place of business is located or in Sacramento County if the filing firm has no place of business within the state. Whether your state does or does not require the filing of a ''fictitious name'' or ''dba'' statement is information you will want to obtain when you inquire regarding the ''how and where'' of filing your claim in Small Claims Court.

The thought that you will be acting as your own attorney should not be inhibiting. This court is not a court where silver-tongued oratory is a requisite. Presenting your case does not demand the skills of a Clarence Darrow. The trial itself is informal and the rules simple:

☐ Be in court on time.

☐ Bring with you all witnesses, books, receipts, and other papers or things to prove your case.

☐ Ask the clerk of the court to issue a subpoena if a witness is reluctant or unwilling to come to court. A subpoena requires the witness to appear.

☐ Be prepared to pay a fee to the witness for his or her court appearance.

☐ Get a court order requiring the necessary records or papers brought to the trial to prove your case, if you do not have them but know where they are.

☐ File a dismissal form with the court clerk, if the case is settled before the trial date or time.

☐ You might receive the court's decision in the mail or someone might hand-deliver it to you in court when the trial is over. The form used for the decision is called The Notice of Entry of Judgment.

☐ The person who wins the case is called the *judgment creditor*; the loser, and the one who owes the money, is called the *judgment debtor*.

☐ You cannot enforce judgment until after the period for filing an appeal has ended. After judgment has been rendered, and if the judgment is appealed in Superior Court by the judgment debtor, both parties may be represented by lawyers.

Other requirements are necessary before the Clerk of the Small Claims Court can accept a filing, (making a final demand on the debtor, etc.). Every jurisdiction should offer some advice and assistance in the preparation of claims cases. In California, it is the Department of Consumer Affairs, Small Claims Advisor, Sacramento. In your city or state there is probably a similar source for information and assistance. If the court in which you would file a claim does not provide such assistance or advice—and I question whether any court that does not permit attorneys to appear would be so insensitive to the needs of litigants—then you should be directed to the appropriate source for such information.

STATUTE OF LIMITATIONS

Collection procedures never should be so poorly organized that an account which you carry as active—a receivables balance on your aged trial balance report—is lost because the statute of limitations has run out. You must be aware of the statute in any state or jurisdiction in which you might want to use Small Claims Court or a conventional civil suit to press for a judgment against the debtor/customer. Take appropriate collection action but initiate it within the period of years prescribed by the appropriate jurisdiction. Virtually no set of circumstances justifies such a level of inattention to the aging of a receivables balance.

If your best in-house collection efforts have not been effective—telephone calls, letters, and a "final demand" letter—then assign the account to your collection service. If the collection service is unable to locate the debtor or determines that there are no assets against which you could hope to levy a judgment, charge the account balance against your company's bad-debt reserve. At that point, you will have made every reasonable effort to collect your company's money.

Under certain circumstances, a debtor might surface after the statute of limitations has seemingly pushed your old account balance—now a bad-debt item—beyond your reach. Unless you are notified that the individual, partnership, or company filed for bankruptcy—and your debt was among those listed and discharged by the bankruptcy court—there is the possibility of life after the statute of limitations. Other pieces also must fit the criteria for reviving the account balance, and it is imperative that you have your company's attorney make the decision. Let him or her tell you whether there is hope, what must be done to make reviving the account a possibility and—if there is a possibility that you can return the debt to the category of a legally-collectible item—are there now any assets against which you could levy a judgment if you obtain one?

Your time is split in too many directions to waste it attempting to revive accounts that are as dead as your bad-debt assignment indicates, or as dead as a judgment and no assets against which to levy it. Unless it is a rare situation, you are well advised, in most instances, to move on past accounts such as the above and focus your time and attention on your active accounts.

PROOF OF SERVICE
(Use separate proof of service for each person served)

1. I served the   CASE NO._____

   Claim of Plaintiff

   b. On defendant (Name):

   c. By serving   (1) ☐ Defendant   (2) ☐ Other (Name and title or relationship to person served):

   d. ☐ By delivery at ☐ home   ☐ business   (1) Date of:
      (2) Time of: (3) Address:

   e. ☐ By mailing   (1) Date of: (2) Place of:
2. Manner of service: (Check proper box)
   a. ☐ **Personal service.** By personally delivering copies. (CCP 415.10)
   b. ☐ **Substituted service on corporation, unincorporated association (including partnership), or public entity.** By leaving, during usual office hours, copies in the office of the person served with the person who apparently was in charge and thereafter mailing (by first-class mail, postage prepaid) copies to the person served at the place where the copies were left. (CCP 415.20(a))
   c. ☐ **Substituted service on natural person, minor, incompetent, or candidate.** By leaving copies at the dwelling house, usual place of abode, or usual place of business of the person served in the presence of a competent member of the household or a person apparently in charge of the office or place of business, at least 16 years of age, who was informed of the general nature of the papers, and thereafter mailing (by first-class mail, postage prepaid) copies to the person served at the place where the copies were left. (CCP 415.20(b)) **(Attach separate declaration or affidavit stating acts relied on to establish reasonable diligence in first attempting personal service.)**
   d. ☐ Other (Specify code section):
      ☐ Additional page is attached.
3. The notice to the person served was completed as follows (CCP 412.30, 415.10, and 474):

   a. ☐ As an individual defendant.
   b. ☐ As the person sued under the fictitious name of:
   c. ☐ On behalf of:
      Under: ☐ CCP 416.10 (Corporation)   ☐ CCP 416.60 (Minor)   ☐ Other:
             ☐ CCP 416.20 (Defunct corporation)   ☐ CCP 416.70 (Incompetent)
             ☐ CCP 416.40 (Association or partnership)   ☐ CCP 416.90 (Individual)
   d. ☐ By personal delivery on (Date):
4. At the time of service I was at least 18 years of age and not a party to this action.
5. Fee for service: $
6. Person serving
   a. ☐ Not a registered California process server.
   b. ☐ Registered California process server.
   c. ☐ Employee or independent contractor of a registered California process server.
   d. ☐ Exempt from registration under Bus. & Prof. Code 22350(b)

   e. ☐ California sheriff, marshal, or constable.
   f. Name, address and telephone number and if applicable, county of registration and number:

I declare under penalty of perjury that the foregoing is true and correct and that this declaration is executed on (Date): . . . . at (Place): . . . . , California.

(For California sheriff, marshal or constable use only)
   I certify that the foregoing is true and correct and that this certificate is executed on (Date): . . . . at (Place): . . . . , California.

_____   _____
        (Signature)   (Signature)

4304 REV 8/83

FIG. 8-15.

MUNICIPAL COURT OF CALIFORNIA, SANTA CLARA COUNTY JUDICIAL DISTRICT, SMALL CLAIMS DIVISION

Case No.

— NOTICE TO DEFENDANT — YOU ARE BEING SUED BY PLAINTIFF	— *AVISO AL DEMANDADO* — *A USTED LO ESTAN DEMANDANDO*
To protect your rights, you must appear in this court on the trial date shown in the table below. You may lose the case if you do not appear. The court may award the plaintiff the amount of the claim and the costs. Your wages, money, and property may be taken without further warning from the court.	*Para proteger sus derechos, usted debe presentarse ante esta corte en la fecha del juicio indicada en el cuadro que aparece a continuación. Si no se presenta, puede perder el caso. La corte puede decidir en favor del demandante por la cantidad del reclamo y los costos. A usted le pueden quitar su salario, su dinero, y otras cosas de su propiedad, sin aviso adicional por parte de esta corte.*

PLAINTIFF/DEMANDANTE *(Name and address of each):*

DEFENDANT/DEMANDADO *(Name and address of each):*

☐ See attached sheet for additional plaintiffs and defendants.

PLAINTIFF'S CLAIM

1. Defendant owes me the sum of $, not including court costs, because *(describe claim and date):*

2. I have asked defendant to pay this money, but it has not been paid.
3. This court is the proper court for the trial because [   ] *(In the box at the left, insert one of the letters from the list marked "Venue Table" on the back of this sheet. If you select D, E, or F, specify additional facts in this space.)*

4. ☐ I have filed more than 12 claims in this court, including this claim, during the previous 12 calendar months.

5. I understand that
   a. I may talk to an attorney about this claim, but I cannot be represented by an attorney at the trial in the small claims court.
   b. I must appear at the time and place of trial and bring all witnesses, books, receipts, and other papers or things to prove my case.
   c. I have no right of appeal on my claim, but I may appeal a claim filed by the defendant in this case.
   d. If I cannot afford to pay the fees for filing or service by a sheriff, marshal, or constable, I may ask that the fees be waived.

6. I have received and read the information sheet explaining some important rights of plaintiffs in the small claims court.

I declare under penalty of perjury under the laws of the State of California that the foregoing is true and correct.
Date:

....
(TYPE OR PRINT NAME)   *(SIGNATURE OF PLAINTIFF)*

ORDER TO DEFENDANT

You must appear in this court on the trial date and at the time LAST SHOWN IN THE BOX BELOW if you do not agree with the plaintiff's claim. Bring all witnesses, books, receipts, and other papers or things with you to support your case.

TRIAL DATE / FECHA DEL JUICIO		DATE	TIME	PLACE	COURT USE
	1.				
	2.				
	3.				
	4.				

Filed on *(date):*   Clerk, by_____, Deputy

— You have a right to a small claims advisor free of charge. Read the information sheet on the reverse. —

Form Approved by the
Judicial Council of California
SC-100 (Rev. January 1, 1985)

PLAINTIFF'S CLAIM AND ORDER TO DEFENDANT
(Small Claims)

Rule 982.7

FIG. 8-16.

MUNICIPAL COURT OF CALIFORNIA, SANTA CLARA COUNTY JUDICIAL DISTRICT, SMALL CLAIMS DIVISION

☐ Palo Alto Facility
270 Grant Ave., PA 94306
(415) 324-0391

☐ Los Gatos Facility
14205 Capri Dr., LG 95030
(408) 866-6331

☐ Gilroy Facility
7350 Rosanna St., GI 95020
(408) 842-3111

☐ San Jose Facility
200 W. Hedding, SJ 95110
(408) 299-2271

☐ Sunnyvale Facility
605 W. El Camino, SV 94087
(408) 739-1502

SMALL CLAIMS CASE NO.

— NOTICE TO PLAINTIFF — YOU ARE BEING SUED BY DEFENDANT	— AVISO AL DEMANDANTE — A USTED LO ESTA DEMANDANDO EL DEMANDADO
To protect your rights, you must appear in this court on the trial date shown in the table below. You may lose the case if you do not appear. The court may award the defendant the amount of the claim and the costs. Your wages, money, and property may be taken without further warning from the court.	Para proteger sus derechos, usted debe presentarse ante esta corte en la fecha del juicio indicada en el cuadro que aparece a continuación. Si no se presenta, puede perder el caso. La corte puede decidir en favor del demandado por la cantidad del reclamo y los costos. A usted le pueden quitar su salario, su dinero, y otras cosas de su propiedad, sin aviso adicional por parte de esta corte.

PLAINTIFF/DEMANDANTE *(Name and address of each)*:

DEFENDANT/DEMANDADO *(Name and address of each)*:

☐ See attached sheet for additional plaintiffs and defendants.

DEFENDANT'S CLAIM

1. Plaintiff owes me the sum of $ _____, not including court costs, because *(describe claim and date)*:

2. I have asked plaintiff to pay this money, but it has not been paid.

3. I understand that
   a. I may talk to an attorney about this claim, but I cannot be represented by an attorney at the trial in the small claims court.
   b. I must appear at the time and place of trial and bring all witnesses, books, receipts, and other papers or things to prove my case.
   c. I have no right of appeal on my claim, but I may appeal a claim filed by the plaintiff in this case.
   d. If I cannot afford to pay the fees for filing or service by a sheriff, marshal, or constable, I may ask that the fees be waived.

4. I have received and read the information sheet explaining some important rights of defendants in the small claims court.

I declare under penalty of perjury under the laws of the State of California that the foregoing is true and correct.
Date:

....
(TYPE OR PRINT NAME)

(SIGNATURE OF DEFENDANT)

ORDER TO PLAINTIFF

You must appear in this court on the trial date and at the time LAST SHOWN IN THE BOX BELOW if you do not agree with the defendant's claim. Bring all witnesses, books, receipts, and other papers or things with you to support your case.

TRIAL DATE FECHA DEL JUICIO		DATE	TIME	PLACE	COURT USE
	1.				
	2.				
	3.				

Filed on *(date)*:

Clerk, by _____, Deputy

— **You have a right to a small claims advisor free of charge.** —

Form Approved by the Judicial Council of California
SC-120 [Rev. January 1, 1985]

DEFENDANT'S CLAIM AND ORDER TO PLAINTIFF
(Small Claims)

Rule 982.7
5171 REV 8/85

FIG. 8-17.

ATTORNEY OR PARTY WITHOUT ATTORNEY *(Name and Address)*:	TELEPHONE NO.:	FOR COURT USE ONLY

ATTORNEY FOR *(Name)*:

NAME OF COURT:
STREET ADDRESS:
MAILING ADDRESS:
CITY AND ZIP CODE:
BRANCH NAME:

PLAINTIFF:

DEFENDANT:

APPLICATION AND ORDER FOR APPEARANCE AND EXAMINATION
☐ ENFORCEMENT OF JUDGMENT   ☐ ATTACHMENT (Third Person)
☐ Judgment Debtor   ☐ Third Person

CASE NUMBER:

ORDER TO APPEAR FOR EXAMINATION

1. TO *(name)*:
2. YOU ARE ORDERED TO APPEAR personally before this court, or before a referee appointed by the court, to
   a. ☐ furnish information to aid in enforcement of a money judgment against you.
   b. ☐ answer concerning property of the judgment debtor in your possession or control or concerning a debt you owe the judgment debtor.
   c. ☐ answer concerning property of the defendant in your possession or control or concerning a debt you owe the defendant that is subject to attachment.

Date: Time: Dept. or Div.:   Rm.:
Address of court ☐ shown above ☐ is:

3. This order may be served by a sheriff, marshal, constable, registered process server, **or** the following specially appointed person *(name)*:

Date: ▶ _____
(SIGNATURE OF JUDGE OR REFEREE)

This order must be served not less than 10 days before the date set for the examination.
IMPORTANT NOTICES ON REVERSE

APPLICATION FOR ORDER TO APPEAR FOR EXAMINATION

1. ☐ Judgment creditor   ☐ Assignee of record   ☐ Plaintiff who has a right to attach order
   applies for an order requiring *(name)*:   to appear and furnish information
   to aid in enforcement of the money judgment or to answer concerning property or debt.
2. The person to be examined is
   ☐ the judgment debtor
   ☐ a third person (1) who has possession or control of property belonging to the judgment debtor or the defendant or (2) who owes the judgment debtor or the defendant more than $250. An affidavit supporting this application under CCP §491.110 or §708.120 is attached.
3. The person to be examined resides or has a place of business in this county or within 150 miles of the place of examination.
4. ☐ This court is **not** the court in which the money judgment is entered or *(attachment only)* the court that issued the writ of attachment. An affidavit supporting an application under CCP §491.150 or §708.160 is attached.
5. ☐ The judgment debtor has been examined within the past 120 days. An affidavit showing good cause for another examination is attached.

I declare under penalty of perjury under the laws of the State of California that the foregoing is true and correct.
Date:

....
(TYPE OR PRINT NAME)   ▶ _____
(SIGNATURE OF DECLARANT)

Form Approved by the
Judicial Council of California
AT-138, EJ-125 [New July 1, 1984]

**APPLICATION AND ORDER
FOR APPEARANCE AND EXAMINATION**
(Attachment—Enforcement of Judgment)

CCP 491.110, 708.110, 708.120

3580 REV 1/85

FIG. 8-18.

APPEARANCE OF JUDGMENT DEBTOR (ENFORCEMENT OF JUDGMENT)

NOTICE TO JUDGMENT DEBTOR If you fail to appear at the time and place specified in this order, you may be subject to arrest and punishment for contempt of court, and the court may make an order requiring you to pay the reasonable attorney fees incurred by the judgment creditor in this proceeding.

**APPEARANCE OF A THIRD PERSON
(ENFORCEMENT OF JUDGMENT)**

(1) NOTICE TO PERSON SERVED If you fail to appear at the time and place specified in this order, you may be subject to arrest and punishment for contempt of court, and the court may make an order requiring you to pay the reasonable attorney fees incurred by the judgment creditor in this proceeding.

(2) NOTICE TO JUDGMENT DEBTOR The person in whose favor the judgment was entered in this action claims that the person to be examined pursuant to this order has possession or control of property which is yours or owes you a debt. This property or debt is as follows *(Describe the property or debt using typewritten capital letters)*:

If you claim that all or any portion of this property or debt is exempt from enforcement of the money judgment, you must file your exemption claim in writing with the court and have a copy personally served on the judgment creditor not later than three days before the date set for the examination. You must appear at the time and place set for the examination to establish your claim of exemption or your exemption may be waived.

APPEARANCE OF A THIRD PERSON (ATTACHMENT)
NOTICE TO PERSON SERVED If you fail to appear at the time and place specified in this order, you may be subject to arrest and punishment for contempt of court, and the court may make an order requiring you to pay the reasonable attorney fees incurred by the plaintiff in this proceeding.

APPEARANCE OF A CORPORATION, PARTNERSHIP, ASSOCIATION, TRUST, OR OTHER ORGANIZATION
It is your duty to designate one or more of the following to appear and be examined: officers, directors, managing agents, or other persons who are familiar with your property and debts.

AT-138, EJ-125
[New July 1, 1984]

APPLICATION AND ORDER FOR APPEARANCE AND EXAMINATION
(Attachment—Enforcement of Judgment)

Page two

Fig. 8-18. Continued.

ATTORNEY OR PARTY WITHOUT ATTORNEY *(Name and Address)*:

☐ Recording requested by and return to:

TELEPHONE NO.:

FOR RECORDER'S USE ONLY

☐ ATTORNEY FOR ☐ JUDGMENT CREDITOR ☐ ASSIGNEE OF RECORD

NAME OF COURT:

STREET ADDRESS:

MAILING ADDRESS:

CITY AND ZIP CODE:

BRANCH NAME:

PLAINTIFF:

DEFENDANT:

ABSTRACT OF JUDGMENT

CASE NUMBER:

FOR COURT USE ONLY

1. ☐ Judgment creditor ☐ Assignee of record
   applies for an abstract of judgment and represents the following:
   a. Judgment debtor's
       Name and last known address

   b. Driver's license no. and state: ☐ unknown.
   c. Social Security number: ☐ unknown.
   d. Summons or notice of entry of sister state judgment was personally served or
      mailed to *(address)*:

   ☐ Information regarding additional judgment debtors is shown on the reverse.

Date:

▶

.... *(TYPE OR PRINT NAME)* ....   *(SIGNATURE OF APPLICANT OR ATTORNEY)*

2. a. ☐ I certify that the following is a true and correct abstract of the judgment entered in this action.
   b. ☐ A certified copy of the judgment is attached.
3. Judgment creditor *(name)*:

4. Judgment debtor *(full name as it appears in judgment)*:

5. a. Judgment entered *(date)*:
   b. Renewal entered *(date)*:
   c. Renewal entered *(date)*:
6. Total amount of judgment as entered or last renewed:
   $
7. ☐ An ☐ execution ☐ attachment lien is endorsed
      on the judgment as follows:
   a. amount: $
   b. in favor of *(name and address)*:

8. A stay of enforcement has
   a. ☐ not been ordered by the court.
   b. ☐ been ordered by the court effective until *(date)*:

9. ☐ This is an installment judgment.

[SEAL]

This abstract issued on
(date):   Clerk, by _____ , Deputy

3568 REV 7/83

Form Adopted by the
Judicial Council of California
982(a)(1) [Rev. July 1, 1983]

ABSTRACT OF JUDGMENT
(CIVIL)

CCP 488.480, 674
700.190

FIG. 8-19.

PLAINTIFF:	CASE NUMBER:
DEFENDANT:	

Information regarding additional judgment debtors:

10. _____   Name and last known address

Driver's license no. & state: ⬜ unknown.
Social Security no.: ⬜ unknown.
Summons was personally served at or mailed to *(address)*:

14. _____   Name and last known address

Driver's license no. & state: ⬜ unknown.
Social Security no.: ⬜ unknown.
Summons was personally served at or mailed to *(address)*:

11. _____   Name and last known address

Driver's license no. & state: ⬜ unknown.
Social Security no.: ⬜ unknown.
Summons was personally served at or mailed to *(address)*:

15. _____   Name and last known address

Driver's license no. & state: ⬜ unknown.
Social Security no.: ⬜ unknown.
Summons was personally served at or mailed to *(address)*:

12. _____   Name and last known address

Driver's license no. & state: ⬜ unknown.
Social Security no.: ⬜ unknown.
Summons was personally served at or mailed to *(address)*:

16. _____   Name and last known address

Driver's license no. & state: ⬜ unknown.
Social Security no.: ⬜ unknown.
Summons was personally served at or mailed to *(address)*:

13. _____   Name and last known address

Driver's license no. & state: ⬜ unknown.
Social Security no.: ⬜ unknown.
Summons was personally served at or mailed to *(address)*:

17. _____   Name and last known address

Driver's license no. & state: ⬜ unknown.
Social Security no.: ⬜ unknown.
Summons was personally served at or mailed to *(address)*:

18. ⬜ Continued on attachment 18.

982(a)(1) [Rev. July 1, 1983]   **ABSTRACT OF JUDGMENT (CIVIL)**   Page two

Fig. 8-19. Continued.

1

144 *Credit Decisions—The Good, the Fair, and the Ugly*

MUNICIPAL COURT OF CALIFORNIA, COUNTY OF SANTA CLARA

NAME OF MUNICIPAL OR JUSTICE DISTRICT	FOR COURT USE ONLY
TITLE OF CASE *(ABBREVIATED)*	
ATTORNEY(S) NAME AND ADDRESS	
	CASE NUMBER
ATTORNEY(S) FOR: TELEPHONE	

**MEMORANDUM OF CREDITS,
ACCRUED INTEREST AND
COSTS AFTER JUDGMENT**

MEMORANDUM OF CREDITS

CREDIT for payments and partial satisfaction of judgment, including direct payments and executions partially satisfied: $.............................
(if none, state none)

INTEREST ACCRUING AFTER JUDGMENT

INTEREST ACCRUING AFTER JUDGMENT at 7% from date of judgment on balances due after dates of payments or credits acknowledged above: $...............................

MEMORANDUM OF COSTS AFTER JUDGMENT

1 COSTS AFTER JUDGMENT CLAIMED ON MEMORANDUM FILED HERETOFORE: .... $......................
2 CLERK'S FEES .... $......................
3 .... $......................
4 SHERIFF OR MARSHAL'S FEES: .... $......................
5 .... $......................
6 SERVING SUPPLEMENTARY PROCEEDINGS: .... $......................
7 .... $......................
8 NOTARY FEES: .... $......................
9 .... $......................
10 .... $......................
11 .... $......................
12 .... $......................
13 .... $......................
14 .... $......................
15 .... $......................
16 .... $......................
17 .... $......................
18 .... $......................
19 .... $......................
20 .... $......................
21 .... $......................
22 .... $......................
23 .... $......................
24 .... $_____
TOTAL $_____

I, the undersigned, say: I am ....
the attorney(s) for the ....
in the above entitled action, that, to the best of my knowledge and belief, the items in the within memorandum are correct and that the said disbursements have been necessarily incurred in said action.
I declare under penalty of perjury that the foregoing is true and correct.

Executed on .... at ...., California.

....
(Signature)

NOTE: A notice of motion to tax costs shall specify the items of the cost bill to which objection is made.

3590 REV 6/81 **MEMORANDUM OF CREDITS, ACCRUED INTEREST AND COSTS AFTER JUDGMENT** Code of Civ. Proc. 682.2, 1033.7, 2015.5 Rule 3(d), Rules for the Municipal Courts.

FIG. 8-20.

DECLARATION OR CERTIFICATE OF SERVICE BY MAIL

C.C.P. Sec. 1010, et seq. 2015.5

DECLARATION OF SERVICE BY MAIL

My .... address is ....
(business/residence)

I am, and was at the time the herein mentioned mailing took place, a citizen of the United States,......................
(employed/resident)
in the County where said mailing occurred, over the age of eighteen years and not a party to the above-en-

titled cause.

On ...., I served the foregoing Memorandum of Costs by depositing a copy there-

of, enclosed in separate, sealed envelope, with the postage thereon fully prepaid, in the United States mail

at .... County of ...., California,
(city or postal area)

each of which envelopes was addressed respectively as follows:

Executed on ...., at ...., California.
(date)   (place)

I declare under penalty of perjury that the foregoing is true and correct.

....
(Signature of Declarant)

ATTORNEY'S CERTIFICATE OF SERVICE

I, the undersigned, certify: that I am an active member of the State Bar of California and not a party to the

above-entitled cause, and my business address as ....

...., California;

that on .... I served the foregoing Memorandum of Costs by depositing a copy

thereof, enclosed in separate, sealed envelope, with the postage thereon fully prepaid, in the United States

mail at ...., County of..,
(city or postal area)

California, each of which envelopes was addressed respectively as follows:

Name: Address:

....
Attorney

ACKNOWLEDGEMENT OF SERVICE

Received copy of the foregoing Memorandum of Costs

on ...., ..., Attorney for.............................

on ...., ..., Attorney for.............................

Fig. 8-20. Continued.

MUNICIPAL COURT OF CALIFORNIA, SANTA CLARA COUNTY JUDICIAL DISTRICT, SMALL CLAIMS DIVISION

☐Palo Alto Facility ☐Los Gatos Facility ☐Gilroy Facility ☐Santa Clara Annex ☐Sunnyvale Facility
270 Grant Ave., PA 94306 14205 Capri Dr., LG 95030 7350 Rosanna St., GI 95020 1675 Lincoln St., SC 95050 605 W. El Camino, SV 94087
(415) 324-0391 (408) 866-8331 (408) 842-3111 (408) 246-0510 (408) 739-1502

SMALL CLAIMS CASE NO.

PLAINTIFF/DEMANDANTE *(Name and address of each)*:

DEFENDANT/DEMANDADO *(Name and address of each)*:

☐ See attached sheet for additional plaintiffs and defendants.

NOTICE OF FILING NOTICE OF APPEAL

TO: ☐ Plaintiff *(name)*:

☐ Defendant *(name)*:

Your small claims case has been APPEALED to the superior court. Do not contact the small claims court about this appeal. The superior court will notify you of the date you should appear in court. The notice of appeal is set forth below.

La decisión hecha por la corte para reclamos judiciales menores en su caso ha sido APELADA ante la corte superior. No se ponga en contacto con la corte para reclamos judiciales menores acerca de esta apelación. La corte superior le notificará la fecha en que usted debe presentarse ante ella. El aviso de la apelación aparece a continuación.

Date: _____ Clerk, by _____, Deputy

NOTICE OF APPEAL

I appeal to the superior court from the small claims judgment or the denial of the motion to vacate the small claims judgment, as provided by law.

DATE APPEAL FILED *(clerk to insert date)*:

▶

(TYPE OR PRINT NAME) .... *(SIGNATURE OF APPELLANT OR APPELLANT'S ATTORNEY)*

CLERK'S CERTIFICATE OF MAILING

I certify that
1. I am not a party to this action.
2. This Notice of Filing Notice of Appeal and Notice of Appeal were mailed first class, postage prepaid, in a sealed envelope to
   ☐ plaintiff
   ☐ defendant
   at the address shown above.
3. The mailing and this certification occurred
   at *(place)*: _____ California,
   on *(date)*:

Clerk, by _____, Deputy

Form Approved by the
Judicial Council of California
SC-140 [Rev. January 1, 1985]

NOTICE OF APPEAL
(Small Claims)

Rule 982.7
6769 REV 6/86

FIG. 8-21.

MUNICIPAL COURT OF CALIFORNIA
SANTA CLARA COUNTY JUDICIAL DISTRICT
SMALL CLAIMS DIVISION

☐Santa Clara Annex
1675 Lincoln St., SC 95050
(408) 246-0510

☐Los Gatos Facility
14205 Capri Dr., LG 95030
(408) 866-8331

☐Gilroy Facility
7350 Rosanna St., GI 95020
(408) 842█6299

☐Palo Alto Facility
270 Grant Ave., PA 94306
(415) 324-0391

☐Sunnyvale Facility
605 W. El Camino, SV 94087
(408) 739-1502

CASE NO. S. C. _____

PLAINTIFF HAS DEMANDED THAT DEFENDANT PAY THE SUM AND IT HAS NOT BEEN PAID.

1. MY NAME (plaintiff) _____

2. MY ADDRESS _____ ZIP_____

3. MY TELEPHONE NUMBER _____ 4. AMOUNT OF CLAIM _____

5. NATURE OF CLAIM _____
_____

6. DATE AND PLACE WHERE DAMAGES OR INJURY OCCURRED, OR WHERE OBLIGATION WAS TO BE

PERFORMED _____

Claim for Automobile Damages: I am _____ **the registered owner of the vehicle**

7. **THIS COURT IS THE PROPER COURT FOR HEARING YOUR CLAIM. SEE INFORMATION FOR PLANTIFF FORM FOR ASSISTANCE AND INDICATE PROPER LETTER IN BOX ☐. FOR FOR G ENTER PROPER NUMBER IN BOX ☐.**

8. (a) If you are suing an individual, give his full name. (b) If you are suing a business firm, give the firm name and the name of the owner. (c) If you are suing a partnership, you must name the partners. (d) If you are suing a corporation, give its full name, and the name of a director of said corporation. (e) If your suit arises out of an automobile accident, you must name the driver and registered owner.

9. I UNDERSTAND I HAVE NO RIGHT OF APPEAL FROM A JUDGMENT ON MY CLAIM

10. MY CLAIM IS AGAINST (defendant)

NAME	ADDRESS	CITY	ZIP

DECLARATION OF NON-MILITARY STATUS

The declarant is the Plaintiff in the annexed and foregoing action, and/or he takes this declaration for said Plaintiff and declares the Defendant, and each of them, of more than one, is not now a person in the Military Service of the United States as defined in Sec. 101 of the Soldiers' and Sailors' Relief Act of 1940, and amendments thereto.
I declare under penalty of perjury that the foregoing is true and correct.

Excuted on_____   _____
                                      SIGNATURE
The declaration under penalty of perjury must be signed in California, or in a state that authorizes use of a declaration in place of an affidavit, otherwise an affidavit is required.

ORDER TO PLAINTIFF TO APPEAR

Your case will be tried on _____ at _____M., in Dept. _____ of said court.

YOU ARE HEREBY DIRECTED TO APPEAR on said date and to bring with you all books, papers and witnesses needed to prove your claim.

> **IMPORTANT Please check the Court Calendar in the lobby of the building for the Department of this Court that will hear this matter.**

REQUEST FOR DISMISSAL

If case is paid or settled before trial, sign below and mail this form to the above entitled court. THIS CASE MAY BE DISMISSED.

Dated: _____   _____
                                   Signature of Plaintiff

361 REV█11/86

FIG. 8-22.

MUNICIPAL COURT OF CALIFORNIA
SANTA CLARA COUNTY JUDICIAL DISTRICT

_____ FACILITY

CASE NO. S. C. _____

— INSTRUCTIONS —

A. If you regularly do business in California for profit under a fictitious business name, you must execute, file, and publish a fictitious business name statement. This is sometimes called a ''dba'' which stands for ''doing business as.'' This requirement applies if you are doing business as an individual, a partnership, a corporation, or an association. The requirement does not apply to nonprofit corporations and associations or certain real estate investment trusts. You must file the fictitious business name statement with the clerk of the county where you have your principal place of business, or in Sacramento County if you have no place of business within the state.

B. If you do business under a fictitious business name and you also wish to file an action in the small claims court, you must declare under penalty of perjury that you have complied with the fictitious business name laws by filling out the form below.

C. If you have not complied with the fictitious business name laws, the court may dismiss your claim. You may be able to refile your claim when you have fulfilled these requirements.

FICTITIOUS BUSINESS NAME DECLARATION

1. I wish to file a claim in the small claims court for a business doing business under the fictitious name of *(specify name and address of business)*:

2. The business is doing business as
   - [ ] an individual
   - [ ] a partnership
   - [ ] a corporation
   - [ ] an association
   - [ ] other *(specify)*:

3. The business has complied with the fictitious business name laws by executing, filing, and publishing a fictitious business name statement. The statement expires on *(date)*:

I declare under penalty of perjury under the laws of the State of California that the foregoing is true and correct.

Date:

▶

. . . . (TYPE OR PRINT NAME) . . . .   (SIGNATURE OF DECLARANT)

Form Approved by the
Judicial Council of California
SC-103 [New January 1, 1986]
🌐 9022

FICTITIOUS BUSINESS NAME DECLARATION
(Small Claims)

Rule 982.7(b)

FIG. 8-23.

Chapter 9

Chapter XI
Bankruptcy

WHEN A COMPANY OR A BUSINESS BECOMES INSOLVENT, IS BEING SUED, AND IS HARD-pressed by creditors and collectors for its payments, it is the usual procedure for that company or business to seek protection from all collection efforts under Chapter XI of the Bankruptcy Act. This procedure allows the company or business to prepare and propose to its creditors an arrangement whereby the company will try—usually over a period of several years—to repay existing creditor obligations while continuing to operate the business under an operations plan that a majority of the creditors and the bankruptcy court have approved. It is a situation that is not loaded with the elements for success, but the insolvency of one of your customers, and the filing of a Chapter XI action does at least bring the matter into the open. Hopefully, it is brought into the open before the business (assets, customer base, will to survive, and key personnel) has eroded to the point where the creditors are looking at nothing more than a hollow shell. If a company has had good management over a period of several years and is in its present predicament because of one or more factors over which it had very little control, the possibility exists that creditors, working together, can help the business turn around. When an insolvency is the result of poor or dishonest management, the creditors will not be impressed with its chances for survival.

When a notice arrives from the appropriate jurisdiction of the United States District Court informing you that one of your customers has filed for protection under Chapter XI of the Bankruptcy Act, it is not the ideal way to start your day. It doesn't help that you might have had strong reasons to be apprehensive about the account, or that you had no advance warning of any major problem(s). At that point, it is too late to take any protective action. You are a *secured creditor* (your receivables protected by a perfected filing under the Uniform Commercial Code or a Mechanic's and Materialman's Lien) or a general or unsecured creditor. If you are secured, there is hope that your company ultimately might recover all, most, or some of the amount owed to it. What happens if your company is an unsecured creditor? Take part in the proceedings and hope for a miracle. The lifeboats are already filled with secured creditors and the life preservers—the company's available assets—would leave little for the unsecured creditors in a liquidation.

BANKRUPTCY PROCEEDINGS

The Bankruptcy Act determines the sequence of the filing and what subsequently occurs. It is a procedure that starts with the filing of the petition by the debtor, the appointment of a receiver of the debtor's property or a trustee in bankruptcy who continues in possession of the debtor's property. The court might appoint an appraiser. The court also will mail notices of the first meeting of creditors from a list of creditors given to the court by the debtor, and they will include a copy of the debtor's proposed "arrangement"—if available at that time. The judge (a referee in bankruptcy court has that stature) presides at all meetings of creditors, examines the debtor (along with creditors and attorneys for the creditors) as to the reasons for the insolvency or inability to meet obligations, hears witnesses on matters relevant to the hearing, and receives the written acceptances (or rejections) of creditors on the proposed arrangement. If, at the first meeting of creditors, the debtor does not present a proposed arrangement the judge will set a time frame within which the debtor must file the "arrangement" (or "plan of arrangement"). The judge then will adjourn the meeting until at least 15 days after the date the debtor must deliver the arrangement to the court. This time frame allows both the court and the creditor's committee to examine the proposed arrangement and make recommendations to the creditors.

What is a creditor's committee? Creditors elect a committee at the first meeting and charge it with serving the interests of creditors large and small. It is customary for the creditor's committee to be composed of three, five, or seven of the major creditors. The number, however, is not fixed and the committee is not closed to one or two of the smaller creditors if their presence is deemed appropriate for a proper balance of large and small creditors. The number of dollars owed to the various creditors usually determines motivation to become a committee member. If you should find yourself in a situation where your company is a major creditor, don't shy away from membership on the committee if you can spare the time necessary to attend meetings. Examining the conduct of the debtor's affairs, the reasons and causes of his or her insolvency and inability to pay, examining and considering documents and arrangements with peer credit managers, negotiating with the debtor regarding the terms of the proposed arrangement—and hopefully bringing the entire process together into an acceptable arrangement for continuing the business under conditions beneficial to all of the creditors—can be an enormously satisfying and an enormously beneficial learning experience.

Whether creditors in a specific Chapter XI are going to be willing to favorably consider any arrangement the debtor offers becomes a matter of the quality of the arrangement—how it addresses debts and obligations incurred prior to the filing—and how the creditors perceive the owner(s) and manager(s). The questions creditors must ask themselves is whether there is anything to salvage, are they willing to do business with the firm if an arrangement is accepted, and perhaps most important to the acceptance of an arrangement, is this management capable of correcting and avoiding the types of mistakes and problems that put the company in its present position? Are the owners or operators of the subject firm or company solid business people who were caught in a situation over which they had little or no control? Is there too little business ability, experience, determination, and integrity to warrant giving these same people a second dance with creditors whose feet are scarred from the first experience? Unless there is a straightforward, clear-cut arrangement that appears to successfully address all of these questions, many of the creditors are going to be reluctant to accept any recommendation for a second chance. The past experiences of individual creditors with this and other Chapter XI accounts will weigh heavily in the decision to give an arrangement a thumbs up or a thumbs down.

Documents and Forms

The notice for a first meeting of creditors should have, on the reverse side, a claim form and instructions for completing and returning it to the court. In some jurisdictions, the claim form might be on a separate sheet of paper, but the relevant point is to be sure you complete and return it promptly. Instances occur when a debtor will fail to list a creditor, either because the debtor disputes the balance allegedly owed or simply overlooked the creditor's account when preparing the list of creditors that must accompany the forms for a Chapter XI filing. Why were you notified of the first meeting of creditors if your firm's name wasn't on the list of creditors given to the court? It could have been on the original list and inadvertently was deleted when the court prepared lists for mailing to creditors. If your firm is listed but is followed or preceded by an asterisk, it indicates that the debtor has questioned the validity of the obligation. If the amount is not listed correctly, you should attach data substantiating the amount of your claim when you return the claim form to the court.

An arrangement is confirmed (becomes effective) when a majority in number of all creditors (or if divided into classes, by a majority of the creditors in each class) whose claims have been approved. A debtor may propose change(s) in any provision of the arrangement at any time before the arrangement is confirmed, but the court will accept changes only if they are satisfied that they do not materially and adversely affect the interest of any creditor who has agreed in writing to accept the arrangement. The debtor cannot have second thoughts that materially affect what has already been accepted and expect the court to go along with it. If the suggested change(s) is valid, conforms to the provisions of the agreement, and poses no threat to the integrity of the whole (or any section thereof), the court will probably agree to it.

The criteria for the court to confirm an arrangement is explicit and uncomplicated. Certainly, the primary factor in any confirmation is that the agreement, and all obligations relating to the procedure and the agreement, are in compliance with the provisions of Chapter XI. It also must be an arrangement that is feasible and in the best interests of creditors in all classes. No evidence can exist that the debtor has been guilty of any acts or has failed to perform any duties that would bar the court from discharging the bankruptcy. Finally, the proposal of the arrangement, and acceptance, must be acts of good faith and conform to what the Bankruptcy Act allows.

You must take other steps as well. Article 1, Section 301, and Article XIII, Section 399 of Chapter XI cover these steps. Dismissal of a Chapter XI filing can come days, weeks, or months after the filing; before, during, and after the proposal and acceptance of an arrangement, and for reasons such: the debtor successfully lived up to the terms and conditions of the arrangement; the debtor was unable to live up to the terms and conditions of the arrangement; the debtor was engaged in some type of fraud. In either of the latter two examples, the court is empowered to reinstate the bankruptcy proceeding, adjudge the debtor as bankrupt, and move on pursuant to the provisions of the Act.

What are the survival statistics for a business that is operating under a continuation arrangement? First, any arrangement carries with it the necessity for creditors to make major concessions regarding account balances owed by the debtor. It is unlikely that any debtor who seeks the protection of a Chapter XI filing has any appreciable liquidity, or prospects for it. Priority creditors (government tax agencies, etc.) and secured creditors almost invariably absorb whatever is available. Frequently that isn't enough to give them a full return on balances owed them. The unsecured creditors are left with no short-term possibility for recovering more than five or ten cents per account dollar, and frequently they receive less than five. Their only hope is that the account has the potential for a turnaround or offers an arrangement with the long-term potential (three to five years or longer) for a small, annual percentage-of-profits dividend. The court would distribute this dividend among any priority creditors with residual balances, secured creditors with larger residual balances, and unsecured creditors with balances probably at 90 or 95 percent of the amount owed when the debtor/customer filed for Chapter XI protection. Chapter XI filings are not a fun and games experience for any of these groups of creditors—priority, secured, or unsecured—with the agony factor rapidly increasing as the class of creditor changes from priority to, and through, unsecured. The secured creditor might not get all his or her money, but however large or small the available dividend, the secured creditor will be *many* dollars ahead of unsecured peers.

I have used the word *nuances* at a couple of other points in the book when describing a subtle or slight degrees of difference between one technique, attitude, or goal and other possibilities. No clear-cut winner is among the classes of creditors in the acceptance of an arrangement or the liquidation of a debtor's assets. Book value means nothing in a liquidation. When the physical assets of a firm are offered for public sale—auction or a prepriced public sale—potential buyers know that the debtor must sell his assets so they will beat the price into the ground. Nickels, dimes, and an occasional quarter will be the ratio of return for each dollar of book value. Of course, you have no guarantee that over the long haul an arrangement will deliver more dollars than a liquidation, but given the plus of honest people who just might have learned their lesson—and learned it well—the probability is greater that you will recoup a higher level of debt-dividend dollars via a solid continuation program than in a liquidation.

In an area that by its very nature is loaded with risks, you still should be better off with what appears to be a well-structured arrangement vs. a zero or near-zero payoff in a liquidation of assets. Unless there are just too many overriding negatives, you probably couldn't lose any more if the court approves an arrangement—and it subsequently didn't succeed—than you would in an early liquidation. If the arrangement enjoys even a modest level of success, your company can benefit from C.O.D. sales and the long-term pleasure of periodic debt-reduction dividends.

The two forms shown in FIGS. 9-1 and 9-2 are examples of the forms sent to creditors by the U.S. Bankruptcy Court having jurisdiction in the matter. The Notice of Hearing (FIG. 9-1) advises creditors that any collection efforts or in-progress legal actions against the petitioner (your customer) are automatically stayed pending a decision in the case. Included is information regarding the date, time, and place of the meeting, and the court's order for a debtor, partners, or a general partner to appear. If the debtor is a corporation, its president or other executive officer must appear for examination by the court and creditors. There is a statement regarding the filing of a Proof Of Claim prior to a time that is fixed by the court. This procedure ensures that the claims of all creditors are included. The debtor might or might not challenge these claims. Ultimately this statement includes the creditors eligibility to participate as secured or unsecured creditors which is determined by the court. The reverse side of the notice is usually the claim form mentioned previously. Complete it, photocopy both sides (Order For Meeting of Creditors and the completed claim form), and send the claim form to the address in the lower left corner of the Order. Also send a stamped, self-addressed envelope with the claim form(s) so the court can stamp the one copy with the receival date and return it to you. This procedure will eliminate any possibility that your claim is not received and entered into the court's case records.

The court will send the Notice Of Hearing (FIG. 9-1) to all creditors of record to advise where and when they will hold the first meeting. Creditors who have a substantial interest in the case usually attend the first meeting. When a creditor company is small and the owner doesn't feel that he or she can be away for the time involved, the owner can wait for the court's summary of the creditor's first meeting. Some owners of small

UNITED STATES BANKRUPTCY COURT

FOR THE NORTHERN DISTRICT OF CALIFORNIA

IN RE:	)	BANKRUPTCY NO. 8-42-16341-Z
XYZ CORPORATION, INC.	)	CHAPTER 11
A CALIFORNIA CORPORATION	)	
	)	
	)	
DEBTOR.	)	
	)	

NOTICE OF HEARING
ON APPLICATION OF DEBTOR-IN-POSSESSION
REQUESTING APPROVAL OF STIPULATION
PERTAINING TO USE OF COLLATERAL PROVIDING FOR ADEQUATE
PROTECTION SECURED BY LIEN ON PROPERTY OF THE ESTATE
UNDER SECTION 364(c), MODIFICATION OF STAY

TO: THE CREDITORS OF THE ABOVE-NAMED DEBTOR AND OTHER PARTIES
IN INTEREST:

NOTICE IS HEREBY GIVEN that XYZ CORPORATION, INC., Debtor-In-Possession herein, has filed an Application with the Court seeking approval of a Stipulation and Agreement between the Debtor and Urban Bank, and that said Application will be heard, considered, and passed upon at the courtroom of the HONORABLE CHARLES C. MONROEL, UNITED STATES BANKRUPTCY JUDGE, ROOM 396, U.S. POST OFFICE BUILDING, NORTH FIRST & ST. JOHN STREETS, SAN JOSE, CALIFORNIA, on: WEDNESDAY, OCTOBER 23 ,1983, AT 2:00 P.M.

The Stipulation and Agreement negotiated between the Debtor and Urban Bank contains a number of provisions, terms and conditions, under which the Debtor will continue to operate its business known as the Centurian Club. Because of the complexity and comprehensive nature of the Stipulation and Agreement between the parties, a copy of the complete Stipulation and Agreement is attached to this notice to provide creditors and parties-in-interest with complete information and details regarding the transaction. Exhibits to the Stipulation are on file with the Court.

Reference is hereby made to all pleadings and documentation on file with the Court with respect to this Chapter 11 case, which information is available for inspection. Creditors or other parties-in-interest having any questions, or wishing additional information regarding the matter, may contact the Debtor's counsel, CARL M. GREEN, GREEN & GREEN, 19 NORTH MARKET STREET, SUITE 168, SAN JOSE, CALIFORNIA 95113, 408 999-9999.

Dated: September 16, 1983

GREEN & GREEN
Attorneys for Debtor and
Debtor-In-Possession

ANY CORRESPONDENCE REQUIRING AN ANSWER FROM THE COURT SHOULD BE ACCOMPANIED BY A STAMPED, SELF-ADDRESSED ENVELOPE.

FIG. 9-1.

UNITED STATES BANKRUPTCY COURT
CENTRAL DISTRICT OF CALIFORNIA - LOS ANGELES
CHAPTER: 11
IN RE:_____ CASE NUMBER:

95103   8723987
U.S. BANKRUPTCY COURT
ROOM 906, U.S. COURTHOUSE
312 NO. SPRING ST.
LOS ANGELES, CA 90012-4701

CHAPTER 11
ORDER FOR MEETING OF CREDITORS, COMBINED WITH NOTICE THEREOF AND OF AUTOMATIC STAY

To the debtor, his creditors and other parties in interest:
    An order for relief under 11 U.S.C. Chapter 11, having been entered on a petition filed by (or against) the above named debtor on   December 27, 1987
IT IS ORDERED, AND NOTICE IS HEREBY GIVEN THAT:
1. A meeting of creditors pursuant to 11 U.S.C., 341 (a) shall be held at:
U. S. TRUSTEE HEARING ROOM   DATE
U. S. FEDERAL BUILDING   JAN. 6, 1988
300 N. LOS ANGELES ST., RM 3114   HOUR
LOS ANGELES, CA   3.15 P.M.
2. The debtor shall appear in person (or, if the debtor is a partnership, by a general partner, or, if the debtor is a corporation, by its president or other executive officer) at that time and place for the purpose of being examined.

ADDRESSEE
XYZ Company, Inc.
5926 Beaker Place
San Jose, CA 95123

YOU ARE FURTHER NOTIFIED THAT:
The meeting may be continued or adjourned from time to time by notice at the meeting without further written notice to creditors.
At the meeting the creditors may file their claims, examine the debtor, and transact such other business as may properly come before the meeting.

As a result of the filing of the petition, certain acts and proceedings against the debtor and his property are stayed as provided in 11 U.S.C. 362(a).

The debtor (or trustee) has filed or will file a list of creditors and equity security holders pursuant to Rule 1007, Any creditor holding a listed claim which is not listed as disputed, contingent, or unliquidated as to amount, may, but need not file a proof of claim in this case. Creditors whose claims are not listed or whose claims are listed as disputed, contingent, or unliquidated as to amount and who desire to participate in the case or share in any distribution must file their proofs of claim on or before the last day fixed for filing a proof of claim. Any creditor who desires to rely on the list has the responsibility for determining that he is accurately listed.

    LOCAL RULE 3001 (B) PROVIDES THAT A PROOF OF CLAIM, INCLUDING AMENDMENTS THEREOF, MAY BE FILED AT ANY TIME PRIOR TO CONFIRMATION OF THE PLAN UNLESS A DIFFERENT TIME IS FIXED BY THE COURT ON NOTICE AS PROVIDED BY BANKRUPTCY RULE 3003 (C) (3).

FILE CLAIM FORM ON THE REVERSE   Dated: DECEMBER 2, 1987   By The Court
SIDE IN DUPLICATE WITH: AT LOS ANGELES, CA
  U.S. BANKRUPTCY COURT   CHARLES A. MILLER, CLERK OF COURT
  ROOM 906, U.S. COURTHOUSE
  312 NO. SPRING ST.
  LOS ANGELES, CA 90012-4701

(Author's Note: The reverse side of the original copy of this Order, and Notice, is the Claim Form. Complete it in duplicate, make a copy for your file, and forward the original and a duplicate as instructed)

FIG. 9-2.

companies (or major company credit managers) who have large balances involved might elect to bring their legal counsel to question the debtor(s), or if they are a large company, they might bring the officer representing the company. A debtor or a debtor's representative also might be represented by counsel.

Subsequent to the first meeting, creditor committee meetings are held at various intervals over what might be weeks or months. Reports of those meetings will come from the court in a form similar to the Notice Of Hearing. The creditor's committee will submit recommendations to the creditors who are then asked to vote for or against one, or many, of the proposals and counterproposals that creditors see on the road to a final decision. This decision ultimately must be a decision between a specific program to continue the business (court and creditor committee supervision for an unspecified period of time, etc.) or a vote opposing any proposed plan of continuation, which is a vote in favor of liquidating the company.

The court may accept or reject the recommendation of the creditors. If it feels that proposed plan of continuation serves the best interests of all creditors, it may impose that decision for a trial period. If it does not think the plan is in the best interests of creditors, it may reject the proposal when the creditor's committee offers it. In the latter case, the creditors never see that proposal. In most situations, the creditors committee only will recommend a plan that has a reasonable chance for success—and the court seldom disagrees.

The example in FIG. 9-3 illustrates a step in the Chapter XI process that, with the Court's permission, will allow the Debtor to remain in possession of the company's assets while working with creditors (in this example the primary creditor is the bank) to effect a turnaround in the fortunes of the business. In this example, the Debtor (who is also the Debtor-in-Possession) and the Secured Party (the bank) are jointly presenting a Stipulation to the Bankruptcy Court in which they request an Order authorizing the Debtor to continue to use collateral (a tennis and athletic club) while providing for appropriate creditor protection. The joint Stipulation requests that the Debtor be authorized to borrow funds to continue operating the business, preserving the collateral.

The financial data that the debtor furnished earlier to the Creditors and the Bankruptcy Court is not repeated in this petition. That data does, however, confirm the statements (paragraphs 3, 4, and 5) contained in the example as it pertains to the Debtor's need to obtain funds to operate the business. The Debtor states that there are currently no funds other than those generated from operations of the club (restaurant, other club facilities, and member fees), and that the Debtor is unable to obtain credit from trade vendors for necessary services and supplies.

The complete Stipulation totals 15 pages and includes a schedule of bank-loan payments, additional protection and security for the Secured Party, the Debtor's use of Collateral and Loan, and a separate account for—and appropriate provisions to exercise control—*excess funds* (money not needed each week to operate the club). A monthly cash budget and financial projection also is available plus the granting of Senior creditor status to the Secured Party (bank) over "all interest(s) and encumbrances which hereafter might be created in favor of third parties."

It isn't necessary to include all 15 pages of the Stipulation for you to understand its purpose. The three pages (first, second, and last) offer enough information for you to recognize the format, and in the future, deal effectively with the Content of a Stipulation offered to a Bankruptcy Court—which again brings to mind a warning that recurs throughout the pages of this book. Recognize the limits of your own knowledge and experience when dealing with anything legal—a document, an interpretation, a question, or a problem. Get your attorney's advice in every situation that is not clear-cut and straightforward within the context of your own knowledge and experience.

(Page One)

FRAZER, CARTER, WALSH,
    BENSON & HARRIS
A Professional Corporation
    Franklin Carter
529 California Street
Suite 1350
San Francisco, California 94111-5879
Telephone: (415) 599-9998

Attorneys for North Bay National Bank

UNITED STATES BANKRUPTCY COURT

FOR THE NORTHERN DISTRICT OF CALIFORNIA

In Re:	)	Bankruptcy No. 5-89-16524 - M
	)	
XYZ CORPORATION, INC.,	)	Chapter 11
A California Corporation	)	
	)	
Debtor	)	
	)	

STIPULATION PERTAINING TO USE OF COLLATERAL PROVIDING FOR ADEQUATE
PROTECTION SECURED BY LIEN ON PROPERTY OF THE ESTATE UNDER s364(c),
MODIFICATION OFSTAY AND ORDER THEREON

TO: THE HONORABLE WILBUR A. HANSEN, BANKRUPTCY JUDGE:

XYZ Corporation, Inc., the Debtor and Debtor-in-Possession herein, and
North Bay National Bank, the Secured Party, apply to this Court for an Order
authorizing use of collateral, providing for adequate protection and the
pledging of collateral in connection therewith, and to borrow funds pursuant
to 11 U.S.C. s364(c) and pledge collateral in connection therewith.

1.   On September 14, 1984, the Debtor filed its Petition under
Chapter 11 herein, and is Debtor-in-Possession.

2.   The Debtor's business consists of a health spa and athletic club.
Debtor is the owner of certain real property, as more particularly described on
the deed of trust attached as part of Exhibit "A" hereto ("Real Property"),
rents, issues and profits, equipment, and proceeds thereof as set forth in
Exhibit "A", (collectively the "Collateral") used in the operation of the

FIG. 9-3.

(Page Two)

business.

3.   The Debtor requires funds to operate said business and to preserve the Collateral.

4.   The Debtor is presently without funds necessary to operate, other than funds generated from the operation of the club, restaurant, other club facilities and member fees.

5.   Other than certain ongoing services and supplies provided by trade vendors, the Debtor is unable to obtain credit on a basis other than under s364(c) of the Bankruptcy Code.

6.   The Secured Party and Debtor acknowledges that the unpaid balance of the loan by Secured Party to Debtor (the "Loan") as of August 7, 1984, including principal and interest only, is $6,945,286. The Secured Party has agreed to consent to use of its Collateral as provided for hereinafter, on a basis that will provide adequate protection and security. In that connection, Debtor and Secured Party have agreed that adequate protection and the necessary security can be provided through use of Collateral secured pursuant to the Loan and the loan documents ("Loan Documents") previously entered into between the Secured Party and the Debtor (copies of which are attached hereto and incorporated by reference herein and are attached as Exhibit "A"), as modified pursuant to the terms of paragraph 7 hereof and this paragraph. Except as expressly modified herein, the Loan Documents shall remain in full force and effect.

7.   The Secured Party and the Debtor hereby agree as follows:

(a) Secured Party consents to the continued use of Collateral by the Debtor, for use by the Debtor as hereinafter set forth, provided that the COurt has approved this Stipulation and the

Fig. 9-3. Continued.

(Page Fifteen)

20.   Nothing herein is intended to create any right on the part of any third party to assume the terms and conditions of this Stipulation and agreement, and Secured Party retains its right to declare all principal, accrued interest, associated fees and charges, immediately due and payable upon the sale or transfer by the Debtor of the Real Property, or any interest therein, or upon any change in the ownership of the shares of stock of Debtor in excess of 25% of the outstanding shares, or effective change in control of the Debtor.

WHEREFORE, the parties hereto pray that this Court enter its Order authorizing the Debtor to use cash collateral, to borrow funds under s364(c) of the Code from the Secured Party pursuant to the terms of this Stipulation, and each of the terms of this Stipulation be authorized, and declaring that the notice and opportunity for hearing which has been given in respect to this Stipulation are appropriate in the particular circumstances.

DATED: November 22, 1984.

NORTH BAY NATIONAL BANK
(Secured Party)

By:_____

Its:_____

DATED: November 22, 1984.

XYZ CORPORATION, INC.
(Debtor)

By:_____

Its:_____

Fig. 9-3. Continued.

Chapter 10

Bad-Debt Account/ Bad-Debt Reserve

ONE OF THE MORE FRUSTRATING EXPERIENCES FOR A CREDIT MANAGER IS THE LOSS OF an account via the filing of a Chapter XI Bankruptcy Petition, and the strong likelihood of an eventual write-off of the balance against the Bad-Debt Reserve. When you recognize a loss, no acceptable correlation exists between profits realized during the number of years you successfully sold the account and the balance owing when the account filed the Chapter XI petition. It's a definite negative, but it is not a negative on which a credit manager should spend an unrealistic amount of time. Whether it was a short or a long-term account, you should examine it for whatever you can learn, then write it off.

SETTING UP A RESERVE

Standard accounting practice calls for firms that offer credit terms to trade accounts to provide annually for bad-debt losses anticipated during the company's upcoming fiscal year. The basis for the provision is a fractional percentage of annual sales, a figure which varies from one firm to another and among the various types of businesses and services. A quarter to one-third of one percent of gross sales is an acceptable annual bad-debt-loss figure for many industries. The credit policy of a firm can be the primary culprit in whether the bad-debt figure is inverted or inflated. Bad-debt losses that are consistently out of phase with industry standards indicate an excessive number of judgmental errors or a credit (and sales) policy that is not providing realistic guidelines to the company's goals or well-being.

At the end of each fiscal year, you should review your aging sheet (Aged Trial Balance Report) for accounts that you have assigned to third-party collection within the past 12 months where there has been little or no collection progress; for accounts that have filed under Chapter XI and offer little hope for any appreciable recovery; for accounts that have gone out of business (failed and skipped town) with no success in tracing the owner; and for accounts that have a balance (or balances) in the maximum past-due columns on your aging sheet and do not respond positively to your in-house collection effort. Any account on your aging report, including the occasional one that never pushed your terms more than 10 or 20 days past terms but went out of business in what seemed midstride, is eligible for your list of current and projected bad-debt write-off items for the current or upcoming fiscal year. You must project by name the accounts you expect will become bad-debt items during the next fiscal year, and thereby ensure that the Bad-Debt Reserve is funded properly to start the new year. You also must add the monthly accrual percentage (or figure) to provide for the unanticipated losses. This figure will sustain the level of your requirement for bad-debt funds throughout the year.

Some fiscal officers like to see a Bad-Debt Reserve account that's so lean it isn't realistic. Others take a more practical approach, particularly when the credit manager has been dealing effectively with the company's accounts for two, three, or more years. Never set a figure that is more than reasonable. The money in a Bad-Debt Reserve account is held hostage from the bottom line of your business and should never be more than a prudent figure based upon past and anticipated experience. Remember also that the unexpected failure of a major account can make a shambles of your bad-debt reserve. Pay close attention to your major accounts at all times and not just when you're evaluating them as a part of your bad-debt projection for the next fiscal year.

If the business is new, you will have no personal track record for setting an appropriate percentage of sales as the guideline criteria for your company's experience. Your own experience with another company in the same industry could be helpful, or an industry association, or national credit group which publishes annual figures for percentages of loss experienced by respondent members. How the industry leaders prepare the industry guideline(s) is relevant to what your company might experience. If the guideline breaks bad-debt-loss experience into the various categories of regional location and/or annual credit sales, it will be far more helpful in relating your experience than a national figure would be that is prepared from firms of all sizes and regional locations.

The formula for determining the bad-debt percentages of sales for a fiscal year is to divide the adjusted gross-annual sales (after returns and credits) into the dollar total of bad-debt losses. Example: Adjusted gross-annual sales of $1,326,000 divided into a bad-debt-loss figure of $33,400 equals a percentage figure of 0.252. At just over one quarter of one percent of sales, this figure is well within acceptable parameters for many businesses and industries. When you have a bad-debt percentage figure for the past two or three years, combine those figures with your current figure, divide by the number of figures used, and come up with one that represents your company's average annual bad-debt experience for those years.

WRITEOFFS

To adequately fund the Bad-Debt Reserve for the upcoming fiscal year, you should prepare your monthly accrual on the basis of the dollar totals of accounts currently on the aging report—accounts that you expect to charge off during the coming fiscal year (Chapter XI's, third-party collection assignments, in-house collections, and any accounts that your analysis of the aging report indicates might be weakening rapidly). Use the projected sales figure for the upcoming fiscal year vs. the total of your list of potential bad-debt accounts to arrive at a dollar figure and percentage of sales. You should review and adjust the monthly accrual figure on a monthly or quarterly basis to ensure that the figure reflects current needs and current analysis. Remember also to include in your calculations for a monthly accrual figure the amount that will be in your Bad-Debt Reserve *after* you write off bad-debt charges for the current year. If, for the upcoming fiscal year, you project a bad-debt percentage of 0.30 against annual sales of $1.5 million, you can decrease the $45,000 that you project as a bad-debt write-off to an accrual of $40,000 (if $5000 is still in the Bad-Debt Reserve after current write-offs). So the monthly accrual figure (with $5000 in the Reserve) will begin at $1200 a month rather than the $1350 that would be required if there were zero funds in the Reserve. Occasionally, you might pull most of what would be a carryover reserve (in this instance $5000) out of the Bad-Debt Reserve and add it to the "bottom line"—into Net Profits—if management feels a need to add more meat to the financials. Whatever the decision regarding carryover money, be sure to provide adequately for your projected write-off of next year's bad debts with an appropriate monthly accrual to your Bad-Debt Reserve.

A cardinal rule exists in the matter of bad-debt accounts, and it goes something like this: No company wants at any time to see a receivables balance become a bad-debt item, but when a balance is lost, it should not be lost in the first few months of the supplier/customer relationship. Virtually every account that fails within a time frame of the first few months is going to take some of your money with it. On the other hand, if the account did business with you for years, the failure will not be a joy, but you should recognize that you made good money from the account over the years of your association. Be especially watchful of your new accounts. Do not let them come in too strong or too fast unless their credentials are impeccable. Should the less-than-impeccable customer try to pressure you into increasing the credit line beyond what you consider an acceptable figure, do not be coerced into going along with something that you know is not right—or is not right for your company.

I have made the following statement elsewhere in this book, but in a chapter dealing with bad-debt accounts and bad debt reserves, it bears repeating. Is the customer always right? The customer is very, very important and you must approach the relationship with the attitude that the customer is usually right, but never is the customer right when he or she is flagrantly abusing the customer/supplier relationship. It is an unacceptable attitude—one that your company does not need and should not tolerate. If your intolerant attitude costs you a relationship with an account that is constantly abusing the customer/supplier relationship, you can do without the aggravation and your company will be better off not doing a credit business with the abuser.

PROVIDING FOR LOSSES

Many companies discussed for a long time the subjects of Bad Debts, Bad Debt-Accounts or Bad-Debt Writeoffs in hushed tones—if at all. A feeling extended from senior management down through the credit department that the possibility of a bad-debt loss was virtually unthinkable. Were their heads in the sand? Absolutely! The percentage of bad-debt loss does not decrease when "head in the sand" is the major defense. Now the subject is addressed openly and realistically. It is recognized as one of the costs of doing business and companies should view it as such. Your company—every company—should have a small, but realistic, loss of receivables dollars each year. If you aren't losing something, your credit policy is *very* restrictive in the selection of accounts or, once you select the accounts, you are not giving many of your accounts the latitude they should have. Your credit policy is, of course, the governing factor, but losing a little occasionally in the interest of making more from an increased level of sales is not a faulted business policy—if you do not allow credit standards to suffer in the process.

Chapter 11

Is It Really
a Contract?

IT WOULD BE DIFFICULT TO POINT A FINGER AT A BUSINESS TRANSACTION IN TODAY'S business world that does not have its' roots in a contract—written or oral. Whether two firms or two individuals do or do not come together for a formal signing of contract documents, usually a real or an implied contractual agreement has its' roots in the standards of a company's products, in the claims the manufacturer makes for them, in the industry standards for performance, or in some other yardstick or combination of guideline levels of quality and/or service. Contracts can be written or oral, real or implied. An improperly or inadequately-written contract can cost your company a tidy bundle if the sleeves of your deal begin to unravel.

ORAL CONTRACTS

Oral contracts are legal. In all but the most simple, concise, and straightforward transaction or deal, you should not use them. Between two men of unimpeachable integrity—two men who have done business for decades and traditionally have looked each other in the eye, struck their "I'll buy these cattle today, all 800 head of them, for 40¢ a pound," and sealed it with a handshake—a case can be made for it. But in too many other circumstances and situations, a disagreement can develop between the parties who contracted orally. Unless impartial witnesses can recall the exact language of the oral contract, it can become a courtroom slugging match with the word of one man or woman attempting to prevail against the word of the other. What happens when more than two people are involved in the oral contract? The more people that are involved in the contract, the more versions of the alleged agreement the court will hear when the matter has to be decided in a courtroom.

WRITTEN CONTRACTS

Today's climate for lawsuits (both capricious and justified) does not lend itself to settling for something as charming—and probably as dangerously archaic—as an oral version of "my word is my bond." It simply does not hold up. I might give you that verbal assurance when we shake hands, and I might believe it, but if later you don't remember the deal exactly as I do, and follow through exactly to my recollection of what was said, I'll sue for what memory tells me is mine. People do not remember the wording of agreements that aren't committed to paper, especially when the remembered version of one party is seriously at odds with what the other (or others) is saying, doing, or delivering.

This chapter is not a course in law—contracts or other areas. I am not only unqualified to teach such a course, but the potential for misguiding people is not something that I care to challenge. What I tell you, however, in this area is to protect yourself and your business (or your employer's business and business assets) at all times. Don't try to do something—as in the law—for which you have no training or experience. When there is a contract to be written, do not attempt to write it yourself unless you are qualified to do so. Get your company's attorney to write any special agreement(s), legal forms, or contracts that you will use from time to time in the course of your business activity, or any other specialized or nonroutine legal work. A mistake in the construction or terminology of a contract or any legal document, can be a disaster. Any competent, experienced credit person should be able to handle flawlessly any routine tasks involving the law. Your company attorney should examine other matters, including the reading and interpreting of any contract or legal document that you do not thoroughly understand before you sign it or accept it. Do not take chances or assume that you understand or are correctly interpreting the subtleties and combinations of legal language.

The best advice ever given to me came out of an early career association with a testy old gentleman who never bothered to look up when I asked him a question. One day I asked him a question about what I thought was a binding contract, and he seemed to bend lower to his desk than usual. "You got a problem with it?" he asked. I replied that I wasn't sure whether it was binding on both parties. Without showing me an eyeball, he impacted the subsequent decades of my professional life. "Have I done or said anything to make you think I'm an attorney?" He didn't want an answer. "We've got an attorney. Get on the goddamn phone and ask him!"

My advice to you—after deleting the expletive—is the same, although I ask you to accept my word that I am looking directly at you as I say it. An owner/credit manager who does not consult his or her company's attorney when a contract or a provision of a contract is unclear is putting the company at unreasonable risk. It is unwise to assume that you know enough regarding applicable law(s) to make a competent judgment regarding the position of your company under the terms of a contract unless you are an attorney or a trained paralegal. If you aren't one or the other, then call your attorney for advice and to prepare your contracts.

BASIC REQUIREMENTS FOR A CONTRACT

A document must meet four basic requirements before it qualifies as a contract. An endless array of other material might be a part of a contract but these are the essentials:

- ☐ Something of value must change hands.
- ☐ The contracting parties must be mentally competent.
- ☐ The subject matter must meet the legal requirements for a contract.
- ☐ There must be an offer and an acceptance.

No amount of extraneous legal jargon will do if it doesn't meet the basic four-point criteria. A contract must offer a promise to do something, a promise not to do something, or that the promisor agrees to make something happen. All of these "somethings" must be between a minimum of two or more people, entities, etc., in order to raise a legal-appearing document to the level of a contract. Cosmetic appeal is great, but if a document doesn't meet the criteria for a contract, it's only masquerading as one.

Chapter 12

Credit Administration— The Support Area of Credit Management

AN OWNER WHO DOES THE CREDIT WORK FOR HIS OR HER SMALL COMPANY MUST AS-sume the responsibility for administrative duties that are not directly related to the basic decision-making responsibility. The owners primary credit management responsibilities are to grant credit lines, approve orders to be released on credit terms, monitor the receivables aging report, and take the appropriate action when accounts begin to become past due. Those areas have dollars and cents impact, and they are of primary importance, but the owner/credit manager also must allow time for the purely adminis-trative areas of the credit and collections responsibility.

The full spectrum of credit administration activities is much more than credit deci-sions and collecting money from past-due accounts. The administrative phase of credit management has responsibility for the support activities and services that keep the com-pany's credit customers satisfied—satisfied with the way you handle shipments, satisfied with the way you process and receive invoices and payments, and satisfied with the speed with which you issue credit memorandums. It is administration's responsibility to deal with pricing errors, errors in quantities allegedly shipped and/or received, and allowed or disallowed discounts. The owner/credit manager must spend time exchanging credit experience and credit information with owners and managers at other companies, must interface with bankers other than his or her own, and must work to improve the tools used to do the total job of credit management. What is Credit Administration? It is that compartment of the owner's mind where changes are phased into existing proce-dures, where new concepts and procedures are tested and accepted or rejected. Credit Administration is, in this context, that phase of credit management which deals with problems and areas other than credit decisions and collection problems. It is the support area of credit management and as such serves an indispensable need.

Although this is a phrase that does not normally warm the heart of an owner, credit administration is overhead in its purest sense. It is, however, a part of your company's total package of administrative overhead that is miniscule in the number of dollars chargeable to it and significant beyond that investment in its contribution to the effectiveness of your total credit management program. No legitimate way exists to escape its demand of time and, if used properly, no way exists to measure the significance of its benefits. Make credit administration—the support area of credit management—your full partner. The time you spend on administration, and thinking about administrative matters, should improve the efficiency of your credit operation and improve your own effectiveness as the manager of your company's credit and collections.

The following topics and forms are typical of administrative tools and areas not directly related to credit decisions or receivables management. Each does, however, have an important support function in the proper flow and continuity of the credit department's work.

RECEIVABLES AND YOUR BANKER

Because most of your company's product(s) sales should be on credit terms, your accounts receivable is one of your biggest and strongest business assets. Bankers react favorably to receivables aging reports that indicate a minimum number of current or potential collection problems. The banker sees it as a valid indicator that you are screening accounts properly before you assign them a credit line, that you are managing them effectively, and that the effective management of your receivables balances is indicative of good business judgment, practices, and management in other areas.

When combined with other data, your Accounts Receivable Aged Trial Balance Report can be one of your strongest and most persuasive documents. If you properly manage your receivables accounts (and also the rest of your company), it is reasonable to expect that your banker will consider favorably an application to borrow against accounts receivable. If such a move is advantageous for your company, it should translate into a borrowing line (or bank credit line) of 70 percent to 80 percent of your currently applicable receivables total, less a probable category of ineligible accounts that show a past-due balance older than 60 or 90 days. The borrowing percentage of eligible receivables will vary from one bank to the next, but it is obvious that the option to use your accounts receivable as collateral for a bank loan is just one more strong reason for maintaining good receivables liquidity.

Most companies depend upon their bank line for some degree of constant financial support. When the business is seasonal, bank support might be indispensable in maintaining satisfactory supplier relationships. Healthy accounts receivable can be the ticket a business needs to guarantee a consistent flow of support financing. What if the business is not impacted by seasonal changes and an internally-generated flow of cash is the primary source of working capital? It is obviously as important that receivables balances maintain a high degree of within-terms (or near-terms) liquidity to perpetuate the flow of cash.

Whether the owner or a designated employee make the credit decisions, the manager of a company's credit accounts occasionally has a credit-related problem that could benefit from the company interfacing with the company's banker. The owner or designated employee should not hesitate to ask the banker for help in getting information from other bankers regarding loan arrangements with current or prospective customers, and the banker's experience with the average balances of commercial and other accounts will assist the owner or other designated employee. Many bankers are reluctant to divulge information to credit managers regarding their relationship with a customer. Your banker has a vested interest in the success of your company. Do not abuse this access route to information held by another banker, but when the need is urgent, do not hesitate to ask for assistance.

REQUEST FOR ADDITIONAL DATA

Not every procedure works exactly as it is set up every time you use it, particularly if there isn't proper followup. In going back through your file folders, you might find occasionally that you assigned an account a credit line on the basis of solid, but incomplete, information. One or two sections of the reference data might be missing and could go unnoticed until a reason exists to sift through account documents and data. To pick up missing information, use the example shown in FIGS. 12-1 and 12-2 to get what you need from the customer.

Unless something unusual or unsettling motivated you to look at information in the file, requesting this information should be a routine procedure. If the reason for requesting the information is not routine, and it is motivated by sudden and persistent rumors of a major problem, move swiftly and decisively to deal with anything that might jeopardize your receivables balance. When rumors begin to build, they might get out of hand quickly. When rumors get out of hand, the infighting between secured and unsecured (general) creditors can become unprofessional. Once a company files a Chapter XI, everything goes "on hold," subject to the rulings of a Referee In Bankruptcy. Until a filing is made, unsecured creditors will be scrambling to get their hands on something—anything of value.

The Request for Additional Information provides space below Business Plan to request data not covered in the preprinted sections. In the tradition of courteous business practice, you should always include a stamped, self-addressed envelope with inquiries of this nature. Many banks and businesses will not reply to your inquiry if you do not include a stamped and self-addressed envelope—and why should they? If the inquiring company is not willing to take the most basic step to ensure a reply, the company receiving the inquiry has no obligation to reply.

PUTTING YOUR COMPANY'S "BEST FOOT FORWARD"

Owners of small businesses must be multidimensional in their approach to company responsibilities. It isn't unusual for an owner to be the company president, general manager, financial officer, production manager, sales manager, and credit manager. If that isn't enough, throw in the additional burden of being the controller, quality control supervisor, and purchasing manager. Any depth of experience is rare in more than two or three of the areas of responsibility that stop at the owner's office door. So when an owner decides to hire a consultant to put the credit function on a solid footing, he or she might ask for advice and guidance in other areas. One need overlaps another in a small company. The absence of broad experience makes it mandatory that the owner/manager know as much about as many things as he or she can—and avail himself or herself of every opportunity to get help.

The following bank presentation package was put together to accommodate a client's request for help. It was successful for that client, has been rewritten twice for other clients, and permission was given for a regional accounting firm to offer it to clients. The format for this familiarization package is a folder indexed to include the seven categories of major interest to the banker. It is an introductory tool that will acquaint a banker with your company's background, product lines, market area(s), financial situation, and other relevant areas of information. The package offers a solid base of facts and information that you can expand readily in a subsequent meeting with an interested banker.

(Date)

The XYZ Company
1400 No Such Boulevard
Anywhere, California

Gentlemen:

A review of the information in your credit file indicates a need to upgrade our decision-making data.

The following list pinpoints information that was either not requested when your account was opened or has become out-dated. In order that we may do the best possible credit job for your company and ours, it is important that we promptly receive the indicated information.

_____   *Current Financials (Statement Of Income/Profit
            and Loss)

_____   Trade References (three major suppliers with whom
            you are currently doing business)

_____   Bank Reference (name, location, telephone num-
            ber and bank officer most familiar with
            your account)

_____   Business Plan

_____

        *This important information will be treated in
            strict confidentiality.

Please address the requested information to the attention of the undersigned.

Sincerely,

Credit Department

FIG. 12-1.

(Date)

Richard Cameron, Controller
The Chestnut Corporation
3652 Wendell Way
Blaney, Nevada

Dear Mr. Cameron:

A current check of the information in our customer credit files
has revealed that many of these files are incomplete. In that
category is our file of information for your company.

The attached Account Information Sheet, when completed and returned with a copy of your most recent financial statement,
will give us the necessary balance of background and current
business information.

Your cooperation is appreciated.

Sincerely,

Credit Manager

CB:ac

FIG. 12-2.

☐ Section 1—Company Background

This section is a one-page synopsis (history) of your company from beginning to current date. Stress the positive factors of ownership, growth, and success, but be straightforward in your presentation of facts.

☐ Section 2—Product Lines

List and briefly describe the company's product lines: proprietary products, private label, nationally-known, or regionally-recognizable nonproprietary product lines. Also work done as a subcontractor furnishing a component part for an item assembled and marketed by another company, etc. (Do not exceed two pages).

☐ Section 3—Market Area(s)

If your company is a manufacturer, processor, distributor, or wholesaler, state the scope of your marketing area, and the concentration of customers in local, intermediate, and distant areas. Illustrate the growth and acceptance of your products and/or services with a series of comparisons—sales figures now vs. two years ago, five years ago, etc. If your growth has been steady in all market areas, make the point in your presentation. If growth has been more obvious in the local (or regional) market area, point out that your small company does not have the personnel (and perhaps has not had the production or distribution facility) to do more than service your own local or regional market.

☐ Section 4—Financial Data

Attach copies of the three most recent annual financial statements and a copy of the most recent quarterly or semiannual profit and loss statement. A brief letter from your accounting firm attesting to the quality of the internal controls and systems would be an appropriate and effective companion piece to the financial data.

☐ Section 5—Benefits To Be Derived From Proposed Loan

The banker will want to know how you propose to use the loan proceeds. A new or enlarged plant facility should enable you to operate more efficiently at a lower cost. Perhaps you will increase production and warehouse facilities, replace or modernize production or processing machinery, or add additional units to provide greater production and warehousing capacity. Emphasize the potential for increasing business and improving the profit percentages.

☐ Section 6—Key Personnel

Of interest to the banker will be the quality and levels of experience that your key people (regardless of how few) bring to the company. If you (owner, manager, etc.) make the decisions in several areas of the company's operations, that is important. If you have one, two, or more experienced people in key positions (production superintendent, quality control, etc.), that is important. Under "other employees" you should list the number of employees by major job classification only.

☐ Section 7—Business Projection - Next 12 Months

In a one-page recap, state what you expect your company to do—sales, growth, and profits—during the next 12 months. Capsulize what level of success, growth, and profits you feel is attainable during the coming 12 months. Explain your reasoning for those projections, and extend the projection to include where you feel the company will be five years from now.

(See following *Business Projection—12 Months*. Also see sample cover letters for familiarization package (FIGS. 12-3 and 12-4).)

BUSINESS PROJECTION—12 MONTHS

We are preparing this Business Projection in lieu of a conventional Business Plan and it covers (in general terms only) the 12-month period subsequent to October 17, 1987.

(Your Company's Letterhead)

October 17, 1987

Mr. Lawrence C. Bartlett, President
North County National Bank
1462 Wayside Boulevard
Oxnard, California

Dear Mr. Bartlett:

The attached familiarization package offers a brief description
of our product lines and customer base, a description of our new
Oxnard processing and packaging facility, a look at our more
than three decades of business success, and a few words regarding
our pattern and philosophy for a carefully controlled growth.

It is our intention to become both participating and contributing
members in the Oxnard business community. To fulfill that expectation, we need the support and services of a community-oriented
bank - one that will help us attain our projected goals via a
sound program of financial support.

Please contact me when you have had an opportunity to review the
attached information.

Sincerely Yours,

(Your Name)
President

FIG. 12-3.

(Your Letterhead)

October 17, 1987

Mr. Lawrence C. Bartlett, President
North County National Bank
1462 Wayside Boulevard
Oxnard, California

Dear Mr. Bartlett:

I greatly appreciate the interest you expressed in this company during our October 12th telephone conversation.

The attached package of information has been put together to show you where we have been, where we are now, where we expect to go - and how we expect to get there.

It will be my pleasure to answer questions or provide additional data. Please contact me at your early convenience.

Sincerely Yours,

(Your Name)
President

FIG. 12-4.

We have used the phrase "in general terms only" because of our current move from Santa Clara to Oxnard and what we anticipate will be a transition period of from 3 to 6 months. This transition periods will see us devoting more than a normal amount of time to bringing production lines to proper levels of efficiency, making appropriate adjustments in materials requirements, preparing the warehouse to accommodate supplies and finished products, and doing our utmost to settle quickly and effectively into the new 28,000 square foot facility.

It is appropriate to note, however, that the transition period will see us actively soliciting the business of several new customers—primarily private-label people who, prior to our move, had contacted us regarding the possibility of packing their product(s) for them. Negotiations that we had put on hold at Santa Clara because we lacked the production and warehouse space to take on meaningful new business can now go forward.

Our position at this point is both advantageous and unique. Very few packers in the area of California that is north of Los Angeles have the capacity or the capability to take on several thousand cases of new business per month. We frequently are contacted by private-label distributors who are almost desperate in their search for a packer who (1) will accept their product or (2) can deliver a satisfactory product—on time and in the required volume. Even more uncertain is the plight of the private-label distributor who is searching for a manufacturer willing to produce a specialty food item in relatively small batches. It is usually very profitable business, but most manufacturers and processors are unwilling to adjust their production schedules to accommodate these smaller orders.

We have the technical skills and the production experience necessary to satisfy the needs of a broad range of customers—from the person with a product idea who retains us to develop and produce that product to, and through, the experienced distributor who brings to us his or her monthly requirement for several thousand cases of product. Happily, we now have the production and warehouse facility to take advantage of these opportunities.

NEGOTIABLE INSTRUMENTS

Although the most common form of negotiable instrument is a check drawn on a bank account, it is by no means the only one. A negotiable instrument might be a check, a promissory note, a bill of exchange, a trade acceptance, a letter of credit, or some other similar "negotiable." What are the special qualities that make an instrument "negotiable?" The guidelines are that it must be in writing, must bear the signature of the maker (or drawer), must promise without condition(s) to pay a specific amount of money, and must be payable on demand or at an established (or determinable) future date. The instrument must be payable to the bearer or to order. When it is written in favor of a drawee, the person or entity addressed must be identified in such a way that the drawer's intent is reasonably clear.

Every person who endorses a negotiable instrument turns that document into a separate contract. Your signature, or the signature of another endorser, turns the negotiable instrument into a new contract—one apart from the maker or other endorsers. You cannot disqualify a negotiable instrument from that category because it bears no date, has no stated dollar amount or other consideration, or has no indication as to where it was drawn or where it is payable. An undated negotiable instrument is considered "dated" as of the date (or time) it was issued. Bank checks are a very familiar type of negotiable instrument, and it is good to know that the rules governing checks apply to other forms of negotiable instruments as well. Words (written or printed) govern figures, and provisions that are in writing control printed ones.

Two general classifications of endorsements exist on negotiable instruments —general or qualified. A general endorsement is given without qualification or reservation. A qualified endorsement is one that, in addition to the endorser's name, has written words (or a written statement) which purports to limit the general liability that would be implied if it were the name alone. Limiting liability is important, and the words ''without recourse'' generally are used to clarify that intent.

One of the less clear-cut areas is the status of a check given to your company in payment of an account balance, marked ''in full of account'' when it does not pay the entire balance. It is not ''in full payment'' if there is no dispute as to the amount the customer owes. In the absence of a dispute regarding the account balance, the creditor (or supplier) is generally safe if he or she deposits the check and contacts the customer for the balance of the money. If, however, there is a dispute between your company and the customer regarding the account balance, *do not* endorse and deposit any check that bears the statement ''in full payment of account,'' or any other statement of similar intent or wording. It is possible that, under the condition of a disputed account balance, you could jeopardize or forfeit your chances of collecting the difference between the ''in full'' check and the disputed account balance. Be very wary of any endorsement on a check or other negotiable instrument that restricts or eliminates your rights or options. Only when there is no question in your mind that the endorsement is acceptable should you add your signature.

FACTORING

Your only peripheral exposure to this form of improving cash flow might have been one that you did not recognize as a part of the ''factoring'' concept. Small advertisements frequently appear in the business and financial sections of daily newspapers in which the advertiser offers to ''buy your invoices for immediate cash.'' The offer might say ''cash within 24 hours, no term contracts to sign, bank-to-bank transfer of funds, and invoices purchased on a nonrecourse basis.'' You certainly would not turn to these sources unless your company is at a point or in a situation where your bank—no bank—will agree to offer the additional funds you need for a short or long term.

Factoring your receivables—whether through an old, and large, factoring firm or through an advertiser such as the type mentioned above—is usually more mostly than the more conventional use of receivables as collateral for a revolving bank loan to augment cash flow. But because of business or economic conditions, your banker might feel that your company's financial and business position will not support an increase in the bank's lending commitment. At that point—and particularly if you are confident that the need to accelerate cash flow will be temporary—factoring your receivables through an established, reputable, factoring firm could be the answer to getting a faster turnaround of your receivables dollars. It is not a form of financing that you should seriously consider (certainly not in most industries) unless bank support—or additional bank support—is available. In the scenario of a relatively short-term need, it is worth exploring.

Factoring of invoices is done on a recourse or a nonrecourse basis. At some point in the discussions, the factor will ask for a list of your accounts and copies of recent receivables aging reports. He will review your experience with the accounts and, from that evaluation, will delete any accounts that are unacceptable. If your discussions with the factor lean toward a relationship where accounts are factored on a *recourse basis* (you guarantee that you will pay the factor within a specified period of time for monies he advances on invoices charged to approved accounts), then the factor will accept more borderline accounts and advance a higher percentage of each invoice total. What is nonrecourse invoicing? The factor assumes responsibility for collecting the full amount of invoices for goods and/or services approved accounts purchase. Because the factor's risk is higher, the percentage advanced to you of each invoice total will be smaller.

SHARING YOUR CREDIT EXPERIENCE

Just as the credit experience of suppliers and bankers is of interest to you, so your experience is of interest to suppliers who have been asked to extend credit terms to some of your customers. It is a two-way street that works effectively only when everyone respects the long-standing necessity of confidentiality among credit grantors. Nothing can more effectively destroy cooperation between credit grantors than for a credit manager to learn that another credit manager has repeated confidential information virtually verbatim to the creditor's customer. (Example: When a similar situation happened some years ago in a group of which I (my company) was a member, we suspended the company from all participation in credit group activities for six months, helped the company find a new corporate credit manager, then fidgeted for an additional year until group members gradually became comfortable when the offending company's new credit manager sat in with us.) Is this behavior unfair? Not at all. The rules of the game are very clear. The legal implications of statements directly attributable to a source, and perhaps distorted for additional effect, are too ominous for any credit group—or individual credit manager—to settle for anything less than total compliance. It is a tradition that has become a compelling necessity—one which amongst credit managers has always had the weight of a manager's personal and professional integrity. I submit that you, as the owner of your company, must agree that no level of peer trust can be more necessary, more demanding, or more clear-cut.

DUPLICATE BANK DEPOSIT

Whether a Duplicate Bank Deposit form has a place in your department or in the relationship between credit and data processing (manual or computerized) depends upon the method you use to receive and process receivables payment checks. You are the person who makes the credit decisions, but you probably have assigned someone to receive the checks, list them for deposit, and make appropriate payment notations on the aging report. If you have assigned a clerical support person to work with you, that person can list checks on the bank deposit form, use the form shown in FIG. 12-5 to list additional relevant payment data, and give the duplicate bank form (with attached remittance advice data) to you. Your clerical support person will make payment notations on the aging report and also will call to your attention such things as unauthorized discounts or a credit taken before your company has issued one. You should retain the Duplicate Bank Deposit form in a credit department file in the event there is some future question regarding the way you applied the payment to the receivables balance.

All commercial bank deposit forms have spaces for data that is important to the bank and its processing of checks. Standard duplicate bank deposit slips fall short of supplying accounts receivable or data processing with the specific additional data necessary to determine whether a check forwarded to clear an invoice does offset that particular item. When you have deposited checks and have not retained any data relevant to individual invoice payments, it can necessitate one or more telephone calls and extra work on the part of people in both companies.

The form is useful for the in-house keypunch operator as the source of information for the daily recording of payments and credits into the data processing system. From the account number on the left side of the page, through the discount adjustment on the

DUPLICATE BANK DEPOSIT

BANK _____

DEPOSIT DATE _____

ACCT. NO.	ACCOUNT NAME	CHECK NO.	INVOICE NO.	INVOICE DATE	INVOICE AMOUNT	FUNDS REMITTED	DISC. ADJUST

(To prepare the form to use in your company or business,   add lines to the bottom of the sheet— or add enough lines to accommodate the maximum number of payment items you receive daily.)

FIG. 12-5.

right, the keypunch operator has the information necessary to work quickly and efficiently to keep receivable balances current.

CASH FORECAST SUMMARY SHEET

This summary sheet is not a tool for the inexperienced or for a credit manager who is not totally familiar with the payment habits of his or her company's major accounts. The positive side is that a person with little experience can incorporate this form into his or her work schedule and anticipate good results. Over a period of six or eight weeks you should begin to come up with some reasonably accurate forecasts. (See FIG. 12-6.)

The first few weeks of projections should be for practice only. Do not try to assign credibility to those early efforts. Look at aged trial balance sheets for the past half-dozen months to confirm your recollection of the paying habits of your major accounts. Try to establish a repetitive payment pattern (discount, always slow 10 to 20 days, etc.) and project for each account the anticipated amount that he should pay during a given week. Add a total for the small accounts to each of the weekly forecast figures, adjust your figures for upcoming weeks on Friday afternoon of each week and continue to fine-tune your knowledge of an account's paying habits. The highest achievable level of accuracy is important to the quality of the projection and how useful it will be to an owner as he or she forecasts cash requirements for the weeks ahead.

If you are not currently doing a forecast, the contribution made by these reports to your company's preparations for dealing with cash-flow needs can be substantial. Larger companies require receivables cash forecasting of their credit manager as a matter of standard practice. It should not be an intimidating forward step if you do it only as an exercise for several weeks, comparing your payments projections for each week against payments received. After several weeks, begin to phase your projections into your fiscal planning, putting more and more reliance on your projections. The prospect of having the benefit of receivables forecasting on a weekly basis should be motivation enough to refine it until it becomes a valuable tool.

Managing credit accounts is not a one-dimensional responsibility. Assigning appropriate credit lines to accounts that you have evaluated from good information, and moving promptly to protect your company's interest when a customer begins to stumble, are your primary credit management responsibilities. Don't underestimate or neglect credit administration—an umbrella that covers the support areas and can help you to put your primary responsibilities in a somewhat more manageable context.

CASH FORECAST SUMMARY SHEET

MONTH OF_____

ACCOUNTS RECEIVABLE BALANCE_____
        (@ end of preceding month)

LESS:

            Credits To Be Issued_____
            Current Balances _____
            Disputed Balances_____
            Samples, Etc.. _____

COLLECTIBLE A/R TOTAL _____

COLLECTIONS BY WEEK (Available Total)	PROJECTED	ACTUAL	DIFFERENCE
Week #1_____	_____	_____	_____
Week #2_____	_____	_____	_____
Week #3_____	_____	_____	_____
Week #4_____	_____	_____	_____
Week #5_____	_____	_____	_____

FIG. **12-6.**

Chapter 13

In Conclusion...

THIS BOOK ADDRESSES THE NEEDS OF THE OWNER OF A SMALL COMPANY—THE ENTRE-preneur who must have the knowledge and capability to handle many jobs successfully. The owner of a small company is one of the last and most to be admired of those who populate an increasingly complex and difficult business climate. Bigger companies have departments for everything. They have departments to handle work that, in a small company, one person handles, frequently as one of three, four, or more areas of daily responsibility. Big companies have on-staff experts and specialists to provide advice in their respective areas of expertise.

What does the owner of a small company have? The constant worry and aggravation of trying to find and retain a market niche that won't be there long if a bigger company decides that the niche is big enough and profitable enough to merit their time and attention. What are the problems of spending long days in a do-it-yourself work environment? No staff and no specialists are available just a couple of office people, a truck driver or two, a warehouseman, some factory employees, a substantial bank obligation, and a desire to succeed in a business environment of his or her own choice. Long hours, production and supplier problems, questions regarding the loyalty and financial stability of customers—are part of a boulder-strewn road to success and the personal choice of almost every owner of a small company. For the owner of a small company, big—really big—is not better. Better is smaller—particularly a "smaller" that has been a family business for generations or a business the present owner has started. Do I admire these owners? They are the single hardest-working group of people I know and they—you, my friends—have my unbounded admiration.

My goal in writing this book was to be helpful in an area where little help is available. I chose the format to allow me to present much of the material as we might talk if one, two, or more of us were to sit around a table discussing the multiple areas and responsibilities of credit management. Sequentially and randomly, we would talk about primary and secondary responsibilities, the types of problems and situations you must be able to recognize and deal with effectively, and how you should go about building your knowledge and skills to the point where you become a confident, capable manager of your company's credit accounts.

Because it is unlikely that many of us will ever sit down together to talk about credit, it is my hope that this book gives to you—in a form that you find quite digestible—much of what you need to know to do a good job with your credit and collections. It should serve you well for several years as a basic credit management guide, a handy refresher, and a valuable reference source. I wish you, my friends, a lifetime of success and an unlimited supply of good credit decisions.

Appendix

FORMS ARE AN IMPORTANT PART OF EVERY CREDIT MANAGER'S KIT FOR DEALING WITH his or her daily problems and decisions. They eliminate any necessity for improvising and generally are successful in containing that urge at a time when improvisation would deliver the least attractive result. Forms are handy, and they're great security blankets. They help to preserve a continuity of established procedures in a variety of decision-making areas of credit at a time when the credit manager is most prone to err in his or her judgments.

Having made a case for forms, let me give an equally strong endorsement for most form letters. Management prepares form letters to deal effectively with the types of routine problems and questions that have only one answer. They deal with the types of questions that occur frequently, rarely require any deviation from the prepared form, and satisfy the questioner's need for information. A few properly written form letters should cover the majority of the things you cannot or should not try to handle on the telephone. If the customer asks for an invoice copy or some other routine piece of information, a form letter will handle it. Eighty percent of the letter is in place when you put it in the typewriter. Fill in one, two, or three blank spaces and send it on its way. There isn't any need to try to prime the creative juices at a time when your major focus should be on credit decisions and credit problems.

Form letters are inappropriate when you are responding to a question or questions posed during a telephone conversation, as a response to a letter of inquiry from a customer or prospective customer, or in any situation that is "first person" in nature and intent. Nothing turns a person off more rapidly than a "mass mailer" response to something that the customer or questioner felt was sufficiently important to warrant writing or telephoning for information. The correspondence might be a letter or telephone call requesting product pamphlets, or a question regarding a credit due on a specific invoice. In both of these hypotheticals, *always* extend the courtesy of a "cover letter" response. Not only is it an appropriate response, but if the inquiry for product pamphlets is not from a current customer, there is the possibility of developing a dialogue with someone who will become one.

Form letters are sensible and appropriate in any circumstance where you need a response in a context that is routine and repetitive. It is not necessarily routine and repetitive with one customer but with your company's body of customers. Any section of the credit responsibility is open to a form letter(s) response if there is no clear-cut need for a personal letter. Your knowledge and sensitivity regarding what constitutes common business courtesy will dictate the appropriate format for your response.

Familiarize yourself with the breakdown of form letters (and forms) that follows. They are broken down into the categories of their usage. You should find them helpful and easy to integrate into your daily procedures.

FORMS

LETTERS

Index